The 'I Wills' of The Psalms

The Determinations of the Man of God as found in some of the 'I Wills' of the Psalms

PHILIP BENNETT POWER

THE BANNER OF TRUTH TRUST

THE BANNER OF TRUTH TRUST
3 Murrayfield Road, Edinburgh, EH 12 6EL
PO Box 621, Carlisle, Pennsylvania 17013, USA

★

First published 1858
First Banner of Truth edition 1985
ISBN 0 85151 445 6

★

Reproduced, printed and bound in Great Britain by
Hazell Watson & Viney Limited,
Member of the BPCC Group,
Aylesbury, Bucks

The 'I Wills' of
The Psalms

PREFACE.

It was the original design of the Author of this volume to have sent forth into the world a little book, containing a few thoughts with respect to each of the subjects which are to be found in the following pages. Hence the first subject treated upon, viz., TRUST, although of equal importance with the rest, is not considered at such length; the style of its treatment also differs somewhat from that of the others. Almost unconsciously to the writer, the little book began to grow and develop into a large one; and all that he can now do, is, to hope that its increased size may make it of increased worth.

Several illustrations have been added to those given in the first edition, especially in the chapter on Prayer. In many of the matters mentioned in these illustrations, the Author has been personally concerned, but he has not deemed it necessary to specify such cases particularly.

The reader will observe that the same persons and facts are frequently referred to in different portions of the volume; this does not, however, involve any real tautology, for such is the fulness of Holy Writ, and such is the variety of application of which each portion of it is susceptible, that, in point of fact, a few incidents and a few characters answer all our need. When we consider how very few are the leading characters which are brought before our notice in Holy Scripture, it seems as though God designed to teach us by the few and not by many, in order that we, as individuals, might be taught or warned by the individual, and not by a class. Hence in part the exceeding preciousness of the individuality of Jesus.

The reader, who is familiar with the book of Psalms, will also observe that many "I wills" are omitted in this volume; amongst these are some which group together under different heads, such as the "I wills" of CONFESSION and HUMILIATION, of WORSHIP, of JOY and REJOICING, of the MIND and HEART, and of OBEDIENCE, together with many which do not range themselves in any distinct order; these the writer preferred leaving untouched, rather than saying but a few words upon them.

The following pages are designed rather to suggest than to teach, to whisper than to speak. Yet all their whisperings are of importance, for their subjects are from the word of God; may they admonish and encourage, may they remind and direct, may they help and confirm the people of the Lord according to their respective needs; may they shew them where they have failed to determine, and where their determinations have come short; and, from time to time, reminded by these pages of these things, may they go on unto perfection, until the fulfilled determinations of time, (accepted in the blood of Christ,) bring to them the fruition of glory in eternity.

CONTENTS.

CHAPTER II.

Ministry and Testimony.

THE "I WILL" OF MINISTRY AND TESTIMONY.

CHAPTER III.

THE "I WILL" OF CONVERSE.

CHAPTER IV.

THE "I WILL" OF CONVERSE.

Continued.

CHAPTER V.

THE "I WILL" OF TEACHING.

CHAPTER VI.

THE "I WILL" OF TEACHING.

Continued.

CHAPTER VII.

Prayer.

CHAPTER VIII.

THE OBJECT OF THE "I WILL" IN PRAYER.

CHAPTER IX.

THE "I WILL" OF PRAYER IN THE TIME OF TROUBLE.

CHAPTER X

THE "I WILL" OF PRAYER IN THE TIME OF TROUBLE.

Continued.

CHAPTER XI.

THE "I WILL" OF PRAYER IN THE TIME OF TROUBLE.

Concluded.

CHAPTER XII.

THE "I WILL" OF CONTINUANCE IN PRAYER.

CHAPTER XIII.

THE "I WILL" OF CONTINUANCE IN PRAYER.

Continued.

CHAPTER XIV.

THE "I WILL" OF EXPECTATION IN PRAYER.

CHAPTER XV.

THE "I WILL" OF INTENSE PRAYER.

CHAPTER XVI.

Action.

CHAPTER XVII.

THE "I WILL" OF HEARTINESS IN ACTION.

CHAPTER XVIII.

THE "I WILL" OF DETERMINATION IN ACTION.

CHAPTER I.

Trust.

The "I Will" of Trust.

Psalm iii, 6. *"For I will not be afraid of ten thousand of people, that have set themselves against me round about."*

Psalm iv, 8. *"I will both lay me down in peace, and sleep, for thou, Lord, only makest me dwell in safety."*

Psalm xxiii, 4. *"Yea, though I walk through the valley of the shadow of death, I will fear no evil; for thou art with me; thy rod and thy staff they comfort me."*

Psalm xliv, 6. *"For I will not trust in my bow, neither shall my sword save me."*

Psalm lv, 16. *"As for me I will call upon God; and the Lord shall save me."*

Psalm lvi, 3. *"What time I am afraid I will trust in thee."*

Psalm lvii, 1. *"Be merciful unto me, O God, be merciful unto me; for my soul trusteth in thee: yea, in the shadow of thy wings will I make my refuge, until these calamities be overpast."*

Psalm lxi, 4. *"I will abide in thy tabernacle for ever, I will trust in the covert of thy wings."*

Psalm lxxxvi, 7. *"In the day of my trouble I will call upon thee, for thou wilt answer me."*

Psalm xci, 2. *"I will say unto the Lord, He is my refuge and my fortress, my God, in him will I trust."*

Psalm cxviii, 6: *"The Lord is on my side; I will not fear: what can man do unto me?"*

SO dull, so wavering are these poor hearts of ours in faith, that very often we will not trust God, even in circumstances in which we would have fully trusted an earthly parent. The dear children of the Lord are continually detecting themselves in unbelief. At one moment they are leaning upon human instrumentality, at another they are wholly at their wit's end; now they are full of terror at an immediate prospect of danger, and now they lose all *rest* in God; all which evils proceed from the want of simple faith, of child-like trust. God loves trust; it honours Him; he who trusts the most shall sorrow least. If there were continual trust there would be continual peace.

Let us first notice THE UNRESERVEDNESS OF TRUST, which we find in the following group of verses.

Psalm iii, 6. *"I will not be afraid of ten thousands of people, that have set themselves against me round about."*

Psalm xxiii, 4. *" Yea, though I walk through the valley of the shadow of death, I will fear no evil, for Thou art with me; Thy rod and Thy staff they comfort me."*

Psalm lv, 16, 17. *"As for me I will call upon God; and the Lord shall save me. Evening, and morning, and at noon, will I pray and cry aloud: and he shall hear my voice."*

Psalm xliv, 6. *" For I will not trust in my bow, neither shall my sword save me."*

The Psalmist will trust, *despite appearances*. He will not be afraid though ten thousands of people have set themselves against him round about. Let us here limit our thoughts to this one idea, "despite appearances." What could look worse to human sight than this array of ten thousands of people? Ruin seemed to stare him in the face; wherever he looked an enemy was to be seen. What was one against ten thousand? It often happens that God's people come into circumstances like this; they say "all these things are against me;" they seem scarce able to count their troubles; they cannot see a loop-hole through which to escape; things look very black indeed. It is great faith and trust which says under these circumstances, "I will not be afraid."

These were the circumstances under which Luther was placed, as he journeyed towards Worms. His friend Spalatin heard it said, by the enemies of the Reformation, that the safe conduct of a heretic ought not to be respected, and became alarmed for the Reformer. "At the moment when the latter was approaching the city, a messenger appeared before him with this advice from the chaplain, 'Do not enter Worms!' And this from his best friend—the elector's confidant—from Spalatin himself! * * * * But Luther, undismayed, turned his eyes upon the messenger, and replied, 'Go and tell your master, that even should there be as many devils in Worms as tiles on the housetops, still I would enter it.' The messenger returned to Worms with this astounding answer. 'I was then undaunted,' said Luther, a few days before his death, 'I feared nothing.'"

At such seasons as these the reasonable men of the world, those who walk by sight and not by faith, will think it reasonable enough that the Christian should be afraid; they themselves would be very low if they were in such a predicament. Weak believers are now ready to make excuses for us, and we are only too ready to make them for ourselves; instead of rising above the weakness of the flesh, we take refuge under it, and use it as an excuse.

But let us think prayerfully for a little while, and we shall see that it should not be thus with us. To trust only when appearances are favourable, is to sail only with the wind and tide, to believe only when we can see. Oh let us follow the example of the Psalmist, and seek that unreservedness of faith which will enable us to trust God, come what will, and to say as he said, "I will not be afraid of ten thousands of people, which have set themselves against me round about."

Helps to unreservedness of trust.

1. Remember how many changes things take, and that they do not always end according to appearances; therefore it does not follow, that because they now look badly, they must of necessity end badly.

2. Remember that all can be turned hither and thither at any moment, and to any extent that God chooses; and if His mind toward us be unchanged, present appearances should not terrify or crush us.

3. Consider the Scripture examples of dark appearances but bright issues.

4. Consider examples within your own experience and knowledge.

5. Remember that any one can trust, or seem to trust God when all things are going on well; that the believer must shew his faith by trusting when things appear to be going ill.

6. Remember that this is a special opportunity for glorifying God, over and above all ordinary ones.

To do all this is hard indeed; but there is great grace for hard requirements, if it be sought.* Let us make

---

* This was St. Paul's experience in 2 Cor. xii, 7—10. "And lest I should be exalted above measure through the abundance of

this prayer, "Lord give me that unreserved faith which will enable me to trust Thee unreservedly, despite all appearances."

The following recent occurrence will perhaps sometimes come into the reader's mind, when he thinks that

the revelations, there was given to me a thorn in the flesh, the messenger of Satan to buffet me, lest I should be exalted above measure. For this thing I besought the Lord thrice, that it might depart from me. And He said unto me, My grace is sufficient for thee; for My strength is made perfect in weakness. Most gladly therefore will I rather glory in my infirmities, that the power of Christ may rest upon me. Therefore I take pleasure in infirmities, in reproaches, in necessities, in persecutions, in distresses for Christ's sake: for when I am weak, then am I strong."

See the unreservedness of trust displayed by Paul in the tempest, in Acts xxvii, 22—25. "And now I exhort you to be of good cheer : for there shall be no loss of any man's life among you, but of the ship. For there stood by me this night the angel of God, whose I am, and whom I serve, saying, fear not, Paul ; thou must be brought before Cæsar : and, lo, God hath given thee all them that sail with thee. Wherefore, sirs, be of good cheer : for I believe God, that it shall be even as it was told me."

Even when circumstances assumed a darker aspect, his faith was unshaken. Verses 33—35. "And while the day was coming on, Paul besought them all to take meat, saying, This day is the fourteenth day that ye have tarried and continued fasting, having taken nothing. Wherefore I pray you to take some meat : for this is for your health : for there shall not an hair fall from the head of any of you. And when he had thus spoken, he took bread, and gave thanks to God in presence of them all : and when he had broken it he began to eat." The result we know, "And so it came to pass, that they escaped all safe to land."

How favourably Paul here contrasts with Peter in Matt. xiv, 30. "But when he saw the wind boisterous, he was afraid; and beginning to sink, he cried, saying, Lord, save me."

ruin is about to be brought upon him by some either apparent or real misfortune:—

A Belgian vessel, called "The Leopold," recently ran, in a violent storm, on a rock, near one of the Falkland Islands, on the coast of Patagonia, and went to pieces. It was supposed that all her crew, nine in number, and their officers, had perished. A letter was, however, subsequently received from one of the crew, named Declerk, announcing that he alone escaped. He swam to an island. He found no inhabitants, and had to live on some bits of bread which had been washed ashore, wild celery, and some birds, which he killed with a stick. Happening to have matches with him, he succeeded in lighting a fire, which he fed with turf. To make his fire burn well, he partly surrounded it with some planks washed ashore from the wreck. One night the wind blew these planks into the fire, and they were consumed. He thought this a *terrible misfortune*, but it was *the means of saving him*. An American ship happened to be passing two miles off, and seeing the rising smoke— an extraordinary thing on a desert island—some of her crew disembarked. They found the poor fellow crouching over the fire, and on hearing his tale, they took him on board.

The Psalmist will also thus trust, *even though all be unknown*.

We find him doing this in Psalm xxiii, 4. "Yea, though I walk through the valley of the shadow of death, I will fear no evil." Here, surely, there is trust the most complete. We dread the unknown far above anything that we can see; a little noise in the dark will terrify, when even great dangers which are visible do not affright: the unknown, with its mystery and uncertainty often fills the heart with anxiety, if not with foreboding and gloom. Here, the Psalmist takes the highest form of the unknown, the aspect which is most terrible to man, and says that even in the midst of it he will trust. What could be so wholly beyond the reach of human experience or speculation, or even imagination, as "the valley of the shadow of death," with all that belonged to it? but the Psalmist makes no reservation against it; he will trust where he cannot see. How often are we terrified at the unknown; even as the disciples were, who "feared as they entered into the cloud;" how often is the uncertainty of the future a harder trial to our faith than the pressure of some present ill! Many dear children of God can trust Him in all *known* evils; but why those fears and forebodings, and sinkings of heart, if they trust Him equally for the *unknown?* How much, alas! do we fall short of the true character of the children of God, in this matter of the unknown. A child practically acts upon the declaration of Christ that "sufficient unto the day is the evil thereof;" we, in this respect far less wise than he, people the unknown with phantoms and speculations, and too often forget our simple trust in God.

Let us seek for grace to exercise a simple trust as regards the future; just to be content with seeing God in it, as the Psalmist was. He said, "I will fear no evil, for Thou art with me; Thy rod and Thy staff they comfort me." Whatever the unknown was, God was in it, and that was enough for him. Oh! how would this simple trust dispel a multitude of fears; how would it rid us of gloomy forebodings; how would it take many of its terrors even from death itself; how would it enable us cheerfully to step onwards into the future; how many heart-aches, how many perplexing thoughts, how many sleepless nights would it save us! The unknown is God's— God is in the unknown; be that enough, O my soul, for thee; say "I will trust, I will not fear; the darkness is no darkness, O my God, to Thee; I will trust without reserve."

Let the very fact of our not being able to concentrate our thoughts upon the unknown, make us concentrate our thoughts upon the truth, that "whatever it may bring forth, God is in it for His people ;" and in that trusting thought, we shall find rest.

Helps to procuring this *trust*.

1. Consider that in all *known* circumstances, God has ever been found equal to His people's. need ; hence there is every reason to believe that He will be thus found in the *unknown* also.

2. Remember that the unknown future contains no chance; its arrangements are all as distinctly made by God, as have been those of the past.

3. Reflect upon the very position in which you are placed. Do your utmost, you *cannot* grapple with, or make provision for, the unknown; therefore, unless you trust God *in* it and *for* it, you never can have peace.

This also is no easy attainment; but if we would live up to our privileges, or honour God fully, we must say with David, "Yea, though I walk through the valley of the shadow of death, I will fear no evil, for Thou art with me, Thy rod and Thy staff they comfort me." We must trust unreservedly, even where all be unknown.

We are further taught by the Psalmist to make God the great object of our trust, *even though the usual human instrumentality of help may be at hand.*

"I will not trust in my bow, neither shall my sword save me," said he in Psalm xliv, 6; and that, after having expressed his belief that great things were about to be accomplished. "Through Thee will we push down our enemies; through Thy name will we tread them under that rise up against us."

Human means and appliances are not to be thrown away as useless or despised, but the temptation of trusting in them must be guarded against. The sword and the bow were surely the fittest things so far as human appliances went, wherewith to go against the enemy: they seemed to make provision for all circumstances of warfare, for distant skirmishing, and for hand to hand engagement; but, whatever they might have been for use, they were valueless as objects of trust.

We are continually prone to lean upon the instrument, to expect much from it, from its tried efficiency, from its suitability to the occasion, from its being apparently providentially ready to our hand; and thus we very often come insensibly to think too much of the instrument; we expect *certain* results from it, as though it had powers and energies of its own. When we succeed, we say, "how admirably the instrument works;" when we do not, we blame the instrument, and say, "how it fails." Satan contrives to hide a snare even in the midst of God's blessings; when God prospers an instrument, Satan is pretty sure to magnify it. We must be very careful ever to put God above the instrument; to keep our reliance specifically upon Him; on no account to lose sight of Him in the instrument. Even in good things, and amongst the children of God, the error of which we are now speaking is too frequently committed.

For example :—how much is expected from a preacher, while little is expected from a recognition of the One by whom the preacher has been sent; how much from human friends, from the advice of certain physicians, from certain well-known and efficacious remedies, and the like, without its being remembered that God makes use of these means, and that they have no virtue in themselves. We shew practical unbelief, when we feel peace because we have certain means at hand, and not because God Himself is near to help. Under these circumstances, the sword and bow are our comfort; we go in Saul's armour; we do not make mention of the living God. It may be that our human instrument is weak; that we have no more than the five smooth stones of the brook, or the handful of meal in a barrel, and the drop of oil in a cruise, but we cling to it nevertheless; we can see it, and sight has ever more power than faith for poor human nature. If we want a blessing upon the means, let us put them in their proper place. They cannot be *absolutely* trusted; in themselves they have the elements of failure, weakness, and miscarriage; they can be depended upon, only so far as faith can recognise God in them; yea, and even more than this, God as able to do without them. In daily life, we too often present the extraordinary spectacle of men trusting in machinery, without recognising its motive power. We cannot expect God to prosper anything which intrudes itself into His place, and detracts from His honour; the bow will be effectual in proportion to our recognition of the fact, that it is He who must direct the arrow's flight; the sword will be powerful in proportion as we recognise the truth, that it is He who gives the strength to grasp its hilt, and skill to whet its edge; to cut, to parry, or to thrust; the means will do most, when the God of means is recognised most. Let us reflect on this, and act upon it in matters of daily life; let us say with David, " I will not trust in my bow, neither shall my sword save me;" and with him, doubtless, we shall be able to add, "But Thou hast saved us from our enemies, and hast put them to shame that hated us."

Helps to attaining a trust which will put God above means. Let us remember that

1. All human means have in them only the virtues which He has bestowed, therefore He can withdraw from them their virtue, or increase that virtue at any moment.

2. No matter how much certain means are in themselves calculated to produce certain ends, a thousand counteracting influences or circumstances may intervene to neutralize or destroy their efficacy, therefore, unless God be above the means, and not dependent upon them, we cannot be sure that all will go well.

3. When all means fail, God is as well able to work as when they abound.

4. Even if the means be at hand, by using them wrongly, or feebly, we may fail in producing the desired result.

5. God will be sure to blast the means if we put them above Him, or make them independent of Him.

Thus He did in the case of Asa, mentioned in 2 Chron. xvi, 12. "And Asa, in the thirty-and-ninth year of his reign, was diseased in his feet, until his disease was exceeding great, yet in his disease he sought not to the Lord, but to the physicians." "Thus saith the Lord, Cursed be the man that trusteth in man, and maketh flesh his arm." Jeremiah xvii, 5.

There remains yet one point to be observed, with reference to the unreservedness of the trust which we should put in God.

In Psalm lv, 16, the Psalmist says, "As for me I will call upon God, and the Lord shall save me." Here we have *cause and effect linked together*, and the Psalmist's unreserved trust in the union of the two; he will call, and the Lord shall save.

It would be blessed indeed for the Lord's people, if they continually exercised the trust expressed in this verse; if they felt, that when they called, He would both answer and save. This trust would bring us gladly to our knees, for we should always feel sure that our labour upon them was not in vain in the Lord; it would dispel a thousand fears; it would give energy to our prayers; it would save us from casting about hither and thither for help; it would simplify many of the intricacies of the spiritual life. While others were rushing to and fro, asking what could be done, and trying one thing and another, we should see our way clearly before us; the use of the "I will" would settle all for us; our trust would bring us peace; we should say, "As for me I will call upon God, and the Lord shall save me." Alas! how often do we call, not as though we expected God to act in our behalf; the utmost we can say is, "I will call, and *perhaps* the Lord will save me;" we do not realize the truth, that effects *must* follow real calling upon God; our prayers are rather trials *whether* the Lord will be gracious unto us, than petitions founded upon the full assurance that He *will* be so. If our feelings were put into words, they would be expressed somewhat thus; "I will call, but I do not know whether the Lord will answer me or not." Oh! for a larger measure of trust in the exercise of prayer. Oh! for a fuller belief that for all spiritual sowing there must be spiritual reaping; that no prayer offered in distress and in faith can come to nought. This faith would give us power with God, and we should prevail; it would give us that spring of energy which is conferred by the prospect of success. See how the *prospect*, or rather the *certainty* of success, sent David forth with a springing step to meet the giant in single fight. "This day will the Lord deliver thee into mine hand, and I will smite thee, and take thine head from thee; and I will give the carcases of the host of the Philistines this day unto the fowls of the air, and to the wild beasts of the earth; that all the earth may know that there is a God in Israel. And all this assembly shall know that the Lord saveth not with sword and spear; for the battle is the Lord's, and He will give you into our hands." 1 Sam. xvii, 46, 47. David acted out this confidence. "David *hasted* and *ran* towards the army to meet the Philistine."

If our trust were such as to give us a belief in the power of prayer, many a thing which now seems impossible would be easy: we should know how to produce great spiritual effects; we should pray with this conviction, "An answer (only in the Lord's way and time) *will surely* come." Let us not be above learning from a little child.

At the time of a great drought, several pious farmers agreed to hold a special meeting to pray for the much needed rain. When the appointed time came, the minister was surprised to see one of his little Sabbath-scholars bringing a huge old family umbrella, and asked

her why she did so on such a lovely morning. The child
gazed at him with evident surprise at the enquiry, and
replied, "why, sir, I thought as we were going to pray
God for rain, *I'd be sure to want the umbrella.*" While
they were praying, the wind rose, and the clear sky
became clouded, which was soon followed by a heavy
thunder-storm, by which those who came unprepared to
the meeting were drenched, while Mary and the minister
were sheltered by the umbrella her faith had led her to
bring.

Here are some practical helps to believing in this
union of cause and effect, in prayer. Let us call to mind

1. The large promises given in Holy Scripture to
prayer.

2. The statements which Holy Scripture makes on
this head.

3. The character of God as a true and faithful God.

4. The many instances of this recorded in Scripture.

5. And also in our own experience.

Thus, then, we have seen something of the Psalmist's
unreservedness of trust. May we aspire to having the
same. May we seek to grow in grace until we can say,
" I will trust the Lord *despite appearances ;* I will trust
in Him *though all be unknown ;* I will trust in Him, and
not in means, though means be ready to my hand ; I
will be sure that *if I call, He will hear ;* that there is an
answer for every prayer."

We have now, in the next place, to consider THE
GREAT OBJECT OF THIS TRUST. *It is* GOD. God *in
personal relationship with the soul ;* God assuming
various aspects, according to that soul's need.

That God does assume a variety of aspects, the soul exercised in spiritual things well knows. It recognises Him as ever the same God, although under different developments of Himself; just as a man knows that a prism is the same prism, although it exhibits different colours under different circumstances, and at different times; or as a man knows that a building is one and the same, though at one time the most prominent object be its massive buttress, and at another its tapering spire. At one time, the prominent idea of God is that of a Father; and at another, that of a Ruler; now, He is the Refuge; and now, the Shadow for the afflicted soul; as is man's need, so is God's development of Himself toward him.

And here, in this book of Psalms, we find determina- tions to trust God in each development of Himself; the Psalmist will not trust Him in one development of Himself, but refuse to do so in another. He does not say, "I will feel safe in Thee as a *Refuge* and a *Fortress*, but I cannot feel so safe only under the *shadow of Thy wing;*" he does not say, "I will trust Thee if Thou drawest me into *the secret of Thy tabernacle,* but I will not trust Thee amid *the ten thousands of the people.*" The "I will" of real, trusting, faith and love, is fixed on God Himself, irrespective of times and seasons. It is well, however, to contemplate the specific characters under which God presents Himself, as in relationship to His people; and to endeavour to attain to that high measure of faith, which will enable us to trust God in each of them.

If we turn to Psalm iii, 6, a passage to which we have already referred, we find the Lord there coming before us, as "the Ruler of the people." Ten thousands swarm around the Psalmist, but he will not be afraid. And the only ground upon which fear could be removed is the supremacy of God; the thought that, however lawless the people were, and however independent in their own mind, He was loftier than them all; He was Ruler in very truth.

Let *us* say, "I will not be afraid, I will trust, because I know that God is ruler over all." Circumstances often arise when it is a blessed thing for God's people to be able thus to trust. Enemies appear in perhaps unexpected quarters; it may be that we find our foes even amongst those of our own household; here and there we find them starting up, and even those whom we hoped would have been on our side prove the most bitter against us; sometimes we become the victims of a series of isolated attacks; and sometimes the enemy comes in like a flood, bursting upon us like a column of soldiers trained to act in concert. Is it not most comforting at such times to be able to trust in God as the "Ruler of the people?" One stronger than their malice or their passions, able to put His hook in their nose, and His bridle in their lips? Why should I be so much afraid of such and such an one, if God be the Ruler of the people? Why should I fear such and such a party, if God can sway and turn their hearts and plans exactly as He will? Why should I compromise principle, either to gain their favour or avert their wrath? Enemies of various kinds we meet with in the world; some who are our enemies on religious grounds, and some who are so for some worldly reasons, yet without any fault of ours. The way to be at peace, no matter what they say, or do, or plot, is to trust God in his character of a Ruler; and then, like the Psalmist of old, we can say, "I will not be afraid of ten thousands of people, which have set themselves against me round about."

We have now to retire for a moment from the strife of tongues, and the open hostility of foes, into the stillness and privacy of the chamber of sleep. Here, also, we find the "I will" of trust. "I will both lay me down in peace, and sleep; for Thou, Lord, only makest me dwell in safety." Psalm iv, 8.

God is here revealed to us as exercising *personal care in the still chamber*. And there is something here which should be inexpressibly sweet to the believer; for this shews the minuteness of God's care, the individuality of His love; how it condescends, and stoops, and acts, not only in great, but also in little spheres; not only where glory might be procured from great results, but where nought is to be had save the gratitude and love of a poor feeble creature, whose life has been protected and preserved, in a period of helplessness and sleep. How blessed would it be if we made a larger recognition of God in the still chamber; if we thought of Him as being there in all hours of illness, of weariness, and pain; if we believed that His interest and care are as much concentrated upon the feeble believer there, as upon His people when in the wider battle field of the strife of tongues. There is something inexpressibly touching in this "laying down" of the Psalmist. In thus lying down, he voluntarily gave up any guardianship of himself; he resigned himself into the hands of another; he did so completely, for, in the absence of all care, he slept; there was here a perfect trust.

Many a believer lies down, but it is not to sleep.
Perhaps he feels safe enough so far as his body is concerned; but cares and anxieties invade the privacy of his
chamber; they come to try his faith and trust; they
threaten, they frighten, and alas! prove too strong for
trust. Many a poor believer might say, "I will lay me
down, but not to sleep." The author met with a touching
instance of this, in the case of an aged minister whom
he visited in severe illness. This worthy man's circumstances were narrow, and his family trials were great;
he said, "the Doctor wants me to sleep, but how can I
sleep with care sitting on my pillow?" It is the
experience of some of the Lord's people, that although
equal to an emergency, or a continued pressure, a
re-action sets in afterwards; and when they come to be
alone, their spirits sink, and they do not realize that
strength from God, or feel that confidence in Him, which
they felt while the pressure was exerting its force.*
We have a remarkable instance of this in the case of
Elijah in 1 Kings, xviii, xix. At the end of the former
chapter he is represented to us as alone confronting the
idolatrous Israelites, the wrath of the king, and the four
hundred and fifty prophets of Baal, and the four hundred
prophets of the grove; in the beginning of the latter he
is a fugitive, running away from the threats of a woman.
When Elijah heard her threat he arose and went for his
life. There is a trial in stillness; and oftentimes the
still chamber makes a larger demand upon loving trust

---

* Ridley's brother offered to remain with him during the night
preceding his martyrdom, but the Bishop declined, saying, that
"he meant to go to bed, and sleep as quietly as ever he did in
his life."

than the battle field. Oh! that we could trust God more and more with personal things. Oh! that He were the God of our chamber, as well as of our temples and houses. Oh! that we could bring Him more and more into the minutiæ of daily life. If we did this, we should experience a measure of rest to which we are, perhaps, strangers now; we should have less dread of the sick chamber; we should have that unharassed mind which conduces most to repose, in body and soul; we should be able to say, " I will lie down and sleep *and leave to-morrow with God!*"

Beloved! Shall we not follow the Psalmist's example; shall not we also say, " I will both lay me down in peace and sleep;" shall not we also surrender ourselves into the holy and personal care of the Lord? Let us observe how loving trust secures rest, and the relaxation of the over-strung soul. The Psalmist would lay him down; he could take rest in God, and God's personal care of him. But how is it with us? If our trust be small, we can seldom thus rest and refresh ourselves in God; we cannot, if I might so speak, enjoy the pleasure of quiet in Him, and with Him; we may be able to walk, run, fight, speak, sing, anything, or everything, but rest.

Let us endeavour, then, more and more, in holy trust to realize the personal and vigilant care of God; to see that He who keepeth Israel shall neither slumber nor sleep. Let us learn as Luther did, who, looking out of his window one summer evening, saw, on a tree at hand, a little bird making his brief and easy dispositions for a night's rest. " Look," said he, " how that little fellow preaches faith to us all. He takes hold of his twig, tucks his head under his wing, and goes to sleep, *leaving*

God to think for him!" God is honoured by such trust, and we, on our part, shall be benefited; and as he who is well rested, comes forth from the privacy of his chamber, refreshed for the trials and labours of the day, and prepared to bear its burden and heat; so we, also, having been drawn aside from all turmoil for awhile, and enjoyed the security and conscious peace which is to be had in the felt presence of being alone with God, may go forth, able to *do* and to *endure* what, otherwise, might have been too much for our overtaxed strength. Jesus says to His people now, even as He did to His disciples of old, "Come ye aside, and rest awhile."

We now turn to Psalm lvii, 1, in which we have God presented to us under another aspect, *as one with over-shadowing wings.* "Be merciful unto me, O God, be merciful unto me; for my soul trusteth in Thee; yea, in the shadow of Thy wings will I make my refuge, until these calamities be overpast." The same idea occurs in Psalm lxi, 4. "I will trust in the covert of Thy wings."

We are all familiar with the image presented to us here, from its use by our blessed Saviour with reference to Jerusalem. "O Jerusalem, Jerusalem, thou that killest the prophets, and stonest them that are sent unto thee, how often would I have gathered thy children together, even as a hen gathereth her chickens under her wings, and ye would not!" Matt. xxiii, 37. And here, as in the care shewn in the sick man's chamber, there is a special personal presence of God, in which the soul finds ground for trust. But there is something peculiarly sweet and precious to the believer in the simile before us now; there is the active interference of love on behalf of an endangered loved one; there is that endangered loved one's faith and trust, making the shadow of the wing, to be sought as the sweet refuge.

Let us observe here, the trust of the Psalmist *in the presence of calamities.* We often pray to be delivered from calamities; we even trust that we shall be; but we do not pray to be made what we should be, in the very presence of the calamities; to live amid them, as long as they last, in the consciousness that we are held and sheltered by God, and can therefore remain in the midst of them, so long as they continue, without any hurt.

This continuing in the presence of the enemy, or of trial brought on by him, will be no more than was the lot of many an ancient worthy, yea, of the Captain of our salvation, Jesus Christ Himself. For forty days and nights, the Saviour was kept in the presence of Satan in the wilderness, and that, under circumstances of special trial, His human nature being weakened by want of food and rest. The furnace was heated seven times more than it was wont to be heated, but Shadrach, Meshach, and Abednego were kept a season amid its flames, (as calm and composed in the presence of the tyrant's last appliances of torture, as they were in the presence of himself,) before their time of deliverance came. And the livelong night did Daniel sit amongst the lions, and when he was taken up out of the den, "no manner of hurt was found upon him, because he believed in his God." They dwelt in the presence of the enemy, because they dwelt in the presence of God. "Thou preparest a table before me,'" says the Psalmist, "in the presence of mine enemies." Psalm xxiii, 5. And the promise of Israel is also ours. "When thou passest through the waters I will be with thee; and through the rivers, they shall not overflow thee; when thou walkest through the fire, thou shalt not be burned; neither shall the flame kindle upon thee." Isaiah xliii, 2.

The hen shelters her chickens under her wings, in the very presence of the enemy. Ah! how do we shrink from the presence of the enemy. We would have the enemy taken away from us, or have ourselves removed from him. We can, perhaps, exercise faith as regards either of these events; but to be able to live safely, and under a consciousness of shelter in his presence, is another thing; this is undoubtedly, a high degree of faith and trust. This we find the Psalmist exercising here; and this may the Lord enable us to exercise also. It is for His glory that we should dwell at times in the presence of our enemies; that we should be there under the shadow of His wing, and in effect, say, "My God can sustain my cause, despite your continual efforts and presence. He need not destroy your activity, and annihilate you, in order to keep me in safety; He can continually and evenly neutralize all your efforts; your intended prey is kept continually in your sight, but you have no power to touch it, or to do it any hurt." Satan is often thus foiled. He has not to go and look for the believer. He has not the satisfaction of saying, "I was crushed by a force so far superior to me, that it was no disgrace to me to be foiled." He has the misery of feeling his impotence against a sheltered believer; of knowing that the prey is, as it were, actually within his reach, and that he cannot touch it. And although this presents no visible spectacle to the human eye, yet we may be assured that it does to that of those, who can see invisible things. How is Satan put to shame before his kindred evil spirits, when the weak believer is actually in his sight, actually before him, and he cannot touch him! How is his impotence against the saints brought forth! How are the promises of God proved good, and His mercies proved true! We may rest assured, that great ends are being accomplished by our being *kept* in the midst of calamities, kept *in* them as well as *from* them. Let us remember this, when we contemplate the passage now before us; let us seek to be kept *in* trial when God calls us thereto, and cultivate, by the help and teaching of the Spirit, that determined trust which shall enable us to say, "In the shadow of Thy wings will I make my refuge, until these calamities be overpast." "I will trust in the covert of Thy wings."

The passage before us has yet further meaning, and brings to our notice not only the preservation of the believer in the midst of calamities, but also his *actual closeness to God.* To be under the shadow or covert of the wing implies closeness; to be under the shadow of God's wing, implies "closeness to God." Let us weigh this well; let us attempt to realize it, and it will bring great peace and assurance to our hearts. We know what a perfect sense of security the child has, from the consciousness of nearness to its parent. One step away from that parent, and all is trembling and tears; but there is no need of these, when the child hides behind the parent, or touches, or holds him. God is close to His people, and is willing that they should both know and feel it. Satan comes close, and the Lord will not be far away; when we realize the closeness of the Evil One, there is no reason why we should not realize the closeness of God also. The stronger faith is, the closer will it ever draw a man to God; and the feeling that we are near God, and that God is near us, will give us peace. There is, perhaps, no sense of security so great as that which man derives in this way. The "covering with the wing" implies an "immediate presence of God, and that in connection with us," which must be of inestimable price, when danger is actually at hand.

Once more : we have here brought before us the idea of *warmth*. While the wing shelters from impending evil, the body infuses some of its own warmth into the sheltered one; and thus, perhaps, the vital heat is restored, the current of which was impeded by the chill which we know comes on with fear. If we act as the Psalmist did, and seek the sheltering wing in real, trusting faith, we also shall find warmth as well as safety. God will impart to us of Himself; our vital heat shall come from heaven. The believer would be saved many and many a cold shiver, if he habitually sought the sheltering wing; many a tremor which shook the soul might thus have been stilled; and many an icy feeling have been thawed; and though natural resources would have supplied no warmth, warmth would have come from God Himself.

All comfort in present calamity is to be had by nearness to God. Such comfort many of the ancient saints possessed. Paul and Silas could even sing praises in their prison-house. Nearness to God will infuse into us that which no nervousness, no fear can chill; in nearness to Him we shall find, that, even in the midst of tribulation, comfort can abound. The Rev. Charles Simeon's life contains a "Memorandum on meeting with injurious treatment," which concludes in these words. " My experience all this day has been, and I hope will yet continue to be, a confirmation of that word, 'Thou wilt hide me in the secret of Thy presence from the strife of tongues.' Insult an angel before the throne, and what would he care about it ? Just such will be my feeling, whilst I am hid in the secret of my Redeemer's presence."

The following thoughts may help some of the Lord's people to hasten under the shadow of His wing, when calamity comes on.

1. At such times the warmth of our love is likely to cool, and by great nearness to God we shall receive fresh heat, which shall hold our soul in life.

2. When the believer shelters himself under God's wing, Satan has to deal with God, rather than with him, and so he becomes sure of deliverance.

3. Any attempts to stand out alone, and fight in our own strength, and with the measure of grace which we possess, apart from the immediate recognition of God, will be sure to bring upon us the consequences of spiritual pride.

4. When close to God, hidden under His wing, the most prominent idea in the believer's mind will be, the immediate nearness and presence of God; and that will bring him peace.

5. There is ever in God, a perfect readiness to receive and shelter us; and that, even after we have been wounded by our own rashness and presumption. If we will but seek the refuge, we shall be sure of welcome.

We now turn to another aspect in which God presents Himself as an object of the believer's trust.

The Psalmist says, in Psalm xci, 2, "I will say of the Lord, He is my refuge and my fortress." The shadow of the wing brought before us the idea of even a mother's care, her love joined with protection; here we have not so much an *active* as a *passive* defence. Resistance, the power of repelling assault, and such like circumstances of war, come prominently before us.

It is beside our present purpose to enter into all the points, in which a similitude exists between God and a fortress; let us rather consider His appearance under this aspect, in relation to the shadow of the wing, which has just come under our notice. There is a strong contrast between the two. We have seen the believer's defence by the watchful eye, by the head turning every way to meet the assault, by the very intensity of life exercising itself on its behalf; (and it is a blessed thought that intensity of life, even of God's life, is in exercise for the sheltered believer;) but now we see the frowning fortress, the thick and battlemented wall; all is still, in the consciousness of mighty strength. The idea before us is the repelling of assault by strength; the trembling creature within the fortress is not presented to our view at all; he is there, that we know;—the presentation is that of the great God Himself, in all His might.

The fortress is an edifice planned for purposes of defence; forethought is to be seen in all its arrangements and contrivances. The hen shielding her chicken, developes the active instinct of nature; the fortress shielding one taking refuge in it, developes forethought, and arrangement, and skill. From the prominence of these various ideas, there is great comfort for the trusting believer. When he thinks of the first, he says to him-

self, "God's-very nature secures His active interference
in my behalf;" when he thinks of the second, he says,
"God's *mind*, as well as God's *nature*, is on my side.
Satan has to contend against God in His forethought,
and His plans, and His arrangements; and as all these
develop infinite wisdom, what prospect has he of being
able to succeed against me?" This thought would at
times be very profitable to us, for we are tempted continually to make our own plans, and to trust in them.
We will construct an entrenchment in the open field, it
shall evidence our skill, and be defended by our valour;
but, alas! our mighty resolutions often end in our defeat.*
But what can Satan, skilled though he be in all spiritual
sieges, as well as personal encounters, do against the
mind of God? There he finds every contingency guarded
against, every avenue closed, every possibility of assault
utterly destroyed; he may survey the fortress, he may
make a demonstration against it, he may, in his madness,

* Thus it was with the Israelites when they attacked the
Amalekites and Canaanites, as recorded in Numbers xiv. "And
they rose up early in the morning, and gat them up into the top
of the mountain, saying, 'Lo, we be here, and will go up unto the
place which the Lord hath promised: for we have sinned.' And
Moses said, 'Wherefore now do ye transgress the commandment
of the Lord? but it shall not prosper. Go not up, for the Lord
is not among you; that ye be not smitten before your enemies.
For the Amalekites and the Canaanites are there before you, and
ye shall fall by the sword: because ye are turned away from the
Lord, therefore the Lord will not be with you. But they presumed to go up unto the hill top: nevertheless the ark of the
covenant of the Lord, and Moses, departed not out of the camp.
Then the Amalekites came down, and the Canaanites which dwelt
in that hill, and smote them, and discomfited them, even unto
Hormah."

even go so far as to venture to assail it, but the fortress must be stormed, before the one taking refuge in it can be hurt. Hear it, O trembling, yet trusting believer; God must cease to be, before the Evil One can take away thy life! Thou art surrounded (if I might so speak) by the arrangements of God; all His foreknowledge and wisdom are keeping thee, all His strength is put forth for thee; surely a realization of this should help thee also to take up the Psalmist's words, and say, "I will say of the Lord, He is my strength, and my fortress."

This idea stands forth, also, by its visibility, in strong contrast to that of the invisible watcher in the still chamber. The fortress is something built, and established, and manifest; it gives an impression of strength from its very appearance; it is a plan carried out into a result. Under this aspect it is our privilege to see our God. When He presents Himself in the aspect of a fortress for His people, He shews himself as simply carrying out His own designs. To love them, to protect them, to save them from the strongest assault, to present an impassable barrier to the utmost efforts of their foe, these are God's designs. He carries them out *in Himself*. As stone cemented to stone, presents to the enemy a front which he cannot successfully assail, so all that makes up the glorious character of God, connected and knit together, presents an obstacle to Satan, against which his utmost efforts cannot prevail. Oh! that we fully realized the strength of the fortress, the refuge which is ours! Oh! that we trusted it as we *should*, nay, let us not say "as we should," but "as it is our privilege to do." God loved His own people from all eternity; God thought *of* them, and *for* them; God intended to manifest Himself on their behalf; He determined that the excellencies which were in Himself should assume a substantial development for them. The believer may not only say, "I know what God *thinks* for me," but also, "I know what he *is* for me." And the more he ponders this, and seeks for the grace of faith, and enlarged trust, the more plainly will the outlines of his mighty fortress begin to be visible; point after point of its great strength will develop itself, as the mists which hang around his spiritual vision disappear; and he will say of the Lord, "He is my refuge and my fortress; my God, in Him will I trust."

It is, further, a source of comfort to the believer to reflect, that that on which he puts his trust is *established* and *immovable*. Changes take place above and around the fortress, but its massive buttresses still stand unmoved, and its battlements frown defiance at the strength of the foe. The clouds above are fleeting past, it may be in silvery brightness, or it may be in pall-like gloom; the leaves are budding, or fading, according to their seasons upon the earth; but there stands the fortress, established and unchanged.

And why is it that many of the Lord's dear people do not realize the great comfort which, from the very fact of God's being their fortress, ought assuredly to be theirs? Because they look at the changes going on all around, and so miss the truth that He is unchangeable. So long as Peter looked at Jesus, all was well; but when his eyes were turned to the waves, and he saw that the sea was boisterous, then his faith began to fail. If we look at the clouds, ever varying, and never continuing in one stay, we are not likely to be impressed with the idea of stability; if we look at the changing leaves and trees, 'continuance' is assuredly not the idea that will come prominently before our minds; but let the aspect of the heavens, or of the seasons, be what they may, there stands the fortress; and 'continuance' is one of the grand ideas connected with it.

We greatly need to have impressed upon our minds, a deep conviction of the firmness, the abiding nature of the character of God. We look at ourselves, and our feelings; and at times, when all seems favorable, take some refuge in them; but then they change, and we are in distress. We look at the effect which time appears to have had on some, who once seemed the greenest in the garden, and we see them verging to decay, their first love having waxed cold; but we look not at God in Christ, unchangeable and unchanged, "the same yesterday, and to-day, and for ever." Let us look at our fortress, and not at what is going on around it, or at the numbers about to come against it, and seek for grace to trust.

The last aspect which we have to notice, in which God presents Himself as the object of His people's trust, is in Psalm cxviii, 6. "The Lord is on my side, I will not fear: what can man do unto me?"

A fresh set of ideas seems brought before us here; embracing, no doubt, many of the points which we have already considered, but distinctive, nevertheless. The reason which the Psalmist gives here for his trusting, or for his not fearing, is the great fact, that the Lord is on his side; and the prominent idea which this brings before us is *Alliance ; the making common cause*, which the great God undoubtedly does, with imperfect, yet with earnest, trusting man.

We know very well, the great anxiety shewn by men, in all their worldly conflicts, to secure the aid of a powerful ally; in their lawsuits, to retain the services of a powerful advocate; or, in their attempts at worldly advancement, to win the friendship and interest of those who can further the aims they have in view. When Herod was highly displeased with them of Tyre and Sidon, they did not venture to approach him until they had made Blastus, the king's chamberlain, their friend. If such and such a person be on their side, men think that all must go well. Who so well off as he who is able to say, "The Lord is on my side?"

The great God Himself, then, makes common cause with His people. We would beg the reader to dwell upon these two words, "common cause." The believer's cause is God's; and why? Because God's cause is the believer's also. This may not appear prominently at first sight. The tried and tempted believer, absorbed in his own necessities, and in the pressure which he is feeling, and the trial he is enduring, may say, "I am the sufferer; I trust indeed that God will help me, but His aid will come as an *external* help; it will be an *outflowing* of His *goodness* towards me." Thus he speaks; but he does not say, "His interests are identified with mine; He will be on my side, because my cause is His cause, and His cause my cause; because we are in relationship, and must have a community of interest."

The realization that the cause of God, and that of the believer are one and the same, will ever make the saint seek, and feel sure of having His help, in hours of trial; he will never feel so sure, as when he knows, that the Lord is working for His own name's sake. Here, then, is a grand position of strength. The believer says, "I know that instead of being in conflict with evil, I might have been left under the power of evil. I know that had I been left to myself, I might have been found in the ranks of those whom I now count as my bitterest foes. But He has called me to the knowledge of the truth, and now His interests are as much concerned as mine; He will help me, not only for my own individual, personal sake, but also for His own sake."

A community of interest is a wonderful bond amongst men; we consider it the strongest guarantee for unity of action; we want no other bond than this; we feel that it stands in the place of all others. We think rightly. Alas! for the selfishness of man, that it should be so. There is another side, however, in which this community of interest is to be looked at; and from this point of view the idea of selfishness is wholly excluded. God cannot be selfish; He has given us one grand proof that He cannot be; He "spared not His own Son, but delivered Him up for us all." In the case now before us, God appears on man's side, not only because He loves man, but because that for which the believer contends is the truth; and for holiness' sake, and truth's sake, God will stand upon his side. God is for truth and for holiness, and the believer has by grace been called into the knowledge of these, and by circumstances, into conflict for them; he cannot, he shall not stand alone, God will be on his side.

It is a matter of great importance to realize this; for it is, under any circumstances, a trying position, to stand alone. We may be, we, no doubt, often are, called upon to stand alone, so far as earthly companionship is con-

cerned. Elijah was in such a position, so was Daniel, so
was David; and many a solitary one in a family, and
many a minister in a dark and dreary district, has known
the bitterness, the difficulty, and the trial of such a
position. We cannot secure ourselves from it. When
we seem best supported by human help, then may come
a sudden stroke, and we may be left to get on as best we
can, with increasing enemies, and thickening clouds. It
is at periods such as these, that men's hearts have often
failed them. They seem to themselves to be deserted as
Uriah was, in the forefront of the battle, that they may
be slain; they say with the prophet, "I only am left, and
they seek my life to take it away;" and at such periods
but one thing can avail them, and that is, the realization
that God is on their side. At such times the people of
the Lord must see into the invisible; they must discern
a helper where man can see none; they must (if they
would avert the direst calamity) be able practically to
say, "The Lord is on my side." If they cannot do this,
we need not wonder if something akin to despair take
possession of their minds. They see the enemy; perhaps he draws out all his forces, on purpose to overwhelm
the poor tried believer with a sight of the fearful odds
which seem to be against him. How can he face such a
multitude alone?

Let God's people, on occasions like these, learn a
lesson from the lilies of the field, and the fowls of the
air; even they are not alone—the first are clothed by
Him, the second are fed by Him. The people of God,
if they read nature aright, might learn much from even
her humblest page; for the bending grass has a voice as
distinct, if not as loud, as the sturdy oak. Myriad

voices ever testify that God is near. This truth was found beautifully realized a little while ago by one of the agents of the London City Mission, who was visiting in one of those courts where the houses are crowded with inhabitants, and where every room is the dwelling of a family. In a lone room at the top of one of these houses, the agent met with an aged woman, whose scanty pittance of half-a-crown a week, was scarcely sufficient for her bare subsistence. He observed, in a broken teapot that stood in the window, a strawberry plant, growing and flourishing. He remarked, from time to time, how it continued to grow, and with what jealous care it was watched and tended. "Your plant flourishes nicely; you will soon have strawberries upon it." "Oh Sir," replied the woman, "it is not for the sake of the fruit that I grow it." "Then why do you take so much care of it?" he inquired. "Well Sir," was the answer, "I am very poor, too poor to keep any living creature; but it is a great comfort to me to have that living plant, for I know it can only live by the power of God; and as I see it live and grow from day to day, it tells me that God is near." A small moss was the means of sustaining the courage of the celebrated traveller Mungo Park. He was robbed by banditti on the 25th of August, 1796, when on his road from Kooma to Sebidooloo, and was stripped of everything. "After they were gone," he says, "I sat for some time looking around me with amazement and terror. Whichever way I turned, nothing appeared but danger and difficulty. I saw myself in the midst of a vast wilderness, in the depth of the rainy season, naked and alone, surrounded by savage animals, and men still more savage. I was five hundred miles from the nearest

European settlement. All these circumstances crowded at once on my recollection, and I confess that my spirits began to fail me. I considered my fate as certain, and that I had no alternative but to lie down and perish. The influence of religion, however, aided and supported me. I reflected that no human prudence or foresight could possibly have averted my present sufferings. I was indeed a stranger in a strange land, yet I was still under the protecting eye of that Providence, who has condescended to call Himself the stranger's Friend. At this moment, painful as my reflections were, the extraordinary beauty of a small moss, in fructification, irresistibly caught my eye. I mention this, to show from what trifling circumstances the mind will sometimes derive consolation; for, though the whole plant was not larger than the top of one of my fingers, I could not contemplate the delicate conformation of its roots, leaves, and capsula, without admiration. 'Can that Being (thought I) who planted, watered, and brought to perfection, in this obscure part of the world, a thing which appears of so small importance, look with unconcern upon the situation and sufferings of creatures formed after His own image? surely not!' Reflections like these would not allow me to despair. I started up, and, disregarding both hunger and fatigue, travelled forward, assured that relief was at hand; and I was not disappointed. In a short time I came to a small village."

And even if the tried and tempted saint be not reduced absolutely to despair, he is at least very likely to be *depressed* to a fearful extent. He may be conscious of his rectitude of purpose; he may be fully convinced of the abstract truth of all for which he has to contend he may believe that God can do great things; but it is all to no purpose if he cannot realize the presence of God on his side. Once let the conviction of this have full power upon the mind, and then the believer becomes strong indeed, and independent of outward circumstances. He may be deserted of his own wife, as Job was; or of his chief friends, as David was; or of those who had companied with him the longest, as Jesus was; but the consciousness that God is on his side will carry him through.

Dear reader! are you sure that God is on your side? Is your case like that of Peter's; though Satan desires to have you that he may sift you as wheat, do you feel that Jesus says of you, "But *I* have prayed for thee, that thy faith fail not?" Have you made peace with God through the blood of the Lamb? Do you love that which He loves, and hate that which He hates? Are you *true* in these feelings, although perhaps very imperfect, and very weak? Do you realize that God has been pleased to bind Himself to you, by your acceptance of the Saviour as your own? Then you, also, like the Psalmist, need not fear what man can do unto you, nor what can be done against you, by those evil spirits which are stronger than man, and work by man. It is highly possible that you may have to stand alone—and yet not alone, for the great God is with you. The fact of His being on your side is everything; in that thought you will find both strength and peace. "If it had not been the Lord who was on our side, now may Israel say; if it had not been the Lord who was on our side, when men rose up against us: then they had swallowed us up quick, when their wrath was kindled against us: then the waters had overwhelmed us, the stream had gone over our soul: then the proud waters had gone over our soul. Blessed be the Lord, who hath not given us as a prey to their teeth. Our soul is escaped as a bird out of the snare of the fowlers: the snare is broken, and we are escaped. Our help is in the name of the Lord, who made heaven and earth." Psalm cxxiv.

The thought of *decisive action*, or taking an active part, is also plainly brought out here. We cannot say that a man is on our side if, when we are hard pressed, and need his aid, he remains passive, and takes no steps on our behalf. The very expression which we are considering now, implies assault, and help given in that assault; one is assailed, or obliged to stand upon his defence, and another is lending him his aid, or prepared so to do.

It cannot be denied that God's people too often forget His activity.* They look upon Him as reigning above, as

---

* It is not uncommon for Satan to keep before the eyes of God's people the value of *their own* activity, while he carefully hides the activity *of God*. The consequence is, trust in self, and distrust of Him, followed by discomfort and distress. Self, and the part self has to play, take up a position in the mind wholly disproportioned to their importance. Whilst called upon to act, and esteeming it an honour to be fellow-workers with God, we should see, also, how He can do without us. The following anecdote may help us to see the value of a common sense view of the activity of God, and may further help us to the enjoyment of that rest spoken of in page 33.

When Bulstrode Whitelock was embarking as Cromwell's envoy to Sweden, in 1653, he was much disturbed in mind as he rested in Harwich on the preceding night, which was very stormy, while he reflected on the distracted state of the nation. It happened that a confidential servant slept in an adjacent bed, who, finding having all resources at His command, yea, as being Himself the one and only resource needed; but not as occupying an *active* position with those who are actually in the fight; hence they look at what *they* can do, and how long *they* can hold out, and what graces *they* have, wherewith to contend; but forget to look for positive and decided action from the One who is on their side. Let us avoid this mistake; let us say, "God will work;" let us expect Him to work, and He assuredly will.

Nor must we forget the idea of *co-operation* which is presented to us here. At first sight, it may seem presumptuous to speak of co-operation with God; but the idea is a scriptural one, as we shall see by referring to 1 Cor. iii, 9. "For we are labourers together with God." The Lord's people are workers together with Him, and He is a worker together with them; they are both in action, and for the same cause.

There is in this fact, something very comforting for our souls. When we are called upon to work, God will work also. He never by circumstances calls any man,

that his master could not sleep, at length said:—"Pray, Sir, will you give me leave to ask you a question?"

"Certainly."

"Pray, Sir, do not you think that God governed the world very well before you came into it?"

"Undoubtedly."

"And pray, Sir, do not you think that He will govern it quite as well, when you are gone out of it?"

"Certainly."

"Then, Sir, pray excuse me, but do not you think you may trust Him to govern it quite as well as long as you live?"

To this question Whitelock had nothing to reply; but, turning about soon fell fast asleep, till he was summoned to embark.

either to resist evil, or to do good, but that He Himself is willing to work together with him. How much readier should we be to enter upon conflict with evil, or to undertake difficult tasks for God, if only we could realize this! The sense of weakness would no longer oppress us; the consciousness of *disproportion to our work* would never daunt us; we should feel that God was with us, and that His present energy pervaded every effort made in humility and faith. Do we not too often fix our thoughts upon what *we ourselves* are doing, upon how *we* are resisting evil, or accomplishing good; do we not practically say, "Am I equal to the task imposed upon me?" Let us remember, that God will work too; that His strength will be in all our efforts; that He will work together with us. It may be that man will not recognise this; that Satan, taking advantage of our weak natures, will try to seduce us into spiritual pride, saying "*You* have done this or that;" but let us recognise God working in us, and we shall thus, at one and the same time, possess humility and strength. The working of God, and the recognition of God, are beautifully brought before us in Isaiah xli, 13, &c. "For *I* the Lord thy God will hold thy right hand, saying unto thee, Fear not, *I* will help thee. Fear not, thou worm Jacob, and ye men of Israel; *I* will help thee, saith the Lord, and thy Redeemer, the Holy One of Israel. Behold, *I* will make thee a new sharp threshing instrument, having teeth: thou shalt thresh the mountains, and beat them small, and shalt make the hills as chaff. Thou shalt fan them, and the wind shall carry them away, and the whirlwind shall scatter them: *and thou shalt rejoice in the* LORD, *and shalt glory in the Holy One of Israel.*"

Let us take care, also, that as God is graciously pleased to be on our side, and to co-operate with us, so also we be ready to be on His side, and to co-operate with Him. It is as true, that in many points He permits us to co-operate with Him, as that He is graciously pleased to co-operate with us. It is through man that He carries out many of His greatest designs upon the earth. Some of these are brought to pass through the instrumentality of those who hate Him; and the wrath of man is made to praise Him; but many through the active work of His own people. The man of God should be ready to co-operate with Him at His first invitation or command; he should not hang back as even Moses did, who would have excused himself by his unreadiness of speech; or as Jonah did, who would even flee from the presence of the Lord; or as Barak did, who lost the honour which might have been his portion, when Sisera was sold into the hand of a woman. So long as we look at ourselves, our feebleness will make us decline the responsibility; but the conciousness that we are but instruments in the hand of God, should make us willing to be wrought with by Him. The case of David is full of teaching for us in this. When he went forth to fight Goliath, he was surely in himself wholly disproportioned to the task; his limbs were not as strong as the giant's; his height was not so great; his practice in warfare was absolutely nothing; true, he had contended with the terrible spring of the lion, and with the crushing embrace of the bear; but these were wholly different from conflict with a man, trained to war from his youth. But despite all this, he went out on the Lord's side; he knew that he was a worker together with God; and he accepted the challenge of the Philistine, as of one who had defied the armies of the living God—as of one whom he would meet in the name of God. It was God, assuredly, who was engaged in that great conflict; it was His eye that marked the place in the giant's forehead, where the fatal missile was to sink; it was His influence that guided it through the air, so that its flight was true for the destined spot; it was His might that energized the arm of David, as he slung forth the smooth stone upon its errand of death. Let the example of this great warrior of God not be lost on us: if we feel that the Lord calls on us to work, we may rest assured, that it is not to do so alone; the strength will be not in the instrument itself, but in the way it is used.

These are some of the practical thoughts resulting from the truth, that God is on His people's side.

1. I never can be left alone, in anything I am called upon to do for God.

2. Nor can I be ever left alone, in any resistance which I have to offer for God.*

---

* Luther was enabled, by the power of simple faith to realize a peace which was not possessed by his fellow labourer Melancthon. The latter seemed overwhelmed at the circumstances in which he was placed. He writes to Luther, " My dwelling is in perpetual tears. My consternation is indescribable. O my father! I do not wish my words to exaggerate my sorrows; but without your consolations it is impossible for me here to enjoy the least peace." Luther traces Melancthon's trouble to a want of simplicity in faith. "As for Melancthon, it is his philosophy that tortures him, and nothing else, for our cause is in the very hands of Him who can say, with unspeakable dignity, 'No one shall pluck it out of my hands.' I would not have it in our hands, and it would not be desirable that it were so. I have had many

3. I must have on my side the full benefit of the heavenly alliance, in God's thought, His resources, His energy.

4. How wonderful the condescension, and the love, which makes the great God stoop to alliance with man!

5. In this I have the pledge of victory.

6. In all courses of action we should seek the assurance that God is on our side.

7. The Lord's being on my side, will be sure to develop itself practically.

Some practical results which should follow :—

1. The falling away of human friends, and the drying up of human resources, should not stop me in my spiritual warfare.

2. I ought to bring as vividly before my mind as I can, the alliance with God, and realize it as a matter of fact; so as to make it confront all the strength that is against me, and compensate for all desertions from me, and weakness in me.

3. In my personal conflicts, I should feel that I do not stand alone; and in active service, that I do not go forth alone.

things in my hands, and I have lost them all, but whatever I have been able to place in God's, I still possess."

On learning that Melancthon's anguish still continued, Luther wrote to him; and these are words that should be preserved :— " Grace and peace in Christ! in Christ, I say, and not in the world, Amen. I hate, with exceeding hatred, those extreme cares which consume you. If the cause is unjust, abandon it; if the cause is just, why should we belie the promises of Him who commanded us to sleep without fear? Can the devil do more than kill us? Christ will not be wanting to the work of justice and of truth. He lives; He reigns; what fear, then, can we have," &c.

4. This one fact, of "The Lord being on my side," should in my estimation far overbalance all the confederacies and alliances against me; when I see them, I should destroy their terrifying influence by a consideration of this. In Psa. lxxxiii, we have brought before us the strong confederacies of the enemy. "They have taken crafty counsel against Thy people, and consulted against Thy hidden ones. They have said, 'Come and let us cut them off from being a nation, that the name of Israel may be no more in remembrance.' For they have consulted together with one consent, they are confederate against Thee. The tabernacles of Edom, and the Ishmaelites; of Moab, and the Hagarenes; Gebal, and Ammon, and Amalek; the Philistines with the inhabitants of Tyre; Assur also is joined with them, they have holpen the children of Lot." Such was the confederacy, it was strong both in men and money; but the Psalmist looks to his God to act against them—he says, "O, my God, make them as the stubble before the wind." And in calling upon God thus to break up the confederacy, and destroy those engaged in it, he reminds Him of former mighty acts. "Do unto them as unto the Midianites; as to Sisera, as to Jabin, at the brook of Kison; which perished at Endor, they became as dung for the earth. Make their nobles like Oreb and like Zeeb: yea, all their princes as Zeba and Zalmunna."

The Lord shews us, in Isa. vii, how easily He can deal with a confederacy. Rezin, the king of Syria, and Pekah, the son of Remaliah, king of Israel, go up toward Jerusalem to war against it, but cannot prevail against it. "And it was told the house of David, saying, Syria is confederate with Ephraim. And his heart was moved, and the heart of his people, as the trees of the wood are moved by the wind. Then said the Lord unto Isaiah, Go forth now to meet Ahaz, thou, and Shear-jashub thy son, at the end of the conduit of the upper pool, in the highway of the fuller's field. And say unto him, Take heed and be quiet: fear not, neither be faint-hearted for the two tails of these smoking fire-brands, for the fierce anger of Rezin with Syria, and of the son of Remaliah. Because Syria, Ephraim, and the son of Remaliah have taken evil counsel against thee, saying, 'Let us go up against Judah and vex it, and let us make a breach therein for us, and set a king in the midst of it, even the son of Tabeal:' thus saith the LORD GOD,"— mark, dear reader, how He will deal with the confederacy —"It shall not stand, neither shall it come to pass. For the head of Syria is Damascus, and the head of Damascus is Rezin, and within three score and five years shall Ephraim be broken, that it be not a people."

Nehemiah was tried by the existence of a confederacy against him, when he undertook the rebuilding of the walls of Jerusalem, but he knew where to go for help. "It came to pass that when Sanballat, and Tobiah, and the Arabians, and the Ammonites, and the Ashdodites, heard that the walls of Jerusalem were made up, and that the breaches began to be stopped, then they were very wroth. And conspired all of them together to come and to fight against Jerusalem, and to hinder us. Nevertheless we made our prayer unto God, and set a watch against them day and night because of them." The conspiracy of Joseph's brethren against him ended in his being promoted so high as to be only second to Pharoah upon his throne.

It may be well to add also a few words upon *the circumstances under which this trust is to be exercised.* A good deal has already been said incidentally on this point; it may, however, be helpful to gather these circumstances together, and look at them by themselves.

In Psa. iii, 6, and also cxviii, 6, the times of danger from man are prominently alluded to. " I will not be afraid," said the Psalmist, " of ten thousands of the people, that have set themselves against me round about;" and again, in Psa. cxviii, 6, he says, " The Lord is on my side, I will not fear what man can do unto me."

Here we have times of danger from men brought prominently before our notice, and the Psalmist's determination to trust God, no matter how imminent the danger might be. Now we must not *under*-rate, even as we should not *over*-rate these dangers from men. When our fellow-men are opposed to us, and threaten us with evil, and proceed to active opposition, we have great need of Trust in God. These visible dangers are likely to exercise a powerful influence upon such frail creatures as we are; they press us closely; they assume a distinctness, and vividness, and reality, which are calculated to daunt the heart; we feel that we have to contend with evil in its activity. When we can plainly see that men are working evil against us, then evil seems to have *embodied* itself against us; we seem to feel that it now has means of working, that it will not remain idle, that we are within its reach; it soon makes itself felt.

At times the struggling believer has to meet with opposition, and the probability of hurt from the very men who should aid and befriend him; he is obliged to

say, "My foes are those of my own household," (see
Matt. x, 36.)   "Yea, mine own familiar friend, in whom I
trusted, which did eat of my bread, hath lifted up his heel
against me," (Psa. xli, 9.) As in the case of David, a wayward child may be the instrument of evil; as in Joseph's,
it may be one's brethren; as in Job's, it may be one's
wife ; and danger is peculiarly appalling when it comes
upon us from those, who from their nearness to us know
all the avenues of our heart, all our circumstances and
habits in life, where and how we can most easily be
hurt.

When evil assumes this present, and this vivid form,
the best way to meet it is by making our Trust do the
same. We must oppose a vivid sight of God, to a vivid
sight of man. And if we do this aright our fear will
soon subside; we shall say with the Psalmist, "I will not
fear what man can do unto me." When Goliath came
forth, there was a special presentation of man, but David
met it with faith; when the eight hundred and fifty
prophets of Baal, and the grove, confronted Elijah on
Carmel, there was a special presentation of man, but
Elijah also met them in the power of faith; when the
armies of Sennacherib came round about Jerusalem,
(Isaiah xxxvi,) and that proud monarch's blasphemous
letter was delivered to Hezekiah, there was also a special
presentation of man, but the king of Judah meets it
with faith, which enables him to oppose to it a special
presentation of God; he owns Sennacherib's might, and
reminds God that it is *He* he is reproaching, (verses 17
and 20,) "Incline Thine ear, O Lord, and hear; open
Thine eyes, O Lord, and see : and hear all the words of
Sennacherib, which hath sent to reproach the living

God. * * Now therefore, O Lord our God, save us from his hand, that all the kingdoms of the earth may know that Thou art the Lord, even Thou only."

No doubt there is much which man can do, to hurt and injure us, so far as this world is concerned. Our Lord Himself tells us this in Luke xii, 4, "And I say unto you, my friends, be not afraid of them that kill the body :"— men can at times proceed even to the last extremity; and if to that, then to other assaults calculated in themselves to terrify or annoy. Our Lord tells us this in Luke xxi, 12, "They shall lay their hands on you and persecute you, delivering you up to the synagogues, and into prisons, bringing you before kings and rulers for my name's sake." See what a description St. Paul gives us of his sufferings in 2 Cor. xi, 23, &c. Amongst other things he tells us that he had "stripes above measure," that he was " often in prisons, and in deaths; five times he received forty stripes save one, thrice was he beaten with rods, once was he stoned;" he knew what it was to experience "perils from robbers and from his own countrymen, perils from the heathen, and perils from false brethren." Our enemies can break in upon, and disturb the peace of our home ; they can hurt our bodies, and our means of livelihood; they can vex and thwart us in many ways. Even if the enemy be not *active* in his opposition, he can do us harm nevertheless, by looking coldly upon us, by engendering suspicion against us, by withdrawing from us some wonted countenance and support; all these are serious things, when we are perhaps placed, to all human appearance, in a position of dependence upon the very persons who treat us thus. May we have grace to meet all this by simple, vivid trust, by seeing God to be for us with the same distinctness that we see man to be against us!

Let us consider also, *the time of helplessness* of the believer. We can imagine no more helpless condition than that of sleep. And what the Psalmist says is this, "I will both lay me down in peace, and sleep, for Thou, Lord, only makest me dwell in safety." Helplessness is one of the great occasions for determined trust.

If we examine the records of Holy Scripture, and the lives of God's people as detailed therein, we shall find the most eminent saints placed from time to time in positions of helplessness. What could be more helpless, as we have just seen, than Jacob's position when he went forth to meet Esau? or than Joseph's, when he lay in Potiphar's prison; or than Jeremiah's, when he was in the bottom of the pit; or than Elijah's, when he stood alone in confronting the prophets of Baal; or than David's, when the people spake of stoning him; and again, when Shimei cursed him and threw dust at him; or than Daniel's, when he was shut up in the lion's den; or than the three children's, when they were thrown down into the burning fiery furnace; or than the disciples', when they were sent forth staff in hand, as sheep amongst wolves?

That we should from time to time find ourselves in a helpless position is no new thing: this is no mere fortuitous falling together of circumstances, but a permitted arrangement of God; He will teach us the perfection of His strength, in the perfection of our weakness. We may rest assured, that we are no less called upon to *realize* our own intrinsic helplessness, than to put forth whatever powers and faculties have been bestowed upon us by God; we have to be taught our utter helplessness, apart from

God, as well as what we should do in the power of God.
The apostle found this sense of personal weakness no bar
to his being strong for the Lord; he did not find it bring
him into such sad circumstances, as would be the natural
consequences of such weakness; he said, "When I am
weak, then am I strong." God had said to him, "My
strength is made perfect in weakness," and he had
realized the truth of that. What we, however, desire
to attain to, is the being able to say, "*I* can do this, *I*
can do that;" we want the personal comfortable feeling
that we are individually equal to this or that; and there
is very often a temptation hidden in this; for Satan, when
once he finds a man working in any feeling of mere personal spiritual strength, soon tries to make him work in
a feeling of personal strength which is natural, and not
spiritual at all. St Paul could say, "I can do all things
through Christ which strengtheneth me;" but oh! that
strengthening of Christ was everything; that was what
he had ever present before his mind.

The child of God, then, must not be surprised, if from
time to time he finds himself in a position of personal
helplessness. At times he may come into this position
in his worldly, and at times in his spiritual circumstances;
but whenever he comes into them the part of faith is to
trust unreservedly.* Let us learn from the words of our

---

* The case of Jacob is a very instructive one in this respect.
(Gen. xxxii. 6.) "His messengers returned, saying, 'We came
to thy brother Esau, and also he cometh to meet thee, and four
hundred men with him.' Then Jacob was greatly afraid and distressed." And no wonder! his two bands were helpless women
and children, with cattle, and in all probability unarmed servants,
and Esau had four hundred men. These two bands of which he

great Teacher Himself, in Psa. xxii, 11, 19, " Be not far
from me, for trouble is near, and there is none to help.
But be not Thou far from me, O Lord, O my strength,
haste Thee to help me."

The recognition of this resting upon God, met with a
notable blessing in the case of Asa. (2 Chr. xiv, 9—15.)
" And there came out against them Zerah the Ethiopian
with an host of a thousand thousand, and three hundred
chariots; and came unto Mareshah. Then Asa went out
against him, and they set the battle in array in the valley
of Zephathah at Mareshah. And Asa cried unto the
Lord his God, and said, ' Lord, it is nothing with Thee
to help, whether with many, or with them that have no
power : help us, O Lord our God; for we rest on Thee,
and in Thy name we go against this multitude. O Lord,

speaks in verse 10 were blessings given, but they were blessings
which he had no power of himself to keep; and this lesson he
had to learn now. God must not only be the one to give blessing,
but also the one to preserve it; the four hundred men would soon
have made havoc of the two bands. Under these circumstances
Jacob acknowledges his fears; he says, " Deliver me, I pray Thee,
from the hand of my brother, from the hand of Esau; for I fear
him, lest he will come and smite me, and the mother with the
children;" but he falls back also in trust upon the old promises of
God; he calls Him the God of his father Abraham, and the God
of his father Isaac, and reminds Him, moreover, of His relationship to himself as a promiser of good; he calls Him " The Lord
which said unto him, ' Return unto thy country, and to thy
kindred, and I will deal well with thee.' And Thou saidst, ' I
will surely do thee good, and make thy seed as the sand of the
sea, which cannot be numbered for multitude.'" Have we the
promises of God as ours; can we plead them? if so, we need not
fear man, he cannot meddle with them.

Thou art our God; let not man prevail against Thee.' So the LORD smote the Ethiopians before Asa, and before Judah; and the Ethiopians fled. And Asa and the people that were with him pursued them unto Gerar: and the Ethiopians were overthrown, that they could not recover themselves; for they were destroyed before the LORD, and before His host; and they carried away very much spoil. And they smote all the cities round about Gerar; for the fear of the Lord came upon them: and they spoiled all the cities; for there was exceeding much spoil in them. They smote also the tents of cattle, and carried away sheep and camels in abundance, and returned to Jerusalem."

And in that of Hezekiah. (Isa. xxxvii, 14—38.) "And Hezekiah received the letter from the hands of the messengers, and read it: and Hezekiah went up unto the house of the LORD, and spread it before the LORD. And Hezekiah prayed unto the LORD, saying, 'O LORD of hosts, God of Israel that dwelleth between the cherubims, Thou art the God, even Thou alone, of all the kingdoms of the earth: Thou hast made heaven and earth. Incline thine ear, O LORD, and hear; open thine eyes, O LORD, and see: and hear all the words of Sennacherib, which hath sent to reproach the living God. Of a truth, LORD, the kings of Assyria have laid waste all the nations and their countries, and have cast their gods into the fire: for they were no gods, but the work of men's hands, wood and stone: therefore they have destroyed them. Now therefore, O LORD our God, save us from his hand, that all the kingdoms of the earth may know that Thou art the LORD, even Thou only.' * * * Because thy rage against Me, and thy tumult, is come up into Mine ears, therefore will I put My hook* in thy nose, and My bridle in thy lips, and I will turn thee back by the way by which thou camest. * * * Therefore thus saith the LORD concerning the king of Assyria, ' He shall not come into this city, nor shoot an arrow there, nor come before it with shields, nor cast a bank against it. By the way that he came, by the same shall he return, and shall not come into this city, saith the LORD. For I will defend this city, to save it for Mine own sake, and for my servant David's sake.' Then the angel of the LORD went forth, and smote in the camp of the Assyrians a hundred and fourscore and five thousand : and when they arose early in the morning, behold, they were all dead corpses. So Sennacherib king of Assyria departed, and went and returned, and dwelt at Nineveh. And it came to pass as he was worshipping in the house of Nisroch his god, that Adrammelech and Sharezer his sons smote him with the sword; and they escaped into the land of Armenia : and Esar-haddon his son reigned in his stead."

Thus was it blessed in them, assuredly it will be also blessed in us.

Now we come to the period when *natural fear comes*

---

* "My hook in thy nose!" What an expressive phrase is this. A bull with a hook in its nose can be led even by a little child. The ferocity of the animal is untamed, his might and strength remain as they were before, but he is powerless, the least plunge or struggle is restrained by the pain of the hook or ring. Thus the Lord often controls wicked men; He leaves them their ferocity of nature, but so puts them under restraint, and that, by apparently unimportant means, that they cannot hurt his people. We must not so much look for the changing of the bull's nature, as for the putting the hook in his nose.

on us. "What time I am afraid," (says the Psalmist in Psa. lvi, 3,) "I will trust in Thee."

There are some persons in the world who seem destitute of fear; they have a natural courage which defies pain, and almost death itself. Such persons are, however, comparatively few; and even they have their weak points, through which fear will occasionally make its way. We are most of us, as we know painfully from experience, subject to natural fear from various causes. Some are afraid of pain. When John Howe's son, a physician, was lancing his leg, Howe enquired what he was doing? and observed "I am not afraid of dying, but I am of pain." The late Sir Robert Peel was engaged with Stephenson the great engineer and others, in making some observations on blood under the microscope. Each furnished some of his blood from a scratch, and at length Stephenson asked for some of Sir Robert's to see what the blood of a politician was like. Sir Robert agreed to furnish it, but shrank several times with such manifest repugnance from the necessary scratch or puncture, that at last the experiment was abandoned, so far as he was concerned. Some are all their life long subject to the fear of death; some are full of nervous dread, lest circumstances should go wrong; some have certain persons as the chief object of their fear; and they never come into contact with them, without having their fears excited. Inevitable pain makes some shrink; and the mere prospect of it has a terrifying effect upon others. Now we may not be able to prevent fear from thus affecting us; this fear may be sinless, although it be an infirmity, and that, one of a distressing kind. There is, however, often more or less sin mixed with human fear, because it often arises, more or less, from want of Trust.

We have many instances in Holy Scripture, of the Lord's people being put into great fear. When Abram was going down into Egypt he was afraid, and that, even though he was surrounded with the promises of God; he says to his wife, "Behold now, I know that thou art a fair woman to look upon; therefore it shall come to pass, when the Egyptians shall see thee, that they shall say, 'This is his wife:' and they will kill me, but they will save thee alive. Say, I pray thee that thou art my sister, that it may be well with me for thy sake, and my soul shall live because of thee." Gen. xii, 11, &c. When Jacob went to meet Esau, he was "greatly afraid, and distressed." Gen. xxxii, 7. We have the terrible effects of a night vision upon Eliphaz, described in Job iv: "In thoughts from visions of the night, when deep sleep falleth upon man, fear came upon me, and trembling, which made all my bones to shake; then a spirit passed before my face, the hair of my flesh stood up." David also, who was pre-eminent for valour, by whose mighty arm the giant had fallen, was thus distressed by his own people, when the Amalekites had invaded Ziklag, and taken away captive the wives, and daughters, and sons of his men; "then David was greatly distressed, for the people spake of stoning him, because the soul of all the people was grieved, every man for his sons and for his daughters, but David encouraged himself in the Lord his God." 1 Sam. xxx, 6. Elijah as we have already seen, was put in fear by Jezebel, as we read in 1 Kings xix, and that after an extraordinary display of courage, "the standing alone against eight hundred and fifty men!"

Now when natural fear comes upon us, our best remedy for it will surely be, simple trust in God. This fear may not be a specific act of unbelief; it may be only the natural consequent of the weakness, or nervousness, of our nature; but the remedy for it is simple trust in God. And let us beware of the temptation of Satan, which would say to us, " God has nothing to do with fear of this kind; He will make no allowances for it; He will feel no sympathy for the man that is afflicted with it; He looks down upon it as weakness; if this fear were a spiritual matter, He would encourage you, and help you out of it, but He cannot be expected to condescend to every petty weakness of your nature." Such thoughts as these are unjust indeed toward God; we are told that " He knoweth whereof we are made;" we know that all things lie open before His eyes, and however unimportant or unfounded our fears may *really* be, He knows that they are of real importance to us; and He acts, not only with reference to His own greatness, but also with reference to our weakness. When Peter, Matt. xiv, 30, " saw the wind boisterous, he was afraid, and beginning to sink, he cried, saying, Lord save me ;" and Jesus did not turn a deaf ear to his distress—" Immediately Jesus stretched forth His hand, and caught him, and said unto him, O thou of little faith, wherefore didst thou doubt?" *Everything* connected with a child of God, whether it belong to his body or his soul, to his temporal or eternal concerns, interests the Most High. " Like as a father pitieth his children, so the Lord pitieth them that fear Him." Psalm ciii, 13. And in this respect, God assuredly deals with His people as a parent does with a child. The child may be alarmed at but a very little thing; perhaps at nothing more than the sight of a strange face, or the sound of an insect, or the falling darkness of the night; there is nothing in all this to be really frightened at, the father well knows; but he tenderly remembers the weakness and the ignorance of the child; he sees that his child is suffering real fear, and therefore he acts accordingly; perhaps pointing out to the little one his error, but certainly soothing him in his fright, and whiling away his sorrow.

When natural fear comes upon us, let us remember this. When we wince in the body, may grace be given to us to commit the body, and its fears, to God; let us not shrink from doing so, under the impression that it is beneath Him to attend to us; He will be gracious to us in the matter of our fears, as well as in that of our wants. Nehemiah committed all to God, when men would have put him in fear; as we read in chapter vi, 9—14. And long before that, when the pressure of direst necessity was upon the Israelites, Moses said unto them, "Fear ye not, stand still and see the salvation of the Lord." Exod. xiv, 13. With us, let the time of natural fear be also the time of trust; let us say with the Psalmist: "What time I am afraid, I will trust in Thee," Psa. lvi, 3; and it shall come to pass that the "Lord will give thee rest from thy sorrow and thy fear, and from the hard bondage wherewith thou wast made to serve," and thou shalt say with the Psalmist, "I sought the Lord, and he heard me, and delivered me from all my fears." Psa. xxxiv, 4.

And before we leave this branch of our subject, let us for a moment recall to mind the human nature of our Lord. The Saviour's body was like ours, subject to pain and suffering of every kind. He had precisely the same natural views of pain that we have; the same shrinkings from it; the actual feelings of human nature concerning it; He did not consider pain an evil, to be philosophically descanted upon, or stoically endured; He knew it to be a portion of the curse; and forasmuch as all the effects of the curse must fall upon Him, pain, without any extraordinary mitigation, was His lot. The prospect of suffering was as terrible to the Saviour in His flesh, as it is to us in ours; for His flesh was the same as ours. Every nerve in His holy body had quick susceptibility; every human instinct shrank back from the pressure of physical suffering. He was very man; and though now in a glorified body, He is very man still, at God's right hand.

Let us not forget that Christ still possesses human sympathies. He remembers well His own human feelings with respect to pain; how His human nature shrank back from the mental anguish of Gethsemane, and the bodily torture of the cross; all these things are before Him; and He knows that His people are even as He was; that they feel as He did; therefore He can sympathize with them, and send them help according to their need. If an angel were sent from heaven to strengthen Him, His people shall not be left destitute of such help as they require; He will deal with them, in their sufferings, in the remembrance of His own. When what we terribly feared is actually upon us; when we say with the Psalmist, in Psalm lxix, "The waters are come in unto my soul, I sink in deep mire where there is no standing, I am come into deep waters where the floods overflow me," we shall not be left alone, if only we have grace to trust.

The Psalmist declares, that he will thus call upon God, when the calamity is actually upon him. "In the day of my trouble I will call upon Thee, for Thou wilt answer me," Psalm lxxxvi, 7. An affecting picture of this day of trouble we have given to us in Psalm cxvi, 3, &c. "The sorrows of death compassed me, and the pains of hell gat hold upon me, I found trouble and sorrow; then called I upon the name of the Lord, O Lord, I beseech Thee deliver my soul." Then what came to pass? "Gracious (says the Psalmist) is the Lord, and righteous, yea, our God is merciful. The Lord preserveth the simple. I was brought low, and He helped me. Return unto thy rest, O my soul, for the Lord hath dealt bountifully with thee; for Thou hast delivered my soul from death, mine eyes from tears, and my feet from falling."

If we were able thus to trust in God, and to stay ourselves upon Him, when the sufferings of pain were actually upon us, we should be able to bear them far better than we have perhaps ever hitherto done.

Thus the martyrs seem to have done, and very wonderful are the histories of their deaths. When we consider their greater pains, and their patience in the midst of them, may we, in our lesser pains, bear all as trusting in a God whose immediate presence we are able to realize and feel. We are told that a young man named Jones, the son of a Welsh Knight, came to Bishop Farrar a few days before he suffered, and lamented the painfulness of the death prepared for him. The Bishop, in faith, relying upon the extraordinary support vouchsafed to those who were thus publicly called to seal their testimony with their blood, told the youth to mark him while suffering that painful death, and if he saw him once stir, then to give no credit to the doctrines he had preached. Foxe adds, "And as he said, so he right well performed the same; for so patiently he stood, that he never moved, but even as he stood holding up his stumps, so still he continued, till one Richard Gravell, with a staff, dashed him upon the head, and struck him down." When the fire was kindled about Dr. Taylor, he held up his hands, and said "Merciful Father of heaven, for Jesus Christ, my Saviour's sake, receive my soul into Thy hands." He stood still in the midst of the flames, without crying or moving, his hands folded together, till Soyce struck him down with a halbert. The particulars of Hooper's death, as given by Foxe, are too shocking to be given here at length; but he endured them all in the strength of God. When three irons were brought for the purpose of fastening him to the stake, he said, "Trouble not yourselves; I doubt not God will give strength sufficient to abide the fire, without these bands; notwithstanding, suspecting the weakness of the flesh, although I have assured confidence in God's strength, do as ye think good." In the fire, Hooper stood praying, "O Jesus, Son of David, have mercy upon me, and receive my soul." And when the fire was spent, he wiped his eyes with his hands, and mildly but earnestly entreated that more fire might be brought. "After suffering inexpressible torments for three quarters of an hour, the martyr, bowing forwards, yielded up the spirit, dying as quietly as a child in his bed." He was indeed strengthened, in answer to his prayer, the concluding words of which were these, "And well seest Thou, my Lord and God, what terrible pains and cruel torments be prepared for Thy creature, such, Lord, as, without Thy strength, none is able to bear, or patiently to endure. But all things that are impossible with man are possible with Thee. Therefore strengthen me of Thy goodness, that when in the fire I break not the rules of patience; or else assuage the terror of the pains, as shall seem most to Thy glory." When the fire was kindled upon the martyr Waid, he was heard to exclaim, "Lord Jesus, receive my soul." And he continued to do so without impatience, standing still, and holding up his hands, clasped together, above his head, as if engaged in prayer, remaining in this attitude "even when he was dead, and altogether roasted, as though they had been stayed up with a prop under them." The account of Latimer at the stake shews us how the bowed down frame can be strengthened for its terrible conflict. We are told that "his mortal frame becoming invigorated at the prospect of the near approach of his journey's end, he no longer appeared a withered, crooked old man, his body crazed and bending under the weight of years, but he stood upright, as comely a Father as one would desire to behold." The case of Thomas Hawkes, who suffered martyrdom at Coggeshall, on June 13th, A.D. 1555, shews us how God can enable His people to bear pain, especially for Him. Shortly before his death, some of his friends, expecting that they should be called to bear a similar testimony to the truth, requested that if the pain of burning were tolerable, so that it could be endured with patience, he would give them a sign by lifting up his hands towards heaven. The trying hour arrived, the martyr was fastened to the stake, and the fire was kindled. His friends anxiously watched for the appointed sign. A long time passed, his skin was shrivelled up by the flames, and his speech taken away, so that all thought he was gone, when suddenly, and contrary to all expectation, he raised up his hands, "burning with a light fire, and with great rejoicing, as it seemed," struck them together three times. At this sign of his stedfastness in the faith, the people shouted with joy, especially his friends. The martyr then sunk down and expired.

And yet how hard the struggle may be in itself we see from the cases of some other martyrs. As Rawlins White was led to the stake, he saw his wife and children stand weeping. The sight of those who were near and dear to him moved him. "Ah, flesh!" exclaimed he, smiting his breast, "wouldst thou hinder me, wouldst thou fain prevail? By God's grace, thou shalt not have the victory." While the smith was fastening him to the stake, he said, "I pray you, good friend, knock in the chain fast, for it may be the flesh will strive mightily; but, O God, of Thy great mercy, give me strength and patience." He also spoke to a person named Dane, who related these particulars, saying that he felt a great struggle between the flesh and the spirit, and entreated, if he began to waver, he would hold up his finger, "and then," said he "I trust I shall remember myself." The conflict between the spirit and the flesh are graphically pourtrayed in the case of George Tankerfield, who was burned at St. Alban's, on August 25th, A. D. 1555. "Being taken to an inn, many persons came to see him, some to dispute with and revile him, while others praised God for his constancy. Sitting down before a fire, he pulled off his shoes and hose, and stretched his leg out to the flame, but quickly withdrew it on feeling the pain. He then shewed to those who stood by, how the flesh persuaded him one way, and the spirit another. "The flesh saith, 'O fool, wilt thou burn and needest not?' The spirit saith, 'Be not afraid, for this is nothing, compared with eternal fire.' The flesh saith, 'Do not leave the company of thy friends and acquaintance, which love thee, and will let thee want nothing.' The spirit saith, 'The company of Jesus Christ, and His glorious presence, doth exceed all earthly friends.' The flesh saith 'Do not shorten thy time, for if thou wilt, thou mayest live much longer.' The spirit saith, 'This life is nothing compared with the life in heaven, which lasteth for ever,'" &c.

What a strength, what a support would it be, if, while enduring pain, we could fix our mind wholly upon God, in Christ; if we spake to Him; if we said some such short sentences as these :—"O Lord, help me to bear this, as one of Thy children should." "O Lord, I would glorify Thee in this pain." "O Lord, undergird me, that I may be able to endure." "O my Father, not my will, but Thine be done." "O Jesus, I would bear it as unto Thee, who didst bear such pain for me." And while thus talking to God, much, perhaps, of the bitterness of the pain will be past; its worst spasms will, perhaps, be tided over; and we shall have the inestimable pleasure of feeling, that we have glorified God in the time of our hardest trial; that, like the three children, we have glorified Him in the fires, and walked in the glowing furnace, even with the Son of man Himself.

Even so, O Lord, enable us to do this! Whenever our trial time comes on—when we have to endure—when the hour of suffering is come—be thou specially at hand, and give Thy special help!

We now conclude this portion of our subject. May we have grace to turn it to practical account. The daily circumstances of life will afford us opportunities enough of glorifying God in Trust, without our waiting for any extraordinary calls upon our faith. Let us remember that the extraordinary circumstances of life are but few; that much of life may slip past without their occurrence; and that if we be not faithful and trusting in that which is little, we are not likely to be so in that which is great. The same spirit which animates the martyr at the stake, enabling him to glorify God amid the fires, may be evinced in the way in which a little pain is endured, or reproach is borne; the same calm Trust which enables the believer to rest peacefully on God, in the little affairs of daily life, is nothing but the exercise, within a narrow circle, of a grace, which, if called upon to move in a wider sphere, would keep the heart in peace, amid the overturning of dynasties, and the wreck of thrones. Let our trust be reared in the humble nursery of our own daily experience, with its ever recurring little wants, and trials, and sorrows; and then, when need be, it will come forth, to do such great things as are required of it; even as Moses came forth from the wilderness to deliver a whole nation from bondage; and David came from his solitary sheep-watching to slay the giant, who had defied the armies of the living God.

CHAPTER II.

Ministry and Testimony.

THE "I WILL" OF MINISTRY AND TESTIMONY.

Psalm ix, 1. *"I will shew forth Thy marvellous works."*

Psalm xxii, 22. *"I will declare Thy name unto my brethren."*

Psalm li, 13. *"Then will I teach transgressors Thy ways, and sinners shall be converted unto Thee."*

Psalm lxxxix, 1. *"With my mouth will I make known Thy faithfulness to all generations."*

Psalm cxlv, 5. *"I will speak of the glorious honour of Thy majesty."*

WE have, in these verses, the determinations of the man of God, with reference to Ministry and Testimony. This subject of Ministry and Testimony is one well worth our consideration in the present day; for to the great loss of the church at large, and also of individual believers, it is but little recognised.

The particulars to which the reader's attention is solicited are these:—the fact that 'the Lord's people are called to Ministry and Testimony;' also, that 'this is not generally recognised in the present day;' further, 'the present aspect of the church of God in this particular;'

and 'the loss which is thus entailed upon the world upon the church, and upon individual believers.'

There are some who may, perhaps, meet us at the very outset with a denial of their being called to exercise any ministry, to give any testimony in the world for God. They have learned the fundamental principles of the Christian faith; they have had some knowledge of the sinfulness of their own hearts; they believe that the blood of Jesus Christ alone can cleanse them from their sin; and being sound in faith, they do not see that they are called upon to be active in life. It may be that such persons are of a contemplative turn of mind; or still more probably, naturally of an inactive disposition; but from whatever cause, so it is, that the world is little the better for their Christianity; and assuredly we might say to them, " We have not so learned Christ."

Selfishness and sloth are, to the eyes of the great and heart-searching God, too plainly marked blemishes of His church, and people upon earth. It is true, there never was more noise made in the world about religion, than there is now; never was there a time, when men could talk louder about their respective views; or pronounce more distinctly the shibboleths of their respective parties; and never was there a time, when there seemed more outward activity in schools, reformatories, charitable societies, and such like agencies for good; but the great energies of the church of God have not been put forth; the inward might of an active faith has not been fully roused; what has been done, has been for the most part done by a few; and while we acknowledge thankfully, that there has been a blessing fully proportioned to the efforts made, we cannot but perceive that the reason why there has not been more blessing, is because the efforts have been so small.

What department is there of Christian labour, that is being worked with the *full* energies of the church of God? What parish, or district, what institution, or society, what family circle is receiving the impulses of Christian ministry in its highest efforts, its very fullest powers? We look around in vain; and were it not, that in the munificence of God, single grains are made to bring forth many more than themselves, the reaping would be even as the sowing, scant and miserable indeed.

Our readers will here remember that we are speaking of the people of God; this fault lies in unnumbered instances at their door; and they cannot allow themselves in this fault without suffering loss. The loss which they shall suffer does not touch their *eternal life,* for "he that believeth on the Son hath everlasting life;" but it does touch and affect *the measure of their future reward.* That glory should be given at all, is of free grace, but the measure of that glory shall be "according to works." We cannot fail in ministry, and testimony, without suffering loss. "Therefore my beloved brethren," says St. Paul in 1 Cor. xv, 58, "be ye stedfast, unmoveable, always abounding in the work of the Lord; forasmuch as ye know that your labour is not in vain in the Lord." "Ye," says St. Peter, 1 Pet. ii, 9, "are a chosen generation, a royal priesthood, an holy nation, a peculiar people, that ye should shew forth the praises of Him, who hath called you out of darkness into His marvellous light." Here the apostles are speaking to true believers —to you, dear reader, if you have embraced Christ; your life is claimed on the ground of having been called

" out of darkness into light;" and that life's labour is made sweet by the blessed truth, that it "is not in vain in the Lord."

But now, let us proceed to take in order three, out of the many losers, by the sloth of God's people, in this matter of Ministry and Testimony. They are

    I.   The Christian himself.

    II. The Church of God.

    III. The world at large.

It may be, that a contemplation of all this loss will stir you, dear reader, on to work!

The child of God is a loser here, and certainly here-after also. Is it not a sweet and blessed feeling, when we are able to render daily service to the one we love? We feel pleasure in being able to *tell* of our love; in being able to *act* it; in shewing it in the unnumbered little opportunities, which continually present themselves in daily life. If love can proclaim its depth in some great deed, it can whisper of it, in all the lesser deeds, which make up the sum of daily life. A little deed, like a gentle whisper, may tell much. We can imagine no greater blow to genuine love, than such a saying as this, "You may feel love, you may rejoice in it, you may nurse it in your bosom, *but you must never shew it.*" How could our human love bear such a restraint as this? How could we bear to feel it ever coming to our lips, and yet those lips never to be permitted to utter a word about it? How could we bear to feel it ever welling upward from the heart to the eye, while that eye was not permitted to beam with one loving look, but was compelled to imprison, as with an impassable barrier of clear thick ice, the warm springs beneath? To be placed in such circumstances, amongst those we love here below, would be hell on earth, and the punishment, proving too severe for mortal frames, would wear us out. And if we be lovers of Christ, if we feel that we owe all to Him, if He have our hearts, how does it come to pass, that we do not come forth in ministry for Him? and not only *for* Him, but *to* Him, for all that is *for* Him is *to* Him also? The woman that brake the alabaster box of ointment loved much, and she anointed the way-worn feet of Jesus, with all that she had most precious; and in most touching *personal* service, she wiped them with the hairs of her head. Her love would have her best bestowed upon her Lord; she ministered to Him of her substance, and of her energies; alas! how many of us are deficient in our ministry, with both of these. In Mary's case there was indeed a personal ministry, a ministry of self. We are told that "she wiped his feet with her hair." A woman's hair is her glory, the greatest adornment of beauty which she has received from God, that about which she gene-rally takes the most care in the attiring of her person; and here we have this loving woman giving that which is her greatest adornment to perform a menial office for Christ. "She wiped his feet with her hair." The feet which had been soiled by travel—the feet which bare the marks of His journeyings to and fro, of houseless wanderings for man's salvation; these, though they were the least honourable portion of His person, were the objects of her care; she poured the ointment on His head and feet, but she wiped also His feet with her hair. And herein she was not left without honour, for was ever any head so distinguished as that which bare away a part of what had anointed Christ? I would rather have had that ointment than the pearly wreath or jewelled crown; that ointment than the warrior's helmet or the victor's laurel; the glory of the diadem is for time, but the glory of an honour like this is for eternity; the crested helm of the warrior is struck down in battle, but the strongest amongst the evil ones could not tear from this disciple the glory of this deed; the chaplet of the victor fades, and his very name becomes erased from the annals of human fame, but the halo of this woman's love shall never perish, and perhaps in her resurrection body it shall be seen, for peculiar love has its own peculiar rewards, and it may be that men shall be rewarded, not only according to the *value*, but also according to the *manner* of their deeds.

But what does this truth teach us? what, save that the very best we have should be ungrudgingly applied by love to do even the most menial deed for Christ. And oh! that we may have greater grace from heaven, never to think anything of Christ's too lowly for our care, anything of ours too good for His lowly work. Nothing is lowly that belongs to Him except His character; everything becomes dignified from the fact of its being connected with Him, the least service that is for Him is greater than the greatest that is for the earth, for He is not only the Son of God, but He is our Lord, our husband, and our king. If it be in itself a wearisome task to teach a dull and wayward child, let us bear in mind that we are teaching it for Him, and then we are invested with more honour than if we were training the noblest genius to become a foremost man in the ranks of intellectual but unsanctified knowledge,—knowledge which is of the world and for it, and never goes beyond.

If it be in itself great weariness in the flesh to climb the almost unending stairs, and keep vigils in the sick chamber during long and silent hours, to listen at times to almost unending complaints, to plod along an unvarying round of duty for which there is little earthly thank; now set Christ, dear reader, between you and all your earthly toils, let them be for Him, then these toils become a burden that is light, and these trials a glory which it is our privilege to be allowed to bear. Think it no small thing to do what might be called little deeds for Christ; it was Jesu's *feet* that Mary wiped with her *hair*.

Let us not forget that Mary bare away with her in her hair a portion of the perfumed ointment which had been poured upon the head of Christ; she did not seek it, she did not immediately intend it; but it clave to her, and what had been bestowed upon her Lord thus in part returns to her again. Thus has it ever been; there is always, as is stated below, a reflex benefit of action for God; we cannot minister to Christ without being benefited ourselves, the honour which we bestow on Him, will cleave of necessity to us. In the very substance with which Mary perfumed the feet of Jesus, was she perfumed in her own hair; she could thus only wipe His feet, but while she was doing so, He all silently and imperceptibly could anoint her head. And has Jesus been ever blest without blessing in turn again? No doubt the world has not seen Him acting, even as no one at this feast saw Him do this, the blessing was between Himself and Mary, our blessing shall be between Jesus and ourselves; it is a law of Christ's kingdom that whosoever spends on Jesus, on him will Jesus spend again, restoring him all that he has given, hallowed by the holy contact into which it has come. Beloved, let us try our love, let us probe deep into it, let us examine it, let us judge it by its fruits; and if we be in no ministry, if we be giving no testimony, let us ask ourselves "how comes this to pass?"

There is another aspect in which this matter is to be viewed. When there is a lack of real ministry and testimony, *we ourselves must suffer loss*. That which we lose is, *"the reflex benefit of action for God."* It is impossible for any man to exercise himself in action for God, without receiving a reflex benefit upon his own soul. The rule of the spiritual kingdom is, that he who waters others shall be watered also himself. God will be no man's debtor, and as the heavens send down again in showers, the moisture which is attracted into them from the earth, by the heat of the sun, so God sends down as blessings upon His people the results of those very energies, which He had drawn forth from them, and attracted upwards to Himself. Never did man do aught for God, but that He in His own way paid him back again. We cannot go forth in any real ministry and testimony for Him, without receiving a blessing ourselves.

Here, however, our reader might say, "This is not altogether borne out by my experience; I have been engaged in such and such acts of ministry, I have given such and such testimony; but I do not see how I myself have been the better for it, or what particular blessing I have had in so doing."*

* A touching instance of the reflex benefit of an act of ministry is given by D'Aubigné in his history of the Reformation. "When Luther had returned to his hotel (after having appeared before

Let us first enquire: what was our motive in ministry and testimony? had you any motive at all? Motives are all important in the spiritual life, and especially in work for God. We can imagine a person in tolerably active ministry, and giving pretty decided testimony, without any motive at all. Suppose a person to be thrown into what is commonly called "religious society;" he may fall into a certain habit of acting from routine, and into a certain formula of speaking, without really living and speaking to God at all. Just as the cameleon takes the

the Emperor in the Diet of Worms) seeking to recruit his body, fatigued by so severe a trial, Spalatin and other friends surrounded him, and all together gave thanks to God. As they were conversing, a servant entered, bearing a silver flagon filled with Eimbeck beer, 'My master,' said he, as he offered it to Luther, 'invites you to refresh yourself with this draught.' 'Who is the prince,' said the Wittemburgh doctor, 'who so graciously remembers me?' It was the aged Duke Eric of Brunswick. The reformer was affected by this present from so powerful a lord, belonging to the Pope's party. 'His Highness,' continued the servant, 'has condescended to taste it before sending it to you.' Upon this Luther, who was thirsty, poured out some of the Duke's beer, and after drinking it, he said: 'as this day Duke Eric has remembered me, so may our Lord Jesus Christ remember him in the hour of his last struggle.' It was a present of trifling value; but Luther desirous of shewing his gratitude to a prince who remembered him at such a moment, gave him such as he had—a prayer. The servant returned with this message to his master. At the moment of his death, the aged Duke called these words to mind, and addressing a young page, Francis of Kramm, who was standing at his bedside, 'take the Bible,' said he, 'and read it to me.' The child read these words of Christ, and the soul of the dying man was comforted. *'Whosoever shall give you a cup of water to drink in my name, because ye belong to Christ, verily I say unto you, he shall not lose his reward.'"*

colour of surrounding objects, or as man drops naturally more or less into the habits of the climate in which he lives, so we are often influenced by the religious society in which we are cast. Under these circumstances, very little passes between God and the soul; we become pieces of spiritual machinery, we miss the connecting link through which blessing should have come. The minister of the gospel, the visitor of the sick, the teacher in the Sunday school, may one and all be at work, but not at work *to* God. That which we must be careful about, above all other things in ministry, is to do it *to* GOD: to let our ministry first be laid before Him; and then, having been consecrated, and having been made powerful by Him, to let it work amongst our fellow men. Our bow of service should arch from earth to heaven, and then back to earth again. Let our ministry pass through the hands of Christ, as did the bread wherewith He fed the five thousand; and then, poor though the provision may be, which we have in ourselves, it will not only do wonders, but come unexhausted out of an effort, in which, humanly speaking, it might have been spent. In all our work for God, let us have Him distinctly before us; let us say, "It is for Thee, O Father, it is for Thee, and for Jesus, and the Spirit:" and this distinctness of purpose will not be without its reward; for a new strength will thus enter into our efforts; God will be in them; we shall feel His pervading presence in them; and we shall be spared that faint-heartedness, which otherwise might have come upon us, and neutralized the effort we were about to make.

The realization of the presence of God is beautifully brought before us in the prayer of Teava one of the

Rarotongan converts in the South Sea. No sooner had the Rarotongans felt the power of the gospel of Christ themselves, than they earnestly desired to take the boon to the islands of the Samoan group. In making known his desire to go as a Christian evangelist to the savage tribes of Samoa, Teava wrote:— "My desire to fulfil Christ's command is very great: He said to his disciples, 'Go ye into all the world.' My heart is compassionating the heathen, who know not the salvation which God has provided for the world. Let me go to those savages. Why is the delay? May God direct us, but my desire for this work is very great." This good man's desire was fulfilled; he was taken to Samoa, he landed in the midst of its savage population; he gained a position at Monono, an influential station, and, besides being one of the most intelligent and consistent pioneers to the European missionaries there, he has been for many years one of their best native assistants in translating, in schools, and in the general work of the station.

A part of a prayer of this excellent teacher has been recorded by Mr. Williams, which he offered to God, on board ship, on his passage to Samoa, which shews the realization of God in effort in ministry. "...... if we fly to heaven," said the good man, addressing God, "there we shall find Thee; if we dwell upon the land, Thou art there also; if we sail on the sea, Thou art there; and this affords us comfort, so that we sail upon the ocean without fear, because Thou, O God, art in our ship."

"The King of our bodies has his subjects, to whom he issues his orders, but if he himself goes with them, his presence stimulates their zeal; they work with energy, they do it soon, they do it well. O Lord, Thou art the King of our spirits; Thou hast issued orders to Thy subjects to do a great work; Thou hast commanded them to go into all the world, and preach the gospel to every creature. We, O Lord, are going upon that errand, and let Thy presence go with us to quicken us, and enable us to persevere in the great work until we die.

"Thou hast said that Thy presence shall go with Thy people even to the end of the world. Fulfil, O Lord, to us this cheering promise. I see, O Lord, a compass in this vessel by which the seamen steer the right course, that we may escape obstruction and danger. Be to us, O Lord, the compass of salvation." *

Let us remember also, to look beyond this world. Here our ministry and testimony may seem to be able to do but little, perhaps not to accomplish anything at all; and because we can trace no results, we may see no use in our going on; but hereafter there are to be diversities of reward; and if we stand not in testimony, we shall lose glory and position; the positive, the enduring property of the other life.

Here let us say a word or two upon the positions, in which ministry is to be carried on. God has placed every one of us in a position; He has ordered, and measured, the diameter of our circle; He has given us our sphere; He has a record of all the opportunities which that sphere affords; and we shall be reckoned with, not concerning matters *beyond* our sphere, but concerning all matters *within* our sphere.

Let us take as an illustration, the case of the mother of a family. The cares of a family are numerous and heavy; and there are many instances, in which it is

* Gems from the Coral Islands

impossible for a mother, and head of a house, to be engaged in much external ministry for God. But if she be willing to serve Him, she need not be disheartened.

Is not home a little world in itself, and is not she, either for good or evil, the grand influence of home, much, most of it taking its tone from her? Would that Christian mothers recognised more, the great opportunities and responsibilities of home ministry; that they saw how the very fact of their influence being concentrated, gave it force! The charge of gunpowder, which occupies but a little space, sends the shot to a long distance; what mother can tell, how far her concentrated influence will send her children, in the career of holiness, and usefulness amongst their fellows. There is ministry in a mother's *look*. It has re-appeared in after life, amid the gleaming eyes which burned with unhallowed fires; and succoured the tempted one by the memory of its solemn, soft, and holy gaze. There is ministry in a mother's *voice*. It has re-echoed, after many years in the chambers of the memory, and warned in deep mysterious tones, as though it now came from another world, and cheered, and soothed, with even more than the power it possessed in earlier days, as though it were privileged to speak with the soft melody of heaven. Yes! there is ministry even in a mother's *touch;* and long after the hand from which it came, is cold in the motionless solitude of the tomb, its impress remains in living power. A mysterious hand from the invisible world traced the sentence of Belteshazzar's ruin; this hand, mysterious and invisible also, leaves imprinted on the heart, words at once of warning and of love—words of most powerful warning, because words of love.

"When I was a little boy," said a good man, "my mother used to bid me kneel beside her, and place her hand upon my head, while she prayed. Ere I was old enough to know her worth, she died, and I was left too much to my own guidance. Like others I was inclined to evil passions, but often felt myself checked, and, as it were, drawn back by a soft hand upon my head. When a young man, I travelled in foreign lands, and was exposed to many temptations. But when I would have yielded, that same hand was upon my head, and I was saved. I seemed to feel its pressure, as in the days of my happy infancy; and sometimes there came with it a solemn voice, saying, 'Do not this great wickedness, my son, nor sin against God.'"

Yes! Christian mothers, God requires testimony and ministry from you, in your own circles. If you be limited to them, by Him, He will accept your home ministry, and He will not leave you without a reward. You shall act upon the world, from the recesses of your own sanctified home; the ministry which you carried on for God upon the child at your knee, shall have a place, not in the annals of the world alone; your sons will perhaps be the fathers of God-fearing, and God-praising families; they will perhaps minister in the public service of the sanctuary; they will salt the society in which they move. It may be, that your daughters, as mothers, will reproduce your influence, the circle widening with every generation; and thus (provided God has limited your circle) shall you, if you minister in it for Him, throw forth circles ever widening more and more, so that you, being dead, shall speak, and live, and move in influence, long after you have departed in the flesh.

Are there not cares, and privations, and many troubles to be borne, from time to time, in the ministry of home? Are there not self-denials to be endured, and exertions to be made? There are—for all such, as would carry on an active ministry for God; as desire to do something more than merely drag through, or discharge duties, which they cannot well avoid.

Thus the individual suffers, when ministry and testimony are neglected. There is another sufferer, also, i.e. *the Church of Christ*. That church must suffer injury, when the Lord's people are not occupying their place; for as in the human body, if one member suffer, all the others suffer with it, so in the church, if one congregation, or one individual be holding back, the church, as a body, suffers loss.

What is this loss? In the first place, the church of God has its power of impression diminished. The church is made up of individuals, and when those individuals are feeble, and of little weight, the church in their locality makes a corresponding feeble impression. A branch of the church need not be large, to do great things; where two or three are gathered together in the name of Christ, there is He in the midst of them. The church of early days was small at first; and even now, some very small branches of the church are making great impressions, and doing great things; their members are in ministry; and here, under the influence of the Spirit, lies the secret of their success.

But let us look for a moment, not at churches great or small, but at *individuals*. How much might be accomplished, by the efforts of even isolated individuals. The man who determines to seize opportunities as they are presented to him, and to work with humble means, when great ones are not entrusted to him, may do wonders in the spiritual world. To write a few texts on a half sheet of note paper, seems but a poor way of doing good, yet see the results of this act of ministry for God. The following account was sent recently to the Secretary of the Religious Tract Society by a gentleman, who confirms its accuracy. It is a true story of Lucknow.

"In the station of———, in the Upper Provinces of India, I was one morning visiting the hospital as usual. As I entered the General Hospital, I was told by one of the men that a young man of the —— Regiment was anxious to speak to me. In the inner ward I found, lying on his chaepoy, in a corner, a new face, and walking up to him, said, 'I am told you wish to see me; I do not recollect the pleasure of having seen you before.' 'No,' he said, 'I have never seen you, yet you seem no stranger, for I have often heard speak of you.' I asked him if he was ill or wounded. 'I am ill,' he replied. He went on to say that he had just come down from Cawnpore. 'Perhaps you would like me to tell you my history. It may be you remember, a long time since, some of our men going into the hospital opposite, as you sat reading to one of the Highlanders. There were some half-dozen or more of them; they went to see a sick comrade. You went up presently to them, and told them how grateful you and all your country-people were to your noble soldiers for so readily coming to protect you all, and how deeply you sympathized with them in the noble cause in which they were now going to take a share. Then you talked to them of the danger which would attend them. You reminded them that life is a

battle-field to all, and asked them if they were soldiers
of Christ, and if they had thought of the probability of
their falling in battle.　I have heard all about that long
talk you had with the men.　Then you gave your Bible
to one, and asked him to read a passage.　He chose the
twenty-third Psalm, and you prayed.　They asked you
for a book or tract to remind them of what had been
said, and you gave all you had in your bag.　But for one
man there was none.　They were to start that afternoon,
so that you had not time to get one.　But you went to
the apothecary, and got pen and paper from him.　When
you came back, you gave this paper to him, telling him
you should look for him in heaven.'　As he said this, the
poor fellow pulled out from the breast of his shirt half a
sheet of note paper, on which I recognised my writing,
though nearly illegible from wear.　On it were written
the 1st, 7th, 10th, 14th, 15th, and 17th verses of the
5th Chapter of the 2nd Corinthians, and that hymn,

'How sweet the name of Jesus sounds.'

'That man,' he continued, 'and I were in the same
company, but he was a day ahead of me.　We met in
Cawnpore, then marched on with the rest to Lucknow.
Whenever we halted, the first thing ―――― did was to take
out his paper, and read it aloud to those who cared to
hear; then he prayed with us.　As we marched he spoke
much of his old father and mother, and only brother, and
wished he could see them once more.　But he was very,
very happy, and ready to go 'home,' if God saw fit.　As
we neared Lucknow he dwelt much on eternity, and said
to me, 'It is very solemn to be walking into death.　I
shall never leave this ill-fated city.'　We had many

fights standing always side by side. I am an orphan; I lost my parents when a child, and was brought up at school. I never had one to love me, and life was indeed a weary burden; yet beyond, all was darker still, for I knew nothing of a Saviour. ———'s reading and words came to my heart—he was so kind to me, and always called me brother. I never loved till I had him. He had found Jesus, and led me to love Him too. I cannot find words to say how I joyed, when at last I felt I had a Friend above. Oh! I never shall forget my joy when I first understood and believed. We had no book, only the paper. We knew it off by heart, and I don't know which of us loved it best. At last, in a dreadful fight in one of the gardens, a ball struck ——— in the chest. Words cannot say my grief when he fell—the only one I had to love me. I knelt by him, till the garden was left in our hands, and then bore him to the doctors. But it was too late—life was almost gone. 'Dear ———,' he said to me, 'I am only going home *first*. We have loved to talk of home together: don't be sorry for me, for I'm so happy.

'How sweet the name of Jesus sounds.'

Read me the words she wrote.' I pulled them out from his bosom, all stained with his blood, as you see, and repeated them. 'Yes,' he said, 'the love of Christ has constrained us. I am almost home. I'll be there to welcome you and her; good-bye, dear——.' And he was gone, but I was left, Oh! it was *so very* bitter! I knelt by him and prayed I might soon follow him. Then I took his paper, and put it in my bosom, where it has been since. I and some of our men buried him in the garden. I have gone through much fighting since, and came down here on duty with a detachment yesterday. They think me only worn with exposure, and tell me I shall be soon well, but I shall never see the sky again. I would like to lie by his side, but it cannot be.' Poor fellow! he cried long and bitterly. I could not speak, but pressed his hand. At length he said, 'So you'll forgive me making so bold in speaking to you. He often spoke of you, and blessed you for leading him to Jesus. And he it was who led me to Jesus. We shall soon be together again, and won't we welcome you when you come home?' We read and prayed together. He was quite calm when I rose from my knees. He was too weak to raise his head even from the pillow, but was quite peaceful and happy. 'I feel,' he said, 'that I shall not be able to think much longer; I have seen such frightful things. Thank God! I have sure and blessed hope in my death. I have seen so many die in fearful terror.' I turned to go. He said, 'Dear——, when I am gone, promise me this paper shall be put in my coffin. It gave me a friend on earth, who led me to a Saviour in heaven.' I promised. Next morning I went to see him, but oh, how sadly altered did I find him? Those soft brown eyes were glassy and lustreless. He was never to know me again. Dysentery in its fearful rapid form had seized him during the night. I took his hand in mine; it was clammy and powerless. Three of the men in the ward came up to me, and said, 'Till sense left him, he was talking of home with Jesus.' They knelt with me in prayer beside the poor sufferer. I went again the next day His body was still there, but his spirit had fled a few minutes previous. He was covered with a blanket, and the coolies were waiting to bear him away. I took his paper from his pillow, where it had been laid, and went to the apothecary, We walked back to the corpse, and he placed it in the hands of the departed. He was buried that evening. I have often thought since, how beautiful was that heavenly love which bound those two dear young soldiers together. How it sweetened their last days on earth. They were indeed friends in Jesus, and though their remains lie parted, yet they are both sleeping in Jesus. Oh, what a glorious resurrection theirs will be in the day of His appearing!"

It seemed but a poor opportunity for usefulness, when on ascending the pulpit, a minister found his congregation to consist of a solitary individual. Such was the case on one occasion when Dr. Beecher, of Cincinnati, was about to preach. The Doctor once engaged to preach for a country minister, on exchange; and the Sunday proved to be excessively stormy, cold, and uncomfortable. It was midwinter, and the snow was piled in heaps all along the roads, so as to make the passage very difficult. Still the minister urged his horse through the drifts, till he reached the church, put the animal into a shed, and went in. As yet, there was no person present; and after looking about, the old gentleman, then young, took his seat in the pulpit. Soon the door opened, and a single individual walked up the aisle, looked about, and took a seat. The hour came for commencing service, but no more hearers. Whether to preach to such an audience or not, was now the question; and it was one that Lyman Beecher was not long in deciding. He felt that he had a duty to perform, and he had no right to refuse to do it, because only one man could reap the benefit of it; and, accordingly, he went through all the services, praying, singing, preaching, and pronouncing the benediction, with only *one* hearer. And, when all was over, he hastened down from his desk, to speak to his "congregation," but he had departed. A circumstance so rare was referred to occasionally; but twenty years after it was brought to the Doctor's mind quite strangely. Travelling somewhere in Ohio, the Doctor alighted from the stage, one day, in a pleasant village, when a gentleman stepped up, and, spoke to him familiarly, calling him by name. "I do not remember you," said the Doctor. "I suppose not," said the stranger, "but we spent two hours alone once in a house, in a storm." "I do not recall it, Sir," said the old man, "pray when was it?" "Do you remember preaching, twenty years ago, in such a place, to a single person?" "Yes, yes," said the Doctor, grasping his hand, "I do indeed; and if you are the man, I have been wishing to see you ever since." "I am the man, Sir, and that sermon saved my soul, made a minister of me, and yonder is my church. The converts of that sermon, Sir, are all over Ohio."

If we cannot do what we *would*, let us do what we can, such is the true spirit of ministry; and he who has this spirit will ever find that he will have as much as ever he can do. The German colporteur in Pennsylvania did what he could in dropping his few tracts, and in years after, they made room for his books. This is his story:—

"I revisited the neighbourhood where, in 1852, I commenced my colporteur labours, and where, on being refused permission to stop at a house over night, I had left a few tracts as I went away, hoping for the blessing of God upon them. I now called at the same house, and found the man reading the Testament. In looking around the room, I saw that the wall behind the glass was papered with tracts. On calling attention to it, the man said, 'Some years ago, a man who carried books and tracts was here, and left us a few to read; but I '—here he stopped, and seemed to hesitate about saying more. I enquired if he had read them. 'No,' said he, 'for at that time I did not believe such things, and therefore pasted them to the wall.' 'Do you now believe them?' I enquired. 'Yes. As often as I approached the wall to look into the glass, I could not help seeing and reading them. It was the same with my wife and children. We were all led to see our sinfulness, and from that time we had no peace until we commenced praying, and continued till we found peace with God through Christ.' He told me that he and his wife and children had joined the church, and that he frequently had expressed a wish to see the man who had given him the tracts. 'If he should come again,' said I, 'what good would it do you?' 'I should like to have some of those good books; I have borrowed several of my neighbours and read them, but could never get any for my own.' Opening my saddle-bags, I informed him that I was the very man, and showed him my books. I cannot describe the joy they felt on that occasion. I had to stay over night with them, and the next morning they bought several dollars' worth of books."

Dear reader, do not try to shift from yourself your share of responsibility as regards ministry. No matter who, or what you be, if you be the Lord's, there is a sphere in which *you* are to act. It is your sphere, God has marked it out as such; and is it, alas, unoccupied, either from never having been entered on at all, or from being deserted after having been wrought in for a time?

You can do something in ministry. Try.

"Children, I want each of you to bring a new scholar to the school with you next Sunday," said the superintendent of a Sunday school to his scholars one day.

"I *can't* get any new scholars," said several of the children to themselves.

"I'll *try* what I can do," was the whispered response of a few others.

One of the latter class went home to his father, and said. "Father, will you go to the Sunday school with me?"

"I can't read, my son," replied the father, with a look of shame.

"Our teachers will teach you, dear father," answered the boy, with respect and feeling in his tones.

"Well, I'll go," said the father.

He went, learned to read, sought and found the Saviour, and at length became a colporteur. Years passed on, and that man had established *four hundred Sunday schools*, into which *thirty-five thousand* children were gathered!

Thus you see what trying did. That boy's effort was like a tiny rill, which soon swells into a brook, and at length becomes a river. His effort, by God's grace, saved his father: and his father being saved, led *thirty-five thousand* children to the Sunday school!

The church, if it awoke to a recognition of the ministry to which it is called, would astonish the world; it is no marvel, if a sleepy church leaves unimpressed a sleepy world. If the world took up a taunting tone toward the church, we could not be surprised; it might say, "yonder is a saint, he tells me that he is called to be a peculiar man; and that in Scripture, his sort are called 'peculiar people;' he says he is to take up his cross daily, and to war with the world, the flesh, and the Devil; but he leads an uncommonly easy life; he does not seem to trouble himself, any more than the rest of us do, about the world, the flesh, and the Devil." The ways of the people of God, are, alas! in the present day too like the ways of the world; the seal is almost as smooth as the wax; and what marvel, if the impression that it leaves, be slight.

We cannot but perceive, that those who hold the pure truths of grace, and see their justification by simple faith in the blood of Jesus, are in many instances of practical activity, and outward ministry, far behind those who distort the truth, and seek, in part at least, to do for themselves what can be done by Christ alone. Well might they say to some who glory in the rectitude of their theology, "shew me thy faith without thy works, and I will shew thee my faith by my works;" they in many instances, put us to shame: and the world, which judges by external evidence, will give the palm to those whose activity they see the most.

See the position in which the church is placed in the aggregate; one might well ask, where is it? here and there we see an isolated individual, or perhaps a little company, ministering *to* Christ, and *for* Him in the world; but where is the great body, the church? Where can we behold its arrayed battalions, where its forces massed for a grand assault upon the powers of evil; where do we see it possessed of power from the very impetus of its weight and numbers? The sight is nowhere to be seen; split into fragments, in many cases inert, and standing aside from ministry, it exists no doubt, but its existence has little influence on the world. May the Lord quicken it, and quicken each of His own people, as members of it; and then, blessings to thousands, and tens of thousands will be the result!

A few words upon *the world*, as the third loser by the non-ministering of many of the people of God, will close this chapter. So long as the church of God takes up a *de*fensive, and not an *of*fensive position, so long will she be occupying a lower position, than that assigned to her by Christ. The position occupied by Christ was aggressive; that marked out for His apostles was aggressive; that occupied by the early church was aggressive. Peter and John refused to be silent, and said, "Whether it be right in the sight of God, to hearken unto you, more than unto God, judge ye, for we cannot but speak the things which we have seen and heard." Acts iv, 19. God has always honoured the aggressive assaults of His church, upon the powers of darkness—a simply defensive church is sure to be despised. The world has a complaint to make against the people of God; they do not, in this ministry and testimony, hold forth the light to a world that lieth in sin; and although the world does not now complain, and wicked men are perhaps glad to be spared the intrusiveness of a troublesome testimony, still a time may come, when these very men will perhaps prefer a charge against the people of the Lord; when they will say, "why did they not testify to us, so that we must at least have been startled; * and perhaps we might not have

* The following speech of a converted Rarotongean, though couched in amusing language, is full of profitable suggestion. In the course of his address he said, "Fathers and Brethren—Last

come into this place of torment?" Yes, perhaps that charge may come, even before they leave the earth. There have been instances of this. Here is one.

For several successive evenings, a beloved and faithful minister preached "Christ, and Him crucified," to an attentive and solemn audience. God's Spirit was there; this was known by the earnest attention, the solemn stillness, the falling tear.

Evening after evening, at the close of the discourse, the pastor invited all who felt concerned for their salvation, to remain for conversation and prayer. Some remained; others went home: some, it may be, in the solitude of their own rooms, to consecrate themselves to the service of Christ; but more, it is to be feared, to drown the voice of conscience, stifle conviction, and harden themselves in their impenitence.

night as I lay on my bed thinking on my present experiences, the cocks began to crow, and all at once a thought came into my mind that they resembled our teachers and missionaries, *they* are always crowing, warning and teaching us from God's word. Papenia came first, and he crowed every morning and evening, making known the sins of the people, and the love of God; then came Wiliameni and Pitimani and Barokote, and they all crowed, all alike and continuously. Ah! it was morning then; and some of you fathers awoke out of your sleep of sin, and you have had a long day, but many of us sleep on; we just heard the sound of the voice, and lifted up our eyelids, but soon folded our hands in our folly, and slept on in sin. It was thus with me, but I am thankful the missionary did not fly away to another land, and leave us to sleep on until death. He remained, and kept on crowing the word of God. But alas! it is noonday now; my morning is passed, yet I rejoice that I have been awakened out of my sleep, and desire to give the remainder of my day to God's service."—*Gems from the Coral Islands.*

One evening, after a faithful sermon, the minister, renewing the invitation to enquirers to remain, narrated the following facts :—

He was awakened at midnight by a message from a young lady sinking in a decline, who wished to see and converse with him. As he entered the room, he noticed a younger sister of the dying one, who was evidently fast following her into eternity. He commenced asking the dying girl of her prospects, and as he did so, the younger sister arose, with a look that said, plainer than words, she did not wish to hear the conversation, and abruptly left the room. But he continued, and was rejoiced to find that the dying girl was leaning on the strong arm of her Beloved, and that, as her feet trod the dark valley, His rod and staff comforted her. And so she died—in hope.

Only a few weeks from her death, he was again sent for; this time to visit the younger sister, who was so soon following the elder to the grave. As he went to her bedside, she looked up with great anxiety, and asked, "Mr. M———, do you remember, when you were here before, and began to talk to my sister about death, I left the room?" "Yes; why did you do so?" "Because I did not wish to hear what you would say; and now see where I am. Oh, Mr. M———, why did you not *follow* me, and *make* me hear?" There was agony, even despair in her tones, as she said it; and then she added, "Oh, it is a dreadful—dreadful thing to die." And before many hours she died—in despair.

"Never, never," said he, "shall I forget that scene, and never shall I cease to urge sinners, even to *follow* them, if need be, that they may be warned of their danger and led to their only Refuge."

Dear reader! let *us* go forth to *our* testimony, and say these " I wills" with all our hearts, and practise them in our daily lives. Let us lose no time, for souls are perishing around, and our own lives are fading fast away; and for aught we know, the night shades of our ministry and testimony may be gathering around us even now!

CHAPTER III.

Ministry and Testimony.

The "I Will" of Converse.

Psalm cxlv, 5. *"I will speak of the glorious honour of Thy majesty."*

THE subject upon which we have here to enter, is THE DIFFERENT FORMS OF MINISTRY AND TESTIMONY brought before us, in the determinations of the Psalmist which we have just read. They may be said to divide themselves into three classes.

I. CONVERSE.

II. TEACHING.

III. MANIFESTATION.

The Psalmist's determination with reference to CONVERSE, will form the subject of our consideration in the present chapter. "I will speak," said he, "of the glorious honour of Thy majesty."

Little need be brought forward, to shew how low is the standard, of the habitual converse of the world. Buying and selling, gossiping and trifling, form the staple subjects of its daily converse. As are men's minds, their hopes, their interests, their enjoyments, and their fears, so also is their conversation. Of the earth, earthy, such is the best description of it; and that it is so, we cannot be surprised. Where the treasure is, there will the heart be also; and where the heart is, there generally will the tongue be too. Of course it is not for a moment to be supposed, that we would shut up all conversation about business, or the ordinary affairs of daily life; most of the children of God, must get their bread by labour as well as others; and to do this, they must mix more or less with the world; but it is one thing to talk with the people of the world, it is another to be worldly in our tone.

That, however, with which we have now to do is, the converse of God's people. Alas! how low, how very low is this oftentimes, in its tone. When the world can, so to speak, make no demands upon us, when we need not speak of its affairs, how frequently do we find ourselves entering with interest upon what is small, and unimportant; instead of upon subjects, calculated to enlarge our knowledge of God, and our love to Christ. In a word, how often do we find ourselves without an aptitude for holy converse—without that abundance of the heart, out of which the mouth should speak—without that readiness in holy things, which would make us turn our conversation in their direction without any *effort*, without any feeling that we were fulfilling a duty, or doing what was right, or performing a task. Laboured conversation on religious matters, is seldom profitable; it is like a tune played by one without an ear; correct indeed in every note, and the time kept with the utmost precision; but the spirit of the composer is not in it; it is like poetry, exact indeed in measure, and in rhyme, but lacking the inspiration, which makes true poetry what it is; it is like a statue with rounded limb, and smoothly chiselled surface, but destitute of that life, which plays in smiles around the lips, and glitters with light in the deep recesses of the eyes; all may be proper and perfect, but alas! all may be also dead. The converse upon religious matters which is pumped with labor from a christian, is very different from that which flows with ease. Better to be silent, and commune with our own hearts, if we feel, from any cause, unwilling to converse on high and holy things; for to *talk* religion is a bad thing.

Let us descend, however, from generalities, to something more particular upon this matter; for when certain points are brought before us with precision, we are more likely to derive some practical benefit; and to bring forth some practical fruit in our daily life.

Let us first take *visiting*. There are many christians who will find, if they will look into the matter, that they have many most unprofitable acquaintances, who, from custom, they are compelled to visit. These acquaintances are not congenial to them; perhaps in the first instance, they never desired to meet them; but they have done so through some of the various changes and chances of life, which are ever throwing us amongst new faces, and making us enter into new relationships. Such persons are unquestionably, at times, a great hindrance; and if the christian can limit their number, so much the better. Many a christian has frittered away in his, or her daily round of calls, not only much valuable time, but also much spiritual strength. A christian can never indulge in trifling of any kind, without deteriorating to some extent.

And here I may point out the position, in which God's ministers are often placed, in this respect. They are expected, as it is called, to visit their people; (I mean the richer portion of them,) and every minister who is alive to his duty, will endeavour to visit rich, as well as poor. But the ideas of the visitor, and visited, are perhaps very different; the former is anxious to do good; it is, perhaps, entirely in a ministerial point of view, he pays his visit; but in nine cases out of ten, he can soon see that this is not the idea of the person on whom he calls. If there be a sick person in the house, then, so far as that individual is concerned, a religious aspect may be put upon the visit; but not so far as others are concerned. Inside the walls of a place of worship, is, in their idea, the place where the minister ought to speak religion; but not in their houses, and not upon a week day. If the minister do not go, he is thought a man that neglects his duty; and many worldly people are piqued, at not being paid the compliment of a call. If he do go, they are perhaps offended at his endeavours to do good; they have certainly done what in them lies, to waste his time; if not to make him as great a trifler as themselves. This was sorely felt by the excellent James Hervey, who for some years before his death, visited very few of the principal persons in the neighbourhood. Being once asked why he so seldom went to see the gentlemen, who yet showed him all possible esteem and respect, he answered, " I can hardly name a polite family, where the conversation ever turns upon the things of God. I hear much frothy and worldly chit-chat, but not a word of Christ; and I am determined not to visit those companies, where there is not room for my Master, as well as for myself." It often happens, that a minister cannot think what has happened to untune his mind, to blunt the fine edge of his spiritual thoughts, and to bring about such like evils; if he turned his attention to this direction, he would sometimes find out whence and how the evil came.

Let us all, henceforth, pay some attention to the visits which we have to pay, or to receive; if we cannot raise the tone of them as high as we would, at least let us prevent them from falling as low as they have a natural tendency to do.

Is it not very painful to listen, from time to time, to the conversation of many who call themselves, and who, perhaps, are, 'the children of God?' It is frequently the merest gossip, it is at times not wanting in the elements of slander, it is just "all about nothing;" when the whole thing is over we are just about as wise as before it began. In every step we take in life we leave a foot-fall behind us; it will not be unprofitable to ask, what footprints have we left in our neighbours' houses? We hope we shall not be misunderstood. If we were to attempt to put a stop to social intercourse, we should be doing what we believe is not according to the mind of God; we would say to God's people, cannot the tone of your visiting be raised?

And to turn from our converse in visiting and company to that of domestic relationship; might we not also profitably ask whether this, too, could not be improved? What speaking is there in our houses of the glorious honour of the majesty of God? Are there not many professing christians' houses in which God, and Christ, and all holy things, are very seldom spoken about?

Are there not many husbands and wives, many brothers and sisters, who never interchange a word upon the highest, and holiest, and noblest themes? Are there not comparatively few who can say, "We take sweet counsel together, and walk in the house of God as friends?" Have not we, alas! not only been backward in leading to holy converse, but do we not feel to our shame that we have damped it, and often been the means of extinguishing it?

And by so doing we have suffered loss; the heat which comes from the friction of mind with mind, has never kindled into a flame; the power of sympathy, which is as great in spiritual as in temporal things, has had no opportunity of gathering, and of putting forth its energies; mind has not been drawn out to mind, and souls have lost that strengthening and comfort, which, had they gone forth together to a common object, might have been theirs. See what a oneness exists between the parents of children, from the very fact, that the father and mother have a common interest, and talk about it as well as act for it. Insensibly they become knit into each other; their own love is drawn out towards each other, while they are spending and being spent upon the common object of their affections. They do not love their children with this design; they do not act together with the view of producing this result; it comes naturally; and just so, when those who dwell together, love the Lord, and talk of Him, their hearts burn within them, as they journey on the road of life; and they are joined together by a peculiar bond; they feel that their interests for eternity are one, that they love the one Saviour, and are travelling on to a common home. May the Lord enable us, henceforth, to sanctify more and more the converse of home! That blessed word will be invested with new and more sacred associations; it will have a fresh halo of light thrown around it, if Jesus occupy his true place in it, as the relation above all others; as the ONE who, with self-existing light, walks amid earth's lesser lights, from the grandsire, whose exhausted flame is glimmering in the socket, down to the last-born child whose feeble life is like the taper that has been just lit. The familiar household words of home will be all the more precious, if our home be Jesus' home, and His be the most familiar name, He the most frequent theme; for wherever He is admitted, He diffuses a fragrance which perfumes all within its reach; whatever He touches He annoints with an oil which forbids the rust to eat, and the heavy wheels of life's daily work to creak.

Oh, I can easily understand how in a household where Jesus is a well-known name, life's weary work is made light, and much of its hard pressure is removed, and much of what must else have proved bitterness, is made sweet.

If Jesus enter into the thoughts and converse of daily life, the servant will not be afraid of profaning His holy name by encouraging a fellow-servant to do that day's work to Him; and the husband will not forget to soothe the anxieties, and to hush the cares, and still the woman's fears, of the one who looks to him for support and counsel, by bringing into their conversations that well-known name, the name of Him who is touched with a feeling of our infirmities, and whose heart is so soft, that it takes the impression of every line of our sorrow; and so responsive, that it echoes every sigh we breathe: and she will be to him, even as he has been to her, and, having been counselled in the name of God, will, by the re-active law, counsel in the same name again; and having been strengthened in His name, will in that name repay, by strengthening in return; and parents will not forget to make Jesus the subject of their teachings to their children, and it may be, that children as they talk of Him, may, in so doing, unwittingly fulfil the great re-active law, and ask some question which will lead the parent into some new, and hitherto undreamed of truth. Thus may Jesus be in our homes on earth, for thus, assuredly will He be in our home in heaven!

And here we have touched but one point, even of Christian converse; and that as a part of the "I will of Ministry and Testimony," but in this one point, how much is contained! The Lord number you, dear reader, amongst those of whom it is said, "Then they that feared the Lord, spake often one to another, and the Lord hearkened and heard it, and a book of remembrance was written before Him, for them that feared the Lord, and that thought upon His name. And they shall be mine, saith the Lord of hosts, in that day when I make up my jewels; and I will spare them, as a man spareth his own son that serveth him."

CHAPTER IV.

THE "I WILL" OF CONVERSE.

(Continued.)

Psalm cxlv, 5. "*I will speak of the glorious honour of Thy majesty.*"

WE must talk much *to* God, we must talk much *with* Him, if we would safely talk much *about* Him. We must have an inner life, out of which the outward life must flow; else our external life of holiness, in all its various streams, whether they be those which take their way through our own home, or the houses of others, will run unevenly, and, at times, run dry.

The secret of an effective holy life in public, will ever prove to be a holy life with God in private; this is the root from which, in due season, will come both leaves and fruit.

And let it be observed, that in this matter of converse, the fruit which is thus brought forth is not, of necessity, the power to speak with *volubility* upon sacred things. There are many eminent Christians who are not great talkers: but though not *abundant* of speech, they are *weighty* in it; and what they bring forth in a *few* words, is often of more value, than the much speaking of other men. Their words are like the large, rich, ripened fruit, which hangs singly upon the tree; and which has absorbed all the strength, and sap, of the branch on which it hangs; the words of others, are at times too plentiful, and like the thick clustering, but immatured fruit, for the swelling and bringing to maturity of which, the branch has not sufficient strength. A few words and weighty, are better than many and weak.

But now to turn more immediately to the matter we have in hand. God, and Christ, and the Spirit, and their honour, and all connected with them, should be the subjects of our converse; not because we ought to speak about them, nor even because it is a privilege so to do; but because we, ourselves, have an *intimate relation to*, and *interest in* them all. We generally speak or *converse* about that, in which we ourselves have an interest; the very fact of our having that interest and relationship, making us come on such a topic. It is personal interest that throws life into conversation; we see a change come over the countenance, and into the tone of voice, and into the very attitude of the body, and the animation of the eye, when the element of personal interest, enters into the conversation in which we are engaged. And when we recall to mind our conversations on holy things, do we not feel how often they have been flat, and cold, how often they have dragged wearily along, because they lacked this very fire of the personal element, this very salt, and seasoning, of individual interest? We have, no doubt, come very short in this respect; and it may be, our very listlessness and formality have done hurt; our coldness and abstraction infected those, who, had we been otherwise, might have caught from our animated eye, a spark of spiritual intelligence; and from our earnest tones, a deeper knowledge of the realities of sacred truth.

Oh! how blessed, how altered will be the condition of God's people in this respect, when they are perfected in glory! Converse upon all that is holy, will then be their delight—converse, with an intelligence far above what they now possess—converse, the interest of which will never flag nor cease; they shall feel in glory that they have a common interest; they shall be near the God, and Christ, to whom they stand in blessed relationship; all the restraints of human corruption, langour, and distraction, shall be removed; and saint shall doubtless communicate with saint, with a freedom, and a largeness, and a depth, of which not even an idea can be formed now. Meanwhile, let us, dear reader, try to improve, and endeavour in a measure, at least, now to attain that, which if we be Christ's, we shall assuredly attain to hereafter. When we converse upon anything connected with God, let us throw our own personal being into our words; let us not content ourselves with *abstract* theories, or truths about Him, and His: surely the christian, who is one with Christ, bone as it were of His bone, and flesh of His flesh, is nearly enough connected with Him, to make him speak with the power of *personal interest*, on every subject in which He is concerned. If this is to be the case, we must seek to have more personal realizations of God in our own souls; that out of the abundance of the heart, the mouth may speak.

But the word which we here translate "speak," is considered by Hebrew critics to include also the idea of "expatiating," "speaking at large;" not merely

" alluding to, incidentally," but " entering into particulars;" as though one took delight, in speaking upon the matter in hand, Now there is something very satisfactory in entering into particulars ; we can often gather light upon a great truth, by having had set before us some of the particulars connected with it; we can often understand what is too high for us, *in* itself and *by* itself, by some examples which bring it within reach of our dull understandings. We are like men who want to attain a height, who have not wings to fly up to it, but who can reach it by going up a ladder, step by step. Particulars are often like the rounds of a ladder, little, it may be, in themselves, but very helpful to us; and to dwell upon particulars is often of use to ourselves; it certainly is to many with whom we converse.

Let us remember, that circumstanced as we are in our present state, we have no faculties for grasping in its simple grandeur the glorious honour of the majesty of God. We know most of God, from what we know of His doings amongst the children of men. Hereafter, the Lord's people shall, no doubt, have much revealed to them of the glorious honour of the majesty of God, which they could now neither bear nor understand; meanwhile they have to know Him chiefly by what He has said and done; and if only our eyes be open, we shall be at no loss to recognise in these, the glorious honour of His majesty.

Perhaps it might be said by some, " What can we know of this ? We move in an humble sphere of life; we never come in contact with the mighty operations of God in nature, nor with anything remarkable in the way of His providence; we have no opportunities of realizing the glorious honour of God's majesty;" but there is no sphere too contracted for this great display; there is no position so low, that in it it will refuse to shine. The fault, dear reader, lies in ourselves; the majesty of the sun is not seen by the eye that is blind; the majesty of God in daily life is veiled, just in proportion to the darkness of our understandings. If God open our eyes, we behold wondrous things; not only out of His law, but in His daily ordering of events. Yes! in these common things, the glorious honour of God's majesty is to be seen; just as His creative majesty is visible, in the formation of the smallest grass-blade or the meanest shell. When our very daily bread comes before us, common as it is, the glorious honour of God's majesty is to be traced in it; for what was every grain of corn of which it was composed, but a separate resurrection from the dead? And how could that have been brought about, save by the glorious majesty of God? Well might the Psalmist say, *"I will meditate also of all Thy work, and talk of Thy doings."*

Let me add, in conclusion, one or two practical directions with reference to the " converse" upon which we have just now been dwelling. If we be God's people, let us shew the world that we have a real interest in everything connected with Him; let them see by our way of speaking of Him, and His, that we love Him, and all connected with Him, in every way. And let us encourage each other, and magnify the majesty and honour of God, by bringing into our familiar converse, the one with the other, the particulars wherein we have found Him gracious, and wherein He has done wondrously for us.

We cannot tell how blessed the result, which may be thus produced. Perhaps some Christian brother, dull of hearing and of seeing, will understand more of His greatness and His goodness; perhaps some little spark, which we have struck from our knowledge or experience, may kindle a flame in him; so that he may say "my heart burns within me on the way." It may be, that making use of our talent, we shall have more given unto us; perhaps we shall be kept from some evil knowledge, or evil train of thought, which, coming up in other conversation, might have done us hurt. Of this we may be sure, that the more our conversation has to do with the glorious honour of the majesty of God, the more will it be free from all that is calculated to debase, or depress the mind: the more will self, in all its varied developments, be excluded: the less will there be of those idle words, for which we must give account.

CHAPTER V.

Ministry and Testimony.

THE "I WILL" OF TEACHING.

Psalm li, 13. *"Then will I teach transgressors Thy ways, and sinners shall be converted unto Thee."*

TEACHING is ennobled by the great fact that God Himself is a Teacher. The three persons of the Trinity—Father, Son, and Holy Ghost—are all presented to us in Holy Scripture in the character of Teachers; yea, not only of teachers, but of laborious Teachers, carrying on their work in the midst of many impediments; and with patience, and wisdom, and skill.

It is a sad fact, that but comparatively few are alive to the vast importance of the position of the teacher. Teaching is looked upon by many almost in the same light as household work, and paid after the same rate; the tutor and the butler are looked upon alike as servants, and the master says, "I will give unto this last, even as unto thee!"

We can never degrade the teacher except at the expense of the person taught; the shaft men so often cruelly let fly, will glance aside, and do some hurt to one they love.

The teacher's mission is from God; and whether this teaching be that of masters, and mistresses in their schools; or that of the mother who clusters her little ones around her knee; or that of the nurse, from whom the infant catches the first meaning of the different tones of the human voice; it is a mission from God: it is en-nobled by God,—and if it be carried on for God,—it will, in eternity, take rank amid the great things which were done by God's people, in time.

The victory which patient teaching has gained over an unruly spirit, will be thought more of than the successful issue of the most protracted siege; the devices by which, with God's blessing, stubbornness of the disposition is melted, and through which the after life becomes full of holy deeds, will be magnified above all that the man of science has done in his laboratory; above all that the skilled artizan has produced from his loom. Christ Himself will, in eternity, as the One who was the Great Teacher, assume the headship of all who were teachers after His example, and for Him; and will acknowledge as His brethren, in this respect, alike the apostle Paul, who wrote "many things hard to be understood," and the poorest Sunday school teacher, who could do little more than teach his infant class how to spell the name of Jesus. Jesus, verily, will not be ashamed to call th   all brethren; they will be accounted the members of a ɔody, of which He is the head.

Surely such a consideration as this, should cheer the heart of many, who are now, it may be, almost tempted to despond. To flesh and blood much of their work is uninteresting; and many of those upon whom they have to carry it on, are disappointing and provoking; but whether they succeed, or whether they do not, if they be teaching as unto the Lord, they are one, in work and interest, with Jesus; and every hour spent in labour, and every effort made, shall hereafter be acknowledged by Him.

Let us now, however, turn from the general subject of the ministry of teaching, to some of the particulars connected with it. Several are suggested to our notice by the passage immediately under consideration. We are all familiar with the cirumstances under which this psalm was written; it is full of fearful realities; the realities of a broken heart; of a deep view of the holiness of God; of the awful nature of sin: there is a living personal earnestness, running through it all, which many, perhaps, of ourselves, have unwittingly acknowledged, by choosing it as the form of words, in which we confessed before God, it may be, our general sinfulness, or more probably, some recent, some decided sin.

It is in a psalm of this character, we find the words, "*Then will I teach transgressors Thy ways;*" and coming, as these words do, after the petitions, that God would "restore to the Psalmist the joy of His salvation, and uphold him with His free Spirit," we have brought before us the great fact, that the Psalmist's teaching will be from *experience;* out of the fulness of his own knowledge of God, he will minister in teaching to others.

We will now assume that the duty of ministering in teaching, is recognised by each of our readers; that you, dear reader, wish to fulfil the whole will of God; and this as well as anything else. Let me, then, direct your attention to the great importance of teaching *out of your own personal experience;* of using your experience for this purpose, and not letting it lie idle. Experience is accounted precious in the world; the man that has it, turns it to account; it is precious also, in the spiritual world; and he who has it, may do good service with it for God. Even the dark experience which a man, unhappily, has had of sin, may be overruled and sanctified, and a jewel be drawn forth from it, just as a precious stone is often drawn from the depths and recesses of a gloomy mine. The precious stone is unconnected with the darkness of the mine, but it comes forth from it; the experience, also, is unconnected with the sin, though it is from it that it is brought out.

Of course no one will misunderstand what I say, and suppose that we would recommend men to do evil that good may come. What we say is this—it seems to be ever the way of God, to draw forth life from death; this He does continually, in the natural world; and by the operation of His wonderful power, and goodness, He does the like in the spiritual world. Death is from man, for sin was his and death came by sin; but resurrection is from God; so sin is of man, the overruling of it is of God; the terrible fall is from himself; the sanctified experience from it, is of the Holy Ghost. And so is the using of that experience also. And what are all the records of the sins of the saints, which we find given us in the Scriptures by the Spirit, but His use of man's dark experience of sin to warn and teach whoever reads? "These things are written for our learning."

Well, then, dear reader, let us use our own experience, and that of others, for the purposes of teaching. Those experiences may be dark ones, of the evil, and chastisement, and misery of sin; or they may be bright ones, of the blessedness of serving God, and of His faithfulness, and truth, and love; but whatever they are, let us not permit them to lie idle. Let us use our own dark experience, *to warn others*, or to *make us pray for them;* we shall have opportunities enough of doing so, if we will. Perhaps those opportunities will be afforded, even amongst those who are near and dear to us, in our daily life. When we see any one hastening to the brink of the pit, into which we have fallen, and in which we have suffered hurt, let us give him the benefit of our experience, and, if possible, save him before he plunge in. And if, unhappily, we cannot do this, oh! remembering what we suffered ourselves, let us pray him out of the pit if we can; let us stand at the mouth of it, and, out of our own experiences, teach him the only way of escape, and, it may be, we shall be the means of rescuing his soul.

Sin is no talent, but the sanctified experience of a sinner, is. Let us use it, along with all other talents, for the One to whom we must give account. A little thought, and searching our own hearts, will shew us how we can in this particular way, teach for God. If we have had experience of gross sin in any form, the way of doing so presents itself, only too plainly, before our eyes; but even if we have not, we need not be at any loss.

Let the mother who was snared in her own young days, by the love of human approbation, teach her children out of the depth of her own experience; and from their youngest days, instruct them to look up to the highest standard of praise, the approbation of their God. Let her shew them that one approving word from Jesus, yea, one sent from Him to them through their own consciences, is better than man's superficial admiration, man's most fulsome praise. Let the one who set her heart too fondly upon human love, only to find that in her case the fair vision was a mirage, the illusive lakes and fountains of which, had not one real drop to slake her parching thirst, teach those who come within her circle of influence, out of the depths of her own wilderness experiences; and let her hand, wasted it may be with life's fever, point others to that One who is the water of life, at which not only the immortal spirit, but even the human affections of the heart, can drink and be refreshed.

Whoever has yielded to pride, or vanity, or worldliness, or selfishness, or foolish habits of thought, or any such like things, can minister out of their experience to others; and do it with the earnestness which experience gives. Who can warn the careless boy, who crowds canvas upon his fragile boat, so well as he who has been himself upset, and snatched, as it were, from the very jaws of a watery death? Who can warn the child of the danger of eating the bright, but poisoned berry, so well as he who had tasted once of the tempting bait, and had writhed in agony from its subtle power, and escaped from its influence barely with his life? None will be so well able to point out pure gold as they who had once believed that all was gold that glittered, but who have now found out their mistake by having become the victims of many a cheat. Let us give our children, and those with whom from time to time we come in contact, the benefit of our experiences, so far as opportunity is afforded; and perhaps from our sorrows they may reap a harvest of joys.

And just one word upon those blessed experiences of

which the Psalmist speaks in the verse immediately preceding the text. *"Restore unto me the joy of Thy salvation, and uphold me with Thy free spirit."* Whatever be our *blessed* experiences, let us put them out to interest for God; let us use them for Him, let us teach out of them.

If so be we have tasted that the Lord is gracious, let us teach others of Him as we have found Him; if He have restored us after we have fallen, let us teach other fallen ones that He is willing to restore them; if He have succoured us in our day of trial, either of body or of soul, let us teach others out of our own experience, and cheer them with the knowledge that the Lord is gracious. "Blessed be God," (says the apostle, in 2 Cor. i, 3,) "even the Father of our Lord Jesus Christ, the Father of mercies and the God of all comfort, who comforteth us in all our tribulation, that we may be able to comfort them which are in any trouble, by the comfort wherewith we ourselves are comforted of God."

If we have been in the garden of the Lord, oh, let, us win others thither, by telling them out of our own experience, how ripe are its fruits, how cool its shade; that there we found the One of whom it is written, "I sat under His shadow with great delight, and His fruit was sweet to my taste." (Canticles ii, 3.)

CHAPTER VI.

THE "I WILL" OF TEACHING.

(Continued.)

Psalm li, 13. *"Then will I teach transgressors Thy ways, and sinners shall be converted unto Thee."*

THE idea of teaching generally includes that of toil. There are, no doubt, many cases when the aptitude and intelligence of the pupil make teaching a pleasant work; but this must be taken as the exception, and not the rule. Teaching generally involves self-denial, as well as toil. Every good and successful teacher has been a painstaking and self-denying man; doing more than his bare duty called upon him to do, and not measuring his exertions simply by his hire. If we might speak of God after the manner of men, He also seems to have taken great pains in teaching the children of men.

Now what I desire to treat of in the present chapter is :—

I. *The painstaking which should be found in all teaching undertaken for God.* And

II. *The necessity of doing the Lord's work fully; not picking and choosing as we like, but taking it as He presents it to us.*

There should be painstaking in all teaching for God. We should be very cautious how we treat as a light thing our ministry of Teaching. That teaching may be in a great congregation, or in a Sunday school, or in our own domestic circle, or perhaps the object of it may be only some one or two friends, who are looking up to us for instruction: but whether those who are taught be high or low, many or few, rich or poor, what our hand findeth to do we should do with our might: though we were but teaching, as it were, the alphabet of religion, we should take pains. The pains connected with teaching may be divided into two classes; the *passive* pains of what we have to undergo; the *active* pains of what we have to do.

There is a great deal to be undergone in teaching. We have *to bear with much*. The stupidity, the inaptitude to learn, the inattention, the forgetfulness, the waywardness, of those we have to teach, are so many dead weights which we have to bear. We are but flesh and blood, and these things weary us, and undoubtedly make our work far harder than otherwise it would be.

Let me, remind you, dear readers, that Jesus, the Great Teacher, and I hope I may say your great example, had to bear with all this; and let me remind you further, that all these are so many trials of endurance; and that the endurance of the saints will add to the lustre and glory of their crown. There is a reward for *endurance*, as well as *action*.

Have we not many instances in Holy Scripture of Christ's endurance in this point? Instead of reviling His disciples for their stupidity, hear how He speaks to them in Matt. xv, 16: "And Jesus said, are ye yet without understanding? do not ye yet understand that whatsoever entereth in at the mouth goeth into the belly, and is cast out into the draught?"   And again in chap. xvi, 6: "Then Jesus said unto them, Take heed and beware of the leaven of the Pharisees and of the Sadducees.   And they reasoned among themselves, saying, It is because we have taken no bread: which when Jesus perceived, he said unto them, O ye of little faith, why reason ye among yourselves, because ye have brought no bread?   Do ye not yet understand, neither remember the five loaves of the five thousand, and how many baskets ye took up?   Neither the seven loaves of the four thousand, and how many baskets ye took up?   How is it that ye do not understand that I spake it not to you concerning bread, that ye should beware of the leaven of the Pharisees and of the Sadducees?   Then understood they how that He bade them not beware of the the leaven of bread, but of the doctrine of the Pharisees and of the Sadducees."   And again in John xi, 11: "These things said He: and after that He saith unto them, Our friend Lazarus sleepeth; but I go that I may awake him out of sleep.   Then saith His disciples, Lord, if he sleep he shall do well.   Howbeit Jesus spake of His death; but they thought that He had spoken of taking of rest in sleep.   Then said Jesus unto them plainly, Lazarus is dead.   And I am glad for your sakes that I was not there, to the intent ye may believe; nevertheless let us go unto him."   Surely the disciple is not above his master, nor the servant above his Lord! Wherever we look we find that endurance in toil meets with its reward.   The greatest discoveries and inventions have been the fruits of long endurance.   At times, men seemed to have the object they desired within their grasp; and then, it receded from them: and with this disappointment came also the temptation to give up: but they endured and gained their end at last. In education above all things, endurance is needed, and is sure to produce its results. Patient endurance in teaching has accomplished more than even the most sanguine could have dared to hope.

At the great day, there will doubtless be seen many wonderful results of simple endurance in ministry; in the ministry of Teaching, and of Testimony. Great things will be found to have been accomplished, without any shining talent, or extraordinary opportunities; with nothing but "the patient continuance in well doing." Our fellow men may have looked upon us, as having a claim to no higher character, than that of a persevering, patient plodder, in the path of duty or of love; they may have despised our want of brilliancy, and talent; we may ourselves have felt painfully conscious, that in these things, we have been far inferior to others; but the reward for patient endurance in labour will, in all probability, be greater than that for the bare use of any talent we might have possessed. It may have been positive enjoyment to use a talent: but it is seldom, or never any enjoyment to endure; the results produced by the sheer exercise of endurance, will be acknowledged to have been purchased at a higher price, than those which have been produced by the exercise of talent. This assuredly ought to be no slight encouragement to those who are possessed of no shining talents. Such persons can do something. They can *endure* in some humble sphere of labour, for Christ; and by such endurance not only act *like* Him, but also act *for* Him. Their talent may be of no more power in itself, than the single drops which trickle down the surface of the rock; but if they, by continuance, can leave a record of their progress, in the channel which they wear away, oh! surely, so can the feeble talent, ever at work, win a record of its endurance, aye, in what will prove more indestructible than the hardest rock itself.*

These, and such as these make up what might be called the passive pains of teaching; there are others which are *active,* and therefore more *acute.*

In teaching, we must *condescend.* We are now, of course, concerned only with spiritual things; and all our remarks must have reference to them. Unless we condescend to men of low estate in knowledge, we shall often not be able to accomplish anything for the soul. There are few who are engaged in spiritual teaching who have not, from time to time, been astonished at the dense ignorance with which they have come into contact; even in the cases of men, who received credit for knowing something of the truths of God. I am not referring now, to ignorance on prophetical views, or abstruse points of doctrine; but upon *fundamental points.* We frequently find instances, where men are very misty upon the great doctrine of justification by faith; and still more

---

* The following fact should be remembered by such as are inclined to despair. "When the celebrated Mr. Milne, the missionary, was preaching, not long before he left England, in the pulpit of his pastor, Mr. Cowie of Huntley, an old man belonging to the church was observed to weep very much. On being questioned as to the cause, he said, ' I remember the day when I took William Milne by the shoulders and turned him out of the Sunday school, for his inveterate obstinacy and stupidity.'"

misty upon the decided distinction, between justification
and sanctification; and the relationship which they bear,
the one to the other. Upon all this we ourselves may
be perfectly clear, we may without intending so to do,
almost look down on those who are misty and confused;
it is one of those cases in which we must condescend;
milk is needed, and we must feed with milk, and not
with meat. Or the ignorance may be in spiritual practice.
A man may have received the truth in his head, but the
measure of his heart's sanctification may be small; the
tone of his spiritual life may be low; he may be allowing
himself in that, which we consider no Christian man
should; this is another case where we must condescend.
Our duty, under such circumstances, is to teach a man
what is better, what is right; to stoop to him, to enlighten
his ignorance, and not to despise him, or pass him by,
or think him not worth teaching, because his point of
attainment is so far beneath our own. We never stoop
to bless another, without picking up a blessing for ourselves; we can never water without being watered; we
can never teach without being taught. Here again Jesus
comes forward as an example. When Philip said to
Jesus, "Lord, shew us the Father, and it sufficeth us,"
Jesus condescends to His disciple's ignorance and answers,
" Have I been so long time with you, and yet hast thou
not known Me, Philip? he that hath seen Me hath seen
the Father; and how sayest thou then shew us the
Father?" John xiv, 9. When the sorrowing disciples
journeyed with Him to Emmaus, they said, " But we
trusted that it had been He which should have redeemed
Israel; and beside all this, to-day is the third day since
these things were done." Then He condescended to

their ignorance; and though He saiɑ unto them, "O fools and slow of heart to believe all that the prophets have spoken. Ought not Christ to have suffered these things, and to enter into His glory?" still He fulfilled towards them His ministry of teaching; for, "Beginning at Moses and all the prophets, He expounded unto them in all the Scriptures the things concerning Himself." Luke xxiv, 27.

Let this, then, encourage us to condescend to teach the rudiments, the alphabet of religion. Let this induce the preacher of the gospel to take up, from time to time, the very plainest things; and to dwell upon the first principles of our most holy faith; and let it induce the man of intellect, or the man of spiritual attainment, not to despise an humble scholar, whether it be in a Sunday school, or in a cottage, or amongst his own children or servants at home. If his Father stoop from heaven, surely he may stoop on earth; it may be that as the Christian rises he will lift up some fellow-Christian from his low estate, at least to the level of himself. On the day of his death, in his eightieth year, Elliott, "the Apostle of the Indians," was found teaching the alphabet to an Indian child at his bedside. "Why not rest from your labours now?" said a friend. "Because," said the venerable man, "I have prayed to God to render me useful in my sphere. He has heard my prayer; for now that I can no longer preach, he leaves me strength enough to teach this poor child his alphabet."

And in this ministry of teaching, let us be willing often to go back, and to go over the same ground again and again. In many cases this is absolutely necessary; the desired effect cannot otherwise be produced. This

the painter has to do with his pictures; this the husbandman has to do with his crops; this God Himself has
done with us. If we have attained to anything, has it
not been by God's teaching us the same thing over and
over again? Have we not continually forgotten even
what we seemed to have learned? Has He not had to
repeat not only old lessons but old chastisements? All
this was God's taking pains with us; and as He has not
thrown us off in our stupidity, we must not throw others
off in theirs. Their precious souls are worth the pains;
let us take them freely and patiently; perhaps we shall
have a great result.*

Let me point out also the great necessity of *not over-
driving in religious knowledge.* There are many who can
take in religious knowledge only very slowly; we may
force them on; we may give them a head knowledge of
great and even deep truths; but they will be like a house
run up in haste, and therefore unsubstantial; they will
be like a tree forced into bearing before its time, and
whose fruit is not natural; they will be like a child, upon
whose weak body there has been placed a load, too

---

* John Wesley's home education, under the tutelage of his
parents themselves, was peculiar, and well calculated to initiate
him early in habits of order and perseverance in accomplishing
any object he might undertake. "Why, my dear," said his father
to his mother, while patiently teaching one of their children
a simple lesson, which it was slow to learn, "why, my dear, do
you tell that dull boy the same thing twenty times over?"
"Because," replied the other, "nineteen times won't do. If I tell
him but nineteen times all my lalour is lost, but the twentieth
secures the object!"

Zeuxis being asked why he was so long about a picture,
answered, "I paint for eternity."

heavy for it to bear. "I have fed you with milk, (said the Apostle,) and not with meat." The Apostle followed the example of his Lord, who said to His Apostles, "I have yet many things to say unto you, but ye cannot bear them now."

There is one point more upon which it will be well to add a few words, *i. e., the necessity of doing the Lord's work fully; not picking and choosing as we like, but taking it as He presents it to us.*

The children of God may rest assured, that the Evil One will tempt them *in* their work, when he cannot tempt them *from* it; a believer may, by the way in which he does work, afford Satan as great an opportunity of triumph, as if he had stood aloof from work altogether.

There is a natural tendency in the heart of man, to shrink from what is painful, and burdensome; and in almost every instance, he has fancies and preferences, which he wishes to indulge; this tendency and these fancies manifest themselves in ministry and testimony, especially in that of teaching. The minister and the district visitor may shrink from visiting the disagreeable people in their respective paths of duty, and give their attention to those with whom it may be pleasant to converse, and from whom, in point of fact, they may learn much themselves; the Sunday school teacher may decline to receive into her class some stupid or unprepossessing child, who should come into it in the ordinary routine of the school's periodic changes, or, perhaps she will visit during the week only the agreeable children or agreeable parents, or, should she be impelled, by a strong sense of duty, to receive the undesired child into her class, perhaps she will slur over her duties towards her, and take less

pains with her than with the rest.   Again, in the matter
of his sermons, the minister may shrink from the rough
hard work of dealing with unconverted men; knowing
well that distinctive preaching must bring with it observation, if not opposition, he may turn to a class of
truths, which may at once edify the godly and leave the
ungodly untouched; he may fall into that dangerous
system, too common in the present day, of calling all,
"Christian brethren," and "beloved brethren," although
they may be well known to be living in open and daring
sin; by so doing he is following his own choice and is
not doing the Lord's work fully, he is choosing for
himself, and he is almost certain to leave that in which,
perhaps the greatest blessings would have been found.

Had we the energy of Whitfield and Hill, and such
men, displayed in the present day, results would doubtless
appear akin to those which followed their ministry; but
he who will minister thus, must expect to be called "an
enthusiast," "a ranter," "a new light," and he may
consider that he has got off well if this be all.*   The

* "When Pickthank had told his tale" against Faithful, in
the Pilgrim's Progress, "the judge directed his speech to the
prisoner at the bar, saying 'Thou runagate, heretic, and traitor,
hast thou heard what these honest gentlemen have witnessed
against thee?'   And when the jury went out, whose names were
Mr. Blindman, Mr. No-good, Mr. Malice, Mr. Love-lust, Mr.
Live-loose, Mr. Heady, Mr. High-mind, Mr. Enmity, Mr. Liar,
Mr. Cruelty, Mr. Hate-light, and Mr. Implacable, every one gave
in his private verdict against him among themselves, and afterwards unanimously concluded to bring him in guilty before the
judge.   And first amongst themselves Mr. Blindman the foreman,
said, I see clearly that this man is a heretic.   Then said Mr. No-
good, away with such a fellow from the earth.   Ay, said Mr.

thin-skinned preacher will bleed at every scratch; and yet, for my part, I have always found those men most respected, and even most followed, who have not paid respect to any person, who have said what they thought, and nailed their colours to the mast. Even the world honours consistency and courage, and the plainest speaker will have, in general, the most hearers. The only part by which a bull can be safely taken is by the horns.

The energy of manner of the late Rowland Hill, and the power of his voice, are said to have been at times overwhelming. While once preaching at Wootton-under-Edge, his country residence, he was carried away by his feelings, and, raising himself to his full height, exclaimed, "Beware, I am in earnest; men call me an enthusiast, but I am not; mine are the words of truth and soberness. When I first came into this part of the country, I was walking on yonder hill; I saw a gravel pit fall in and bury three human beings alive. I lifted

Malice, for I hate the very look of him. Then said Mr. Love-lust, I could never endure him. Nor I, said Mr. Live-loose, for he would be always condemning my way. Hang him, said Mr. Heady. A sorry scrub, said Mr. High-mind. My heart riseth against him, said Mr. Enmity. He is a rogue, said Mr. Liar. Hanging is too good for him, said Mr. Cruelty, Let us despatch him out of the way, said Mr. Hate-light. Then said Mr. Implacable, Might I have all the world given me, I could not be reconciled to him; therefore let us forthwith bring him in guilty of death."

Christians who are in testimony for God, do not always hear the world's, and perhaps their own ungodly neighbours' opinions of them, but the above would salute their ears full often, if men spoke out what they inwardly think, and what they say amongst themselves.

up my voice so loud that I was heard to the town below,
a distance of a mile. Help came, and rescued two of the
poor sufferers. No one called me an enthusiast then;
and when I see eternal destruction ready to fall upon
poor sinners, and about to entomb them irrevocably
in an eternal mass of woe, and call on them to escape by
repenting and fleeing to Christ, shall I be called an
enthusiast? No, sinner, I am not an enthusiast in so
doing." A shipbuilder on being asked what he thought
of Whitfield, replied, "Every Sunday that I go to my
parish church I can build a ship from stem to stern
under the sermon; but under Mr. Whitfield I could not
lay a single plank."

In all ministry, whether its special development be
teaching, or anything else, Christ Jesus is to be our
example. And what is the example which He sets us
here? Jesus did his Father's work fully; He shrank
from no part of it; He did not decline any portion of it;
He came into contact with sinners; yea, He died with
one on the right hand, and another on the left. If any
one was warranted in declining contact with the sinner,
that ONE, assuredly, was Christ. Sin was to Him essen-
tially odious; odious in a way in which it never can be
to us; we cannot know its depths—He did; we cannot
detect the individuals in whom its worst developments
are dwelling—He knew them as soon as they came near
Him; moreover, our nature being sinful in itself, does
not recoil instinctively, as His did, when evil is at hand.
The presence of sin was suffering to Him—it is not
always so to us; the presence of sin could not lie hidden
from Him—it may be wholly undetected by us. When
we think of all this, and then, that the testimony con-

cerning Him was, "This man receiveth sinners, and eateth with them," how can we pretend to be in ministry, after His example, and yet act altogether differently from the way in which He did.

Jesus never shrank from any sinner, when He could minister to him in teaching. True! He left the Pharisees, and Sadducees, and Scribes, and such like cavillers, who wanted to gainsay, and not to be taught; but He went out into the highways of life; He conversed with the worst He found there, and invited them to come in. Zaccheus found Jesus willing to look upon him; the Samaritan woman found him willing to converse with her; and again, and again, did He return to minister to, and to teach the crowd; to bear with the captious questions of some, with the hard unbelief and pitiless scorn of others. How could He have been the man of sorrows, and acquainted with grief, if He had so chosen His path in life, as not to touch one piercing thorn, or tread upon one rough edged stone?

And as Jesus did, so did His apostles also. They verily did not pretend to choose the smooth; they certainly did not pretend to avoid the rough. Had they done so, they need not have gone through their great fight of afflictions; we may also add, their ministry would have been without its glorious results.

Common observation ought to teach us, how impossible it is to avoid the rough, if we would succeed in any great enterprize. No conqueror brings to a successful issue the war in which he is engaged, without encountering many difficulties; and those, over and above what he has to meet on the field of bloody strife itself. No sailor can bring his vessel to port, after a long voyage, without having had to weather some storms, and reef his sails in some tempestuous gales. The shopkeeper, in his daily transactions of business, has to take the rough with the smooth; the artizan must do the same, even with the material upon which he works. Shall the Christian be the only one who is exempted from all rough work, and who is not to be called upon for an exercise of patience and of skill? Let the Christian know that much of this rough work from which he shrinks, is absolutely necessary for his soul's health. Carefully refined food, would be deleterious to the body; and God has mixed the coarse and fine, in due proportions, so that both, together, nourish and expand the frame; and so, carefully refined circumstances, and spheres of action, would be deleterious to the soul, and God has mingled the rough and smooth: and he who takes them, as God gives them, will be robust in his spiritual frame, and well developed in all the graces of the soul. For our own sakes, then, dear reader, let us not reject anything whereunto we are called; let us not look for fancy spheres of duty, fancy school children, fancy sick people, fancy poor people; picked cases for our convenience, or, to speak more plainly, for our sloth; rather let us be prepared to endure hardness, for Christ; let us simply ask that our sphere, and all in it, be allotted by the ONE whose we are, and whom we wish to serve; and let us go forth to fill it, saying determinately, in the strength of the Holy Ghost, "I will."

CHAPTER VII.

Prayer.

Psalm xxviii, 1. *"Unto Thee will I cry, O Lord, my rock, be not silent to me: lest, if Thou be silent to me, I become like them that go down into the pit."*

Psalm lv, 16, 17. *"As for me, I will call upon God, and the Lord shall save me: evening, and morning, and at noon, will I pray and cry aloud: and He shall hear my voice."*

Psalm lxi, 2. *"From the end of the earth will I cry unto Thee, when my heart is overwhelmed: lead me to the rock that is higher than I."*

Psalm lxiii, 1. *"O God, Thou art my God, early will I seek Thee; my soul thirsteth for Thee, my flesh longeth for Thee, in a dry and thirsty land where no water is."*

Psalm lxxxvi, 7. *"In the day of my trouble I will call upon Thee, for Thou wilt answer me."*

Psalm cxxi, 1. *"I will lift up mine eyes unto the hills, from whence cometh my help."*

WE hear much, we see much of the mighty powers which God has put into the hands of man, as regards the natural world. Wheresoever we turn, we find ourselves surrounded with the evidences of this power in construction, in invention, and in imitation. Scarce a day passes, in which we are not presented with something which has more or less of the claims of novelty; with some new discovery, or else some application or combination of powers already known. To this, man is not blind; he appreciates, he uses every new and mighty engine, as it is presented to him: and whether it be chloroform, to blunt the acuteness of his pain; or electricity, to flash his messages to the ends of the world; or steam to whirl him over the earth's surface, and do in his factories the work of thousands of hands; he hears, sees, speaks about, and uses the mighty powers which God has put within his reach.

We hear but little, however, of the mighty powers which God has put into man's hands, so far as the spiritual world is concerned. The prevailing aspect of God's people is one of weakness, often one of despondency; they feel the pressure of the world, they see difficulties to be overcome, they realize their own inherent weakness—there is much despondency, by reason of the realization of their own feebleness; there is little vigour, by reason of the non-realization of the mighty efficacy of faith and prayer.

Faith and Prayer! Could we but realize, and put into operation, the powers contained in these, the two great forces of the spiritual world, we should, in our collective and individual capacity, be very different from what we are; we should know and feel that we had the key of heaven's treasure, and the lever of heaven's strength; we should " be strong in the Lord, and in the power of His might," we should be prepared, for great deeds, both of action and resistance, in the spiritual life; we should never dream of failure, we should never miss real success. The Lord give you dear reader, power in prayer.

Now, first of all, it will be encouraging to note some of the Scripture statements, which show the power that God has linked to prayer.

"Elias was a man subject to like passions as we are, and he prayed earnestly that it might not rain; and it rained not on the earth by the space of three years and six months." James v, 17.

"Elijah cried unto the Lord, and said, O Lord my God, hast Thou also brought evil upon the widow with whom I sojourn, by slaying her son? And he stretched himself upon the child three times, and cried unto the Lord, and said, O Lord my God, I pray Thee let this child's soul come into him again. And the Lord heard the voice of Elijah; and the soul of the child came into him again." 1 Kings xvii, 20—22.

"Asa cried unto the Lord his God, and said, Lord, it is nothing with Thee to help, whether with many, or with them that have no power: help us, O Lord our God; for we rest on Thee, and in Thy name we go against this multitude. O Lord, Thou art our God; let not man prevail against Thee. So the Lord smote the Ethiopians before Asa, and before Judah; and the Ethiopians fled." 2 Chron. xiv, 11, 12.

"Jabez called on the God of Israel, saying, O that Thou wouldst bless me indeed, and enlarge my coast, and that Thine hand might be with me, and that Thou wouldst keep me from evil, that it may not grieve me. And God granted him that which he requested." 1 Chron. iv, 10.

"The angel said unto Zacharias, Fear not, Zacharias, for thy prayer is heard; and thy wife Elizabeth shall bear thee a son." Luke i, 13.

"Then shall ye call upon Me, and ye shall go and pray unto Me, and I will hearken unto you. And ye shall seek Me, and find Me, when ye shall search for Me with all your heart. And I will be found of you, saith the Lord: and I will turn away your captivity, and I will gather you from all the nations, and from all the places whither I have driven you, saith the Lord; and I will bring you again into the place whence I caused you to be carried away captive." Jer. xxix, 12—14.

"And he said, O Lord God of my master Abraham, I pray Thee, send me good speed this day, and show kindness unto my master Abraham. Behold I stand by the well of water * * * and let it come to pass, that the damsel to whom I shall say, 'let down thy pitcher, I pray thee, that I may drink;' and she shall say, 'drink, and I will give thy camels drink also:' let the same be she that Thou hast appointed for Thy servant Isaac; and thereby shall I know that Thou hast shewed kindness unto my master. And it came to pass, before he had done speaking, that Rebekah came out," &c. Gen. xxiv, 12—15.

These are some examples of the power of prayer, but Scripture might be said to teem with them in almost every page.

Wonderful, indeed, is what can be done by prayer. By it the hungry have been fed, and the naked clothed, and the sick healed; heaven has been unlocked, and hell shut up: by it God's people have been strengthened, and their enemies weakened; brands, half burnt, have been plucked from the fire; and difficulties, otherwise insurmountable, have been overcome: great battles have been won by it; great loads have been moved by it; great burdens have been sustained by it; and yet, is it not wonderful, that, although we know all this, we often have to drag ourselves to prayer, and feel listless and heartless when on our knees. Satan knows the power of prayer, and doubtless does all he can to weaken us in it, to make it a burden to us. Good need has the man of God to make a determination, and say "I will."

It may not be amiss to say a few words upon the nature of the prayer on which we are now about to dwell.

How comes a man to pray at all? 'The light of nature' will teach a man to pray. Some pray to the sun and moon, some to the devil, some to angels and saints, and to the virgin Mary; with scarce an exception, all members of the human family have some object to which they pray. But in addition to this, the teaching of the light of nature, there is 'the teaching of parents.' We are from our infancy taught to pray; almost all of us, as soon as we are able to lisp anything, begin to say some form of prayer. Advanced as the reader may now, perhaps, be in life, he may possibly remember the time when he knelt at his mother's knee, and uttered, after her, the first petitions which he addressed to the throne of grace. How often do these early memories cling to us, when the intervening events of life fade and pass away!

I would address a word or two to mothers, upon this all important subject, of their children's prayers. We continually find children taught a certain form of prayer, which they unvaryingly repeat, morning and evening; and which only, too often, becomes a mere matter of repetition, a form of words. This may be, this, doubtless, *is*, productive of mischievous consequences; a child becomes insensibly a mere piece of machinery, performing its accustomed round of work; or a parrot repeating certain sentences which it does not understand. That a child should in part be taught what to say, is very right; but the evil consists in confining it to the form. Let us remember that a child lives in a perfect little world of its own; that it has its griefs and joys, which are as real as our own—as important to it, as ours are to us; it has its little wants, desires, and fears; and to repress its prayers on all these subjects, and turn them into another channel, is to introduce the leaven of unreality, into the very beginning of its spiritual life. Let prayer, above all things, be real; let a child mean what it says; let it have an interest in the prayer it offers up; let it not be forced to *say prayers* about things which it cannot understand, and in which it cannot possibly take any interest. For my own part, I should much rather hear my child pray to God, with all her heart, that to-morrow might be a fine day, so that she may be able to enjoy an expected treat, than to hear her utter some words about the conversion of the heathen, or a similar subject, which, from her age, she could not possibly understand.

If I might make a suggestion to parents upon this subject, I would say, when your child has uttered its simple form of prayer, every word of which you should take care that it understands, not only permit, but encourage it to offer up prayer to God in its own words, and about its own interests. Do not be shocked, or offended, if the request be about a trifle; remember that trifles are the great events of a child's life; a broken wheel of a little cart is as important to it, as the breaking of a bank may be to you. Because the child *is* a child, its little sorrows are real to it; let its prayers be real to;

then it will grow up with a real interest in prayer; it will look upon prayer as a *practical working* thing; it will, in all probability, escape much of that formalism which is so detrimental, so dangerous to the soul. A parent will, of course, shew a child when, and where its petitions are not right; but, above all things, take care that the child understands.

'Conventional habit' has also something to do with prayer. Public worship, and family worship, and morning and evening prayer, are, to a certain extent, customary; thus people get into what might be called the routine of saying prayers; and this " prayer saying " is, often, only too like any of the other customs of daily life; it would be missed because it is a custom; it would be missed from the *outer*, but not from the *inner* life of man.

It will be readily understood that it is not such prayer we have now to consider. That which alone is worthy of the name of prayer, is something widely different; it is the fruit of the operation of the Holy Ghost within the heart; it is a reality derived from personal need; it is soul work.

And what are we to say of such prayer as this? Is it not that the child of God has, very often, to put a holy violence upon himself, to bring himself thus to pray. It may seem anomalous, but so it is; the Christian has often to be very determined with himself, to bring himself to his knees, to make him avail himself of the privileges and blessing of prayer. It may not be amiss to consider, a little more at large, these impediments of which we have to complain.

The first to be noticed is

Natural Inaptitude. By nature we are unapt to pray, we have no natural drawings to this holy exercise, we

turn against it.   How often have we experienced this
inaptitude ourselves? our souls have been as sickly and
disinclined for prayer, as the body often is sickly and
disinclined for food; we have turned *from* it, happy are
we if we have not turned *against* it.   It is by no means
uncommon to hear true Christian people complain, that
for many days they have not been really able to pray.
They knew not why, they could not even guess why;
but their hearts were dull and cold, and refused to
respond to anything save the stern command of duty.
All this is lamentable, no one laments it more than the
Christian himself; experience, however, shews us that it
is true, and Natural Inaptitude must be numbered
amongst our serious impediments to prayer.

To know this, may be in itself of no inconsiderable
value to the striving, and perhaps sorrowing, child of
God.   Instead of going to pray in his own strength, and
expecting the power of prayer to keep alive within him,
simply from his own habit of praying, the Christian
will say "I need continual influencings of the Holy
Ghost, I need an energy which will counterbalance the
inertium of my own nature, I need a gift of prayer, I
need something above nature, even springs and impulses
from heaven."   It is under the blessed influences of
such impulses, that we shall say "I will," in this matter
of prayer, and not only say it, but act it also.   We shall
pray, despite our dull heavy natures; we shall rise above
the weight of the flesh and all belonging to it, its dull
and heavy inertium will be overcome.

Some there are who are often kept from prayer by
*the great difficulty they experience in putting their
thoughts into the form of words.*   This inaptitude is

used by the Evil One, to act upon the soul, and further his designs with reference to increasing the difficulty of prayer. Men are ashamed of the poverty of their language, they are oppressed with the difficulty of clothing their ideas, and so they are often restrained from prayer. Now as God does not look at a man's clothes, but at the man himself, so he looks not at the words, but at the ideas and feelings, of a man's prayer; be the words never so poor He will understand them, He will never misunderstand them.

Some years ago, one of the North American Indians, a chief, visited our country, and at several large meetings told his story. That story was given in something like the following words :—

"I was a worshipper of the sun, and moon, and stars, some fourteen years ago, when I heard a missionary preach of a beautiful heaven, into which, he said, all the righteous should enter, and of a dreadful hell, into which all the wicked must be cast. I asked, 'Is there any chance of a Chippewa Indian getting to heaven?' I was told, 'Oh yes, heaven is open to all who believe in Jesus, God's Son, if we come through Him we shall find a warm welcome and a ready entrance.' I was glad at this, for my sins began to trouble me; I was like one of our Indian deer, when it is shot by the hunter; it flies over the hills and prairies until it becomes weary with its exertions and faint with loss of blood; it falls down, and turns first on one side, and then on the other side, and at last it dies. Thus it was with me, the pain in my heart rankled sorely, and I could get no rest from its smart. But I prayed to God: however, I thought God would only hear me if I prayed to Him in the English

language. I did not know much English, but I said,
'Oh Christ, have mercy upon me, poor sinner, poor
Indian.' About that time I was asked out to dine.
Before dinner a blessing was asked in the English language, 'Ah,' I thought, 'God understands that;' but
after dinner, thanks were returned in the Chippewa
language, and I thought, 'If God understands your
Chippewa, He will understand mine.' I went home, I
crept up into a little hayloft, and in my native tongue, I
poured out my heart before the Lord, I said with Jacob,
'Oh Christ, I will not let Thee go except Thou bless me,'
and before the day broke, my heart was full of joy
unspeakable and full of glory." The results of this
prayer we cannot omit. "I then strove to make known
to my fellow-men the blessedness of the Gospel I had
received, I established a school, and, among other scholars,
I had thirty married women, who taught their husbands
at night what they had learned during the day. I had,
however, but one spelling book and one Testament.
My spelling book I took to pieces and gave a leaf to
each scholar, my Bible was passed from hand to hand.
Our progress was very slow, so I thought I would come
to the country whence the Bibles came, to look out for
help. And now, my dear friends, I have told my tale,
and I want to ask you if you will give me some
Bibles and spelling books to take back to my dear
children." The response of the hall to this appeal was,
"We will! we will!" And soon afterwards, freighted with
a large supply, the Indian went back to his own country,
and lived and laboured for Christ. Can we doubt that a
blessing accompanied such labours? We may be sure
that every Bible and spelling book went forth with the

power of prayer resting upon them; what work they did, eternity will tell.

Inherent Unbelief is another sore impediment to prayer. Now it might seem strange to speak of this, in connection with the children of God. If *they* be not believers, who are? if they have not faith, who has? They undoubtedly have faith, and in that faith, they live; but with faith enough for eternal life, there exist, also, remnants enough of unbelief, to vex and keep back the believers soul in a thousand ways. Unbelief many a time keeps the believer from the throne of grace; he wants something which he knows God *can* give him, but he has not the faith which can make him ask for it *joyfully*, because *believingly*, upon his knees. Oh! if we had a living, ever present, full, rich faith, with what joy should we often pray! We should be sure of being heard; we should go to our knees in the full expectation of being about to receive some good thing. What keeps us back from large petitions? What makes us pray with that feeling of insecurity, which causes *wavering* in prayer; which makes us think that we are as unlikely, as likely, to get what we desire? It is the remnant of unbelief. This unbelief takes the life out of many of our prayers: it shakes us, and gives us that feeling of uncertainty, which damps our earnestness; it makes our hand too unsteady to lay hold of, and to bear away a full cup of blessing. And many a time, it keeps us from praying at all. Because we are not sure of God's answering us, of course as He thinks best, but nevertheless of answering, we are daunted from trying, and unbelief gradually works its way, until it passes from the point in hand, to other things also, and does us amazing hurt.

Must we not meet this unbelief with a brave and determined "I Will;" must we not meet it with a full resolution to act against it? Surely, it does not become the Christian, to succumb to this unbelief; to let it triumph over him : to let it keep him from prayer, by which alone the desired blessing is to be had; let him now nerve himself for conflict; let him prepare himself to act, in spite of his unbelief; and coming determinately to prayer, in prayer he shall receive fresh strength; in it his faith will grow, and the victory shall be obtained. There are remnants of unbelief, in the holiest of the saints of God, clinging to them even to the last; and, as they mount higher and higher in their desires, seeking more and more from God, these remnants will endeavour to work hindrance to the spirit in its flights, and will call forth the believer's determined "I will."

We must not suppose that unbelief is easily beaten out of the field; it will try and hurt, so long as we are at this side of the grave. And it is well for us to be on our guard, with reference to this, for we are liable to be deceived; even our very progress in faith may be used, by unbelief, to work out its own ends.

The course of its proceeding will probably be this. We have attained to a certain measure of belief in prayer—we can pray for certain classes of things, fully believing that God will answer our prayer—we are happy in that faith—we enjoy the comfort of it; and in doing so, will scarce believe that there is unbelief still within our heart. But, suddenly we are taken out of *our accustomed beat and sphere* in prayer; a *fresh class* of subjects comes before us; perhaps they involve our making larger requests of God, than have ever hitherto been the case;

perhaps these requests require more immediate answers, than any we have ever hitherto preferred; they bring us more quickly *to a point;* they lead us into subjects in which there is not so much *likelihood* of an answer as there was in more ordinary things. Now we see how much unbelief clings around us still; how, the moment our faith is led out of its accustomed beat, and made to stand upon its own resources, upon its inherent vitality and strength, it begins to waver; it is good to be creatures of habit, in faith, but we must be something more also, or in sudden emergencies, in all higher flights, we shall fail.

Thus, when we think well of our faith in prayer, we become tried, and are found to come short; and hence, dear reader, the necessity for a stern, and determined "I will." "It is no use to pray about such and such a thing," says unbelief; "I will," says the man of God; and then, the battle with unbelief brings down upon the knees; prayer after prayer, is troubled and weakened by it; but in the power of the SPIRIT, the battle is fought, and the day is won. After this the Christian, in all probability, stands on ground higher than any on which he ever stood before; and is found not only to have gained a victory in conflict, but also to have accumulated strength for some more stern combat, yet to come.

The natural tendency to do the most for ourselves, independently of God, is another great impediment to prayer; for prayer is an acknowledgment of dependence; and from this cause, also, the Christian is summoned to prepare himself to utter a determined "I will."

An attempt at independence, was the ruin of our forefather Adam; and it has ruined many of his sons.

Independence of God is one development of pride; and oftentimes, almost unknown to the believer, exists in him, to a greater or less degree. "I am rich, and increased with goods, and have need of nothing," is often said by one, who, in the estimation of Christ, is wretched, and miserable, and poor, and blind, and naked. Rev. iii, 17.

We can easily understand, how a believer needs some degree of watchfulness over himself, in order to keep his heart determinately in a prayerful state. We are required, while in the flesh, to *act*—we have to think *how* to act—we have to follow, in our minds, the *results* of action—we have to appear, as prominent actors in the scenes of life; and we have to do with others, who are tangible actors also; moreover, we have natural energies, and judgment; and we have appliances at hand, and so forth; and the natural tendency of all these is, to make us busy in them, and in our efforts to help ourselves, and while thus engaged, to forget how much we need to be helped by God.

There is something very sweet to the natural man, in independence; and in so far as the Christian has remnants of the natural man, thus far will independence be sweet to him. Satan, who is ever ready to ground a temptation to evil upon a good foundation, or at least, upon one seemingly good, is prepared to do so here. He says, "Why carry all those trumpery little things to God?" he says, "God meant you to help yourself, why don't you do so?" and he adds a great deal more of the same stamp. Of course he never tells us that God is our Father, and interested in the most minute of our affairs; nor does he tell us, that He never intended us to put the machinery of life in the place of Himself, the great living, guiding power; nor, that acting *without* Him will soon lead us to acting *independently* of Him; all this would be beside Satan's purpose; and under the pretence of cultivating a manly spirit of self-reliance, he will make us, if he can, live, and move, and act, independently of God; of God sought, and acknowledged in prayer.

It sometimes happens that God allows His people to try this independence—this was the case when the Gibeonites were received, as we read in Joshua ix, 14. "And the men took of their victuals, and asked not counsel at the mouth of the Lord." The result we know; they were miserably deceived. God will allow His people to be workmen *under Him,* but not independently of Him. And because of this, we must use these words, "I will." "I will pray, in using such and such an instrument; I will pray for success and skill; I will not allow myself to be led astray by the fairness of appearances; I will not think that the end is secured, because the means for accomplishing it seem of surpassing strength; I will not allow God to be hidden from mine eyes, by all these material things; I will use them in a spirit of prayer."

Let us but observe, and act on this, and we shall find that we shall not be confounded. The God whom we practically acknowledge in prayer, will be sure to acknowledge us practically, by giving us cause for praise; "in all thy ways acknowledge Him, and He shall direct thy paths." Prov. iii, 6.

There is in man *a natural tendency to keep from alone and immediate connection with God;* and to overcome this, often requires the expressed determination, "I will."

We have, in all probability, experienced something of

this ourselves. In our hours of trial and difficulty, we have sought the sympathy of our fellow-man; when evil tidings came, we have written off to some dear friend to come to us, or we have gone to him; we had not as yet learned to go alone, and to go immediately, before God. It is not that at such times we desire to bear our sorrows by ourselves, for we seek for sympathy and support; nor is it that we want to hide them from God, and disconnect ourselves from Him; it is simply that we have not attained to such a knowledge of Him, and such experiences of Him as our truest friend, as would draw us at once to Him, to tell Him everything, either about what we wish to do, or have to bear. Here we must bring in the determined "I will;" we must say, "*I will* take counsel of Him in the solitude of prayer; *I will* tell Him everything, as it were, face to face; I will do as Hezekiah did, I will spread my letter before the Lord."

Did you ever, dear reader, spread a letter before the Lord; literally take the vexing sheet, and open it out before Him, and say to Him, "Behold, O Lord, what I have received, and teach me what to do; or help me that I may bear; or give me wisdom that I may answer," as the case may be? Few of our readers escape letters with evil tidings, letters of provocation, or annoyance, or disappointment; when the postman raps at the door, who can tell what tidings he brings? There is but one way of being prepared for whatever the day may bring forth; it is by being able to refer all to God; by knowing that in humble trust we may bring *every*thing before Him in prayer. This is the preparation of which the Psalmist speaks in Psa. cxii, 7. "He shall not be afraid of evil tidings; his heart is fixed, trusting in the Lord." We are prepared for everything, if we feel that we can bring all before the Most High; if we can go in alone unto Him, and hear what he will say concerning it. Let me recommend you, dear reader, to go in with your letters before the Lord; to spread them as literally before him, as you would before a friend; to point with your finger, as you pray, to the very passages which trouble you most; and in such an exercise as this, there will be a reality which will speak even to your own soul. The matter will be between God and you : and you may be sure you will have a realization that it is so. But in order to pray thus, bringing yourself and your affairs into immediate connection with God, you must, by His grace, be a man of holy determination; able in these matters to say, "I Will."

There is yet one point more upon which it will be well to touch, as calling for this fixed determination in prayer. We are sometimes backward *because of our own known, and felt, imperfection in prayer.* Man is generally averse to doing what he does with difficulty, or what he feels he does badly; and this natural feeling enters into prayer. We often feel discouraged, when we think of our luke-warmness and our wandering in prayer; we feel at times, it is only mockery or formality to pray, when we think how miserable our prayers are; and Satan is sure to help on such thoughts as these, and say, "God will not listen to you," and "if you can do no better than you have done lately, you may as well let prayer alone." The consequence is, that the Christian very often is put on a wrong tack altogether; he waits until he can work himself up into a better frame of mind for prayer, until he thinks he can pray better; and whilst thus engaged, with his mind turned in upon himself, he gets weaker instead of stronger, which is precisely the result that Satan wishes to bring about.

Dear reader, be encouraged to come to God, *just as you are;* with all your imperfections, with all your shortcomings. Nothing can atone for the presence of these in your past prayers save the blood of the blessed Jesus, who has already atoned for them, if so be that your prayers were offered through Him. Let us remember that He, the Perfect One, will do away with our imperfections; and if the heart be right with God, Jesus will take care that the prayer be right also. Our past imperfections, instead of making us backward, should rather spur us forward, in order that such imperfections should be overcome; let us put ourselves under restraint, and bringing with us Jesus, the One through whom all prayer is heard, determine in the power of the Spirit, and say "I will."

CHAPTER VIII.

THE OBJECT OF THE "I WILL" IN PRAYER.

Psalm xxviii, 1. *" Unto Thee will I cry, O Lord my rock: be not silent to me; lest, if Thou be silent to me, I become like them that go down into the pit."*

THE verses which we have to consider in reference to prayer, present the supplications of the man of God before us, in several different aspects. More than one of these aspects, is frequently found in the same verse; we shall therefore have to recur to some passages, even after they have been specially treated of, as presenting to us *fresh* teaching, in this all important matter of prayer. Thus Psalm lv, 16, 17, gives us the time of trouble, in which prayer is made; and no less than three characteristics of that prayer, namely " Faithful Expectation," " Intensity," and " Continuance." " As for me, I will call upon God; and the Lord shall save me. Evening, and morning, and at noon, will I pray, and cry aloud: and He shall hear my voice." The time of prayer was a troublous one. He says, that " the Lord shall *save* him." The prayer was made in faithful expectation—" the Lord *shall* save "—the Lord " *shall* hear my voice." The prayer was characterized by intensity—I will "pray and *cry aloud.*" And also with long continuance—"*evening,* and *morning,* and *at noon.*"

We shall limit our thoughts in this chapter, to the consideration of God *as the great* OBJECT *of prayer, in the troublous time.*

Prayer is here made in trouble, in which, all earthly solacing would be but vain. It is evident that the trouble is great; that it is beyond the reach of ordinary alleviation; that it will depress into the very lowest depths, unless help be afforded from God Himself; if He be silent, the Psalmist will be "like one, that goes down into the pit."

Now earthly solace is not to be despised. The sympathy of our fellow man, especially if it come from a kindred heart, is sweet to most; and even the rough sympathy of those, who are not in many things kindred with ourselves, but who, nevertheless, are drawn forth to us by our woes, is grateful to us in our sorrowing hours. Whilst, however, human sympathy is not to be spoken of with depreciation, it must also be spoken of with truth. Its powers are limited—it often tires and fails—there are woes, both spiritual and temporal, which it cannot reach. This has been experienced by every one who has been in deep sorrow, either of body or of soul; they have been cast loose from man; the tie of communion, the connecting link with their fellows, seems to have been severed; and they have been placed alone. How often is it the case that this has been done, in order that the way might be made clear for God, and God alone, to act.

It must not be supposed that at such seasons earthly solace is silent, in the abstract No! the voice of sympathy is heard by the outward ear, but it cannot penetrate to the heart; kindly looks are bright, as the sunbeams in their radiance, but they fall upon an icy surface, which may reflect them, but does not receive them; the depths remaining as frost-bound as they were before. Many a word of sympathy, and sustaining, and consolation, has fallen, not only upon the outward ear, but has reached the judgment, and yet never reached the heart. The lip has responded to it; so has the mind; but the heart has been silent; it has not heard itself addressed, it has nothing therefore to answer.

It might not be amiss to remind the reader, that if he undertake the task of comforter, or sympathizer, he must expect to find this. There are times when we feel inclined to be disappointed, at the little success of our sympathizing efforts; we feel half inclined to be displeased with the sorrowing one, because he will not be comforted; it is not enough for us that he receives our sympathy, we want something more; we want to see some effect from it. If, indeed, we wish to be wise sympathizers, let us be content to spend our sympathy, without *seeing* any result; let us learn to be silent with the silent ones; to shew them that we, in some measure, take in their sorrows; that we are feeling they have a depth of woe, which we cannot fathom. Such silence is eloquence, and has much more likelihood of reaching the heart in time, if indeed it ever can be reached by human sympathy, than if we lavished many words at a season when the heart had no capacity for taking in words at all. Job's friends did more for him when " they sat down with him upon the ground seven days and seven nights, and none spake a word unto him, for they saw that his grief was very great," than when they exhausted upon him all their arguments. Job ii, 13. The sympathy of silence is, alas! but little understood.

At such seasons at these, God shuts us up unto Himself; He takes us into the wilderness, where our eye can light upon nothing that delights us; where our ear can hear no sound that pleases us; He removes from us all the ordinary occupations of life, so that there is nothing to divert us; we have no resource except it be in Him.

At such seasons of trouble as these, the soul often feels as though it can be spoken to by God; or, perhaps, half-numbed, it scarce feels as though it can. When the soul feels as though it can be spoken to by God, it realizes that there is One who has access to the hidden springs of its being; One who has a voice, which can penetrate where human voice cannot reach; if He will speak, it will be to say, what will suit the soul's sad case. Such a belief is, under circumstances like these, very conducive to prayer; the eye is turned simply upon God; the afflicted one asks Him to speak, and believes that He will. But it is not always thus; grief and trouble sometimes numb, and half stupify the afflicted one; he thinks that his woe is beyond the reach of any, whether it be God or man; he feels so blunted that he can scarce receive any comfort; he has now no courage to look upward; and unless God give, at least, so much quickening, as will make that man believe that something can be done for him, disastrous results ensue.

In your trouble, dear reader, may it be ever given to you to retain the sensitive powers of the heart; far better is it to retain sensitiveness, and the capacity for being acted upon by God, than to be numbed, and for a long time to bear the heavy oppression of the heart, as well as, subsequently, the stingings which accompany the return of sensation. As we naturally seek for help, where we believe it is to be found, so the bare fact of realizing that God *can* help us, will in itself lead our minds upward to Him, who, in man's trouble, is not looked up to in vain.

The points, then, upon which we shall now dwell, are these:—

The heart's fixing upon God.
The heart's desire from God.
The heart's dependence upon God; and
The heart's hopelessness apart from God.

"Unto *Thee*," says the Psalmist, "do I cry." Now it is of the utmost importance that we should have a *definite object* on which to fix our thoughts. Man, at the best of times, has but little power for realizing abstractions; but least of all in his time of sorrow. Then he is helpless; then he needs every possible aid; and if his mind wander in vacancy, it will soon weary, and sink down exhausted. God has graciously taken care that this need not be done. He has so manifested Himself to man in His word, that the afflicted one can fix his mind's eye on Him, as the definite object of his faith, and hope, and prayer. "Call unto *Me*, and *I* will answer thee, and shew thee great and mighty things which thou knowest not." Jer. xxxiii, 3. This was what the Psalmist did; and the definiteness of God, as the object of his trust in prayer, is very clearly marked. "Unto Thee lift I up mine eyes, O Thou that dwellest in the heavens. Behold, as the eyes of servants look unto the hand of their masters, and as the eyes of a maiden unto the hand of her mistress, so our eyes wait upon the Lord our God, until that He have mercy upon us." Psalm cxxiii, 1, 2.

And specially great is the privilege of the *Christian* in this matter. He can fix his eye on Jesus; he, without any very great stretch of imagination, can picture that Holy One looking down upon him; listening to him; feeling for him; preparing to answer him. Dear reader, in the time of your trouble, do not roam; do not send out your sighs into vacancy; do not let your thoughts wander, as though they were looking for some one on whom to fix; for some one to whom you could tell the story of your heart's need, and desolation. Fix your heart, as the Psalmist did, and say, " Unto *Thee* will I cry." What a comfort is it to the child, that he can run and tell his sorrows, or his fears to his parent; that he can go at once to the living sympathizer, or helper, as the case may be; thus many woes have been lightened; many evils been averted. Such comfort may be ours, if we know where to take our troubles; on whom to lay them; to whom to confide everything connected with them.

Let us, as speedily as possible, seek to obtain this personal definite view of God, if we have it not as yet; many reasons combine to make it most advantageous so to do. For, first, should trouble come upon us speedily, how dreadful will it be to have then to learn that we are practically without resource. We believe, indeed, that there is One who can sympathize with, and help us, but we do not know where to find Him, we have not been used to speak personally with Him, we cannot go upon experience, all our knowledge we have to acquire. And while things are in this state, considerable mischief

is going on, we have to bear our load *alone;* we have to
bear it, not sitting down, but *going about* seeking for one
to help us; and under these circumstances the burden
must be the heavier. Much valuable time is thus lost,
wounds are being galled and opened, instead of mollified
and closed, the heart is being crushed under its own
weakness, instead of being lightened by reposing on
heavenly strength. Moreover, while turning hither and
thither, there is a danger of our being led far astray.
Satan will be sure to be at hand, and ready to lead us
away from God instead of to Him. That soul is in a
dangerous case, which is found wandering about by
Satan in the day of trouble; he has refuges of his own,
to which to lead it; and many a poor stricken one has
been thus deceived, and has plunged into his pitfalls, by
way of *drowning* sorrows, which Jesus would have *taken*
and borne Himself.

Oh! how happy is that man, who feels and knows that
when trouble comes, he cannot be bewildered and
confused by the stroke, no matter how heavy it may be.
Sorrow-stricken he will be, sorrow-stricken God may
intend him to be, but he has his resource, and he *knows*
it, and will avail himself of it. His is no vague theory
of the general sympathy of God for man; his is a knowledge of God, as a personal and feeling God; he says
with the Psalmist, " Unto *Thee* will I cry."

And that object is the right one. What terrible
mistakes do men often make in their choice of a friend!
Some cannot understand our case; some will take base
advantage of it; some, meaning well, will wholly mislead
us; and, after all, the heart, with the addition of some
fresh bitter experience, may be thrown back upon itself.

The present is the time for learning, that God is the One on whom to fix the heart, in the day of trouble. We shall always learn something fresh of God, when looking to Him in our troublous time; but it is not then that we should begin to seek Him; we should be able to go to Him as a tried, as a well-known God; as One who is not now to be *tried*, but rather to be *depended*, and *leant upon*. It is one thing to have attained to making an effort to lean on the right one for help; it is another to be able to dispense with effort, and to *repose* on Him.

Such, then is the heart's fixing upon God; we may rest assured that such heart fixing is well pleasing to Him. He loves His people to come first and straight to Him; He wills to be the One to come uppermost in their minds, when they need a friend—He is honoured in this trust; and those that honour Him, He will honour in return; when He is the first object of His people's thought, in their time of trouble, He will shew them that the confidence they repose in Him, by coming to Him first in prayer, is not misplaced.

Let us next observe *what the heart desires from God*. It is that He would speak. "Be not silent unto me." Under these circumstances, when we make our prayer, we desire that God would let us know tnat He hears us—and that he would appear for us—and that He would say, He is our Father.

And what do we desire God to say? We want Him to let us know that He hears us; we want to hear Him speak as distinctly to us, as we feel that we have spoken to Him. We want *to know, not only by faith* that we have been heard, but *by God's having spoken to us, on the very subject whereupon we have spoken to Him.* When we feel thus assured that God has heard us, we can with the deepest confidence, leave the whole matter about which we have been praying, in His hands. Perhaps an answer cannot come for a long time; perhaps things, meanwhile, seem working in a contrary way; it may be, that there is no direct appearance at all of God upon the scene; still faith will hold up and be strong; and there will be comfort in the heart, from the felt consciousness that God has heard our cry about the matter, and that He has told us so. We shall say to ourselves, "God knows all about it; God has in point of fact told me so; therefore I am in peace." And let it be enough for us that God tells us this, when He will perhaps tell us no more; let us not want to try and induce Him to speak much, when it is His will to speak but little—the best answer we can have at certain times is simply the statement that "He hears;" by this answer to our prayer He at once encourages, and exercises our faith. "It is said," says Rutherford, "speaking of the Saviour's delay in responding to the request of the Syrophenician woman, 'He *answered* not a word;' but it is not said, He *heard* not a word. These two differ much. Christ often heareth when he doth not answer— His *not* answering *is an answer*, and speaks thus—'pray on, go on and cry, for the Lord holdeth His door fast bolted, not to keep you out, but that you may knock, and knock, and it shall be opened.'"

But what if God be silent, and continue so for a lengthened time? Has this ever been the experience of a believer? It undoubtedly has; and men have risen from their knees, not knowing whether they had been heard or not. These are seasons of peculiar distress, to the praying people of God; and they have to take up the words which we find a little further on, in the verse, "lest if Thou be silent unto me, I be like unto them that go down into the pit."

Many of God's people have, from time to time, been oppressed in prayer with the feeling, that God has not heard them; that their prayers have never pierced the skies at all, but have fallen back heavily upon themselves; depression has come over their hearts; they have prayed in vain.

There is a peculiar depression consequent upon the feeling of not having been heard; a depression, distinct from that which accompanies the thought, that God may not grant our requests. In the present instance, we appear thrown back upon ourselves; our labour, it may be our agony in prayer, seems useless; we almost think ourselves thrown out of our connection with the spiritual world—unable to gain even a hearing, no matter what the consequence of that hearing might be. By supposing ourselves similarly circumstanced in matters of daily life, we can easily understand how painful this state of things is—happy are we if we do not understand it from actual experience!

Suppose the suitor cannot get a hearing for his case from the judge; suppose that applications for help are written, again and again, and no answer comes in return; at least, to say that they have been received; suppose we have offended some one that we love, and that now, repentant and distressed, we address letters of sorrow for the past, but that no acknowledgement leads us to know that they have been opened, or even received; we can imagine the numbing, and distressing influence on the heart.

If only we could get a hearing, we think that all would be well, or at any rate, that matters would be better than they are now; we might be able successfully to plead our cause, or, if we could not, ours would be at least the satisfaction of knowing that we had left no stone unturned, and that things would have been different if only we could have been heard. It is more depressing and irritating not to be able to get a hearing, than to succeed in getting one, and then to fail in obtaining our desires.

Now what the soul often wants in prayer, is just this *assurance of being heard.* If only the petitioner can feel that every word he says, every thought he has upon the matter in hand, really enters into the ears of God, one half his difficulties are passed, he can experience more comfort, and exercise more power in prayer.

It is indeed of the utmost importance that we should feel that we are being heard; one sentence uttered under this consciousness, is of more power than many when it is not present.

We shall be greatly helped in this matter, if, when we go to prayer, we take pains about being sure that we come into the very presence of God.* If we be sure that

* This may not be an unfitting place to make an observation upon the great value of mental realization in prayer, and some of the aids thereto. Very many find great difficulty in making prayer, as matter of fact a transaction, as any of the ordinary proceedings of daily life; Satan uses the sacredness of prayer to destroy its reality; with consummate craft he removes it from

we are in His presence, we must also be sure that we are
heard. That time is well occupied, which we spend *in
the act of coming into* the Divine presence. True, some
can find themselves there in a moment, but some cannot:

what is customary and real, to what is speculative and ideal. Let
us make prayer a common transaction between ourselves and our
God; until we do so, it will never exercise a matter of fact influence, a *working* power. The author knows a minister who
finds it very helpful to act as well as pray his prayers; *e g.,* if
an unpleasant or perplexing letter comes, he spreads it open upon
the chair or table at which he is kneeling, and he points with his
finger to the passages in question, and prays about them. If he
has to preach, he lays his hand in prayer upon his forehead and
says, " O Lord, anoint my thoughts, that I may be able to think
aright on the subject on which I am now about to preach "—he
passes his hand across his lips, and says, "O Lord, anoint my
lips, that wise words may come forth from them, and prudent and
skilful words, that I may not only know what to say, but how to
say it; that no unadvised word may come forth from my mouth;"
—he opens his waistcoat and lays his hand upon his heart, and
says, " O God, give right affections here, give warmth of feeling,
and love, and fervour," &c. . . and thus he has the consciousness
that, so far as he himself is concerned, he has really sought God's
influences in prayer. Then, with regard to the congregation—in
his mind's eye he takes in, not the whole church, but one side of
the aisle, and he prays for those who will be there; then for the
other side, and so on, for the different parts of the church; then
when the time comes for him to preach, and he looks down from
his pulpit, he feels that he has prayed for all.

If the reader have a letter of importance to write, let him put
the unwritten sheet of paper before him; let him point to *it*, before
the Lord, and say, " O Lord, teach me what to write on this
paper;"—if he be going to distribute a bundle of tracts, let him
bring the tracts *themselves* before God, and put his hands upon
them and pray *over them;* if the mother have a child that grieves
her, let her creep quietly into its room when it is sleeping at night,

and there is no reason why a man should not pause before he begins to pray, and solemnly perform the act of approach in his own mind, and thus reverentially proceed into the presence of the Most High. When sure that we are in His presence, and that we are addressing Him, we then, as has been said, feel sure that we are heard.

But we seek for more than this; our heart's desire is that *God will speak to us*, and thus *let us know that He hears us;* we say " Be not silent unto me."

Now, when God gives us an inward witness that our prayer has been heard, that witness brings peace to our hearts. God may not say, " I will grant this petition," but He does, in point of fact, say, " It now rests with me; I know thy desires;" and then, if we know anything of Him at all, we feel that He will send such an answer as is for our truest good.

There is great sustaining influence in the realization that God has heard us; in His having said even no more than this, " I have heard thee." If things seem to be going wrong in the matter concerning which we have prayed, we shall feel we know that God has it before Him, because He witnessed to our hearts that he heard us about it; if there be long delays, and the heart seem

and pray *over it*, and *point to it*, before the Lord, and say, "O Lord, for *this* child I ask," &c. And in the common things of daily life, this embodying of prayer will be very useful—let the sick man hold his medicine in his hand and pray over it—let the teacher spread her books before the Lord, and say over them, " Lord help me to communicate the knowledge I am to impart," &c.; and thus, and thus only, we bring the might of heaven into the little things of daily life, and live in the enjoyment of a privilege which is surely ours.

inclined to become sick under the influence of "hope
deferred," we shall stay ourselves upon this thought,
" God has said to me that He listened to my supplications
on this point." When once we are certain that God
has heard us about any matter, there we must leave it,
results are with Him ; and being willing to leave results
with Him, we are entitled to seek the full assurance that
He has listened to us, by His own witness to us on the
point.

Another part of the heart's desire is, that *God would
appear for us in these circumstances.*

Now this appearance need not have reference to the
outer world at all. The desire of the Psalmist is, that
God would speak to *him*. " *Be not silent unto* ME." He
wants to hear God assure him, that He is noting all the
circumstances of his case ; and this voice need not, for
purposes of comfort, go beyond himself. What powerful
comfort there is in the thought that God has spoken to
our soul ; that He has spoken with reference to the
points, in which we are at that moment troubled ; that
He has thus made His appearance on our behalf. At
the sound of this voice, our fears are stilled ; and if we
cannot attain to being joyful, we are at least in peace ;
the appearance of circumstances may have in no wise
changed : our own resources may have in no wise increased ; but God has spoken to us, and in this our heart
finds rest.

Let us not want immediate displays of active interference ; let us rest in the fact of having heard the voice
of God, in answer to our prayers. If we know God
aright, that fact will involve many others. We shall

have His secret; we shall know that it is impossible for God to *hear* and not to *act*, and so we shall wait patiently until He work, how and when He please.

The heart's *dependence upon God*, is another point prominently brought before us here. The Lord seems to be everything to the Psalmist in his trouble. "Unto THEE will I cry, lest if THOU be silent unto me, I become like them that go down into the pit."

This dependence is well pleasing in the sight of God. Man does not often like to find his fellow man leaning upon him, much less, throwing himself wholly upon him; he is afraid of the drag that will be made upon his resources; he does not like to be clogged, and embarrassed with a helpless creature. But it is not so with God. Infinite in His resources, He never can be embarrassed; the larger the demand made on Him, the better pleased He is.

If we had deep realizations of God's wealth, and of His desire to see men draw largely upon it, we should know more of heart dependence, than we do now; but the truth is, that we, imperceptibly perhaps to ourselves, measure God by our own little standard; and so fail to lean upon Him, with that thorough dependence which He loves. Not long since, a considerable sum of money was wanted for a special purpose, in which God's cause was concerned; and a worthy man, when conversed with about it, and told that it was confidently expected from the Lord, answered, that it was expecting too much from God; the homely phrase used meaning, that it was " pushing God too hard ! " This worthy man's idea was by no means an uncommon one: many think that it is *exacting*, to expect much from God; that it is not modest to expect too much from Him; in a word, that He, the Infinite One, should be dealt with as though He were finite, as though He could be exhausted by our petitions. Concentrated dependence is what God likes to see in His people. Dependence of the deepest, and most perfect kind; dependence concentrated upon Him. He loves His people to feel that "if He be silent unto them, they become like them that go down into the pit."

And this mention of the pit introduces us to the last point, which is to be noticed in this chapter, viz., *The heart's hopelessness apart from God*. "Lest if Thou be silent unto me, I become like them that go down into the pit."

The word "pit," taken by itself, may mean any kind of pit; but in the phrase in which it is here and elsewhere found, it means the place of the departed, either of their bodies or souls. The sense, then, of what the Psalmist says is this, "Unless Thou, O Lord, wilt hearken to my cry, I cannot be sustained even in life; there is no hope for me upon earth."

We shrink, in all probability, from being reduced to such a state as this; we cannot bear to have to say, "Attend unto my cry, for I am brought very low," but it is necessary that we should come to this. The last resource of the heart of poor fallen man is God; He should be the first, He is the last; and as long as there is anything for the heart to lean upon or hope from, it will not go to Him. Even God's own people are prone to forget this; and, from time to time, grounds of human hope imperceptibly take the place of the One great object of hope, God, the all-sufficient God Himself.

There is no doubt but that God sees it expedient from time to time, as the Great Physician, to reduce His patients very low; to make them *feel* what they knew well enough in theory, viz., that without Him, they are utterly undone. At such seasons, visions of the pit seem to come before their eyes; they seem shut up to it, and there is little likelihood of escaping from it. These are terrible times, but they are also times of immense spiritual acquisition; we sometimes learn more of God in them, than in the evenly flowing events of one half our lives. We know that in our ordinary lives, there are periods of very short duration in which we seem to learn more than we had learned in years previously. When death has taken away some one very near our heart, we seem to live a whole lifetime in a very few days or hours, and not only to live but to learn in proportion. I can well understand a man's saying " I learned more in those few hours than in all my life beside;" it may be that then, for the first time, such an one was shut up between God and the pit, and obliged to cast himself upon Him, in a way which he had never done before. There are times in which the spiritual man will age many years in a few short hours. And this will just shew us how little we can gauge another man's spiritual experience, and how presumptuous it is for us to sit in judgment upon it. " Is not this the carpenter's son?" say the Jews, " whence then hath He these things! and they were offended at Him." They knew not His communion with the Father, and how different it was from theirs. And much the same form of question is asked by some, with regard to those for whose knowledge and experiences they cannot account. They know that such an one could not have *grown* into his present advanced state; how is it then that, all at once, he has made such a stride in spiritual things? He has seen the pit, he has seen no deliverer from the pit but God alone; he has been brought into such terrible nearness to that pit that he must go into it unless God interfere on his behalf; let us be assured that there are seasons, when five minutes are more pregnant with deep spiritual teaching, than thrice as many years. Jesus lived far more than an ordinary lifetime of sorrow, in the moments of his bitter agony in Gethsemane. Spiritual life may be measured by intensity as well as length.

Let your heart then, dear reader, fix itself upon God; say, "Unto Thee will I cry, O Lord my rock." Let your heart's desire be from Him, that He would speak to you; say, "Be not silent unto me." Let your heart's dependence be upon Him, yea, let your heart be hopeless apart from Him; say, "lest if Thou be silent unto me, I become like them that go down into the pit." Thus cast yourself upon God, and He will accept the trust, and He will keep you from the deep, dark, dungeon-pit of despair; and if, for His glory, there be any pit into which you have to descend, He will not be silent to you; He will not leave you nor forsake you; but will walk with you in furnace fires heated seven-fold more than is their wont, and sit with you, even amid all the horrors of the lions' den.

CHAPTER IX.

THE "I WILL" OF PRAYER IN THE TIME OF TROUBLE.

Psalm lv, 16, 17. "As for me I will call upon God, and the Lord shall save me. Evening, morning, and at noon, will I pray, and cry aloud: and He shall hear my voice."

DAVID was a man who not only worshipped God, but who lived and walked with him also. His communion and his prayer were morning, noon, and evening—when the sun was rising, when it was hot, and when it was setting—he lived with God, and so he lived in a spirit of prayer.

David, then, could well say the "I will" which we are about to consider now; so also could Christ, to whom prophetically this psalm belongs.

In the days of His flesh, our Lord called evening, morning, and at noon, upon His Father; He cried aloud; and we know that He was heard. Thus much we know of Jesus, that He prayed continually: that He remained all night upon the mountain side in prayer; but how little do we know of His " cryings aloud." Such as are revealed to us, may, perhaps, give us a clue to what many others were; the bitter cries of Gethsemane were not strange sounds in the ears of God; many such had, doubtless, come before His throne from the mountain side, on which His Son was keeping His lonely vigil, of meditation and prayer—and not only from the solitude of the mountain side, but also from the crowded haunts of the resorts of men. When Jesus sighed, when He looked up to heaven, little, or it may be, nothing was heard by human ear; but a loud voice was heard before the Father's throne in heaven. "I know," said Jesus, "that Thou hearest me always." "Evening, morning, and at noon will I pray, and cry aloud: and He shall hear my voice."

Humbly and at a great distance, no doubt, must Jesus' people ever follow Him; still we may, yea, we must follow Him on earth, even as we hope to follow Him to that place whither He is gone before; and so we also, it is to be hoped, can take up this 'I Will' of Jesus, and of David, and say, "As for me, I will call upon God, and the Lord shall save me. Evening, and morning, and at noon, will I pray and cry aloud; and the Lord shall hear my voice." Feebly and imperfectly, owing to the weakness of the flesh, will we carry out such a declaration as this; but our feebleness must not deter us from entering on it. Of that feebleness God will take no account in wrath, but much account in pity; so much, that we may in all faith take up the Psalmist's words, and say, "And He shall hear my voice."

There are some points of practical instruction brought before us here, from which we may gather teaching, in matters connected with our ordinary spiritual life.

Observe, I. *The standing out in strong distinctiveness,* "As for me."

Circumstances were now about as bad as they well could be. The voice of the enemy was heard; the oppression of the wicked was felt: "they cast iniquity upon me," says the Psalmist, "in wrath they hate me." And these circumstances became aggravated by the fact, that some of the actors upon the scene, were those who ought to have occupied the position of friends. "It was not an enemy that reproached me, then I could have borne it; neither was it he that hated me, that did magnify himself against me, then I would have hid myself from him; but it was thou, a man mine equal, my guide, and mine acquaintance. We took sweet counsel together, and walked unto the house of God in company."

Let us here, first of all, observe that *there is no disarming of malice by compromise.* Had the Psalmist chosen to compromise, he might often, no doubt, have disarmed the enmity of his foes; had Jesus chosen to compromise, he also might have done the same. A half-and-half man, a half-and-half creed, will never meet with violent opposition or enmity from the world. Even what might be called a three-quarters man will escape without very much hurt. It is the out-and-out Christian, and the out-and-out creed that the world hates. Making compromises is an old trade of Satan's; it is one at which he shews consummate skill; he is willing to be large and liberal; he will concede far more than, at first sight, any one would suppose; in fact, he will go so far as to say, " You may be nine-tenths Christ's, if only, as regards the remaining tenth, you will agree to be mine."

The man of God must pray for grace, never even to listen to the smallest word on the subject of compromise.

He ought to nail his colors to the mast, and not listen, even for a moment, to any terms upon which those colors are to be struck. "No surrender!" No compromise!" These should be the mottos, and the watchwords under which he fights.

Let us see how some of the ancient saints and martyrs dealt with the endeavours which were made to induce them to a compromise. "When Polycarp was apprehended, and was on his way to the tribunal, the irenarch Herod, and his father Nicetes, met him, and, taking him up into their chariot, began to advise him, asking, 'What harm is it to say, Lord Cæsar! and to sacrifice, and be safe?' At first he was silent; but being pressed, he said, 'I will not follow your advice.' When they could not persuade him, they treated him abusively, and thrust him out of the chariot; so that in falling he bruised his thigh. But he, still unmoved, as if he had suffered nothing, went on cheerfully, under the conduct of his guards, to the Stadium. There, the tumult being so great that few could hear anything, a voice from heaven said to Polycarp, as he entered on the Stadium, 'Be strong, Polycarp, and behave yourself like a man.' None saw the speaker, but many of us heard his voice. When he was brought to the tribunal, there was a great tumult, as soon as it was generally understood that Polycarp was apprehended. The proconsul asked him if he were Polycarp; to which he assented. The former then began to exhort him :— 'Have pity on thy own great age'—and the like. 'Swear by the fortune of Cæsar—repent—say 'Take away the atheists.'' Polycarp, with a grave aspect, beholding all the multitude, waving his hand to them, and looking up to heaven, said, 'Take away the atheists.'

The proconsul urging him, and saying, 'Swear, and I will release thee; reproach Christ.' Polycarp said, 'Eighty and six years have I served Him, and He hath never wronged me; and how can I blaspheme my King who hath saved me?' The proconsul still urging, 'Swear by the fortune of Cæsar,' Polycarp said, 'If you still vainly contend to make me 'swear by the fortune of Cæsar,' as you speak, affecting an ignorance of my real character, hear me frankly declaring what I am :— I am a Christian, and if you desire to know the Christian doctrine, assign me a day, and hear.' The proconsul said, 'Persuade the people.' Polycarp said, 'I have thought proper to address you, for we are taught to pay to magistracies, and powers appointed by God, all honour, which is consistent with a good conscience.' 'I have wild beasts,' says the proconsul; 'I will expose you to them, unless you repent.' 'Call them,' replies the martyr; 'our minds are not to be changed, from the better to the worse; but it is a good thing to be changed from evil to good.' 'I will tame your spirit by fire,' says the other, 'since you despise the wild beasts, unless you repent.' 'You threaten me with fire,' answers Polycarp, 'which burns for a moment, and will be soon extinct; but you are ignorant of the future judgment, and of the fire of eternal punishment, reserved for the ungodly. But why do you delay? Do what you please.'"

To swear by "the fortune of Cæsar" seemed but a small concession, how much less evil did it appear than cursing Christ; but the Christian martyr would hear of no concession at all, and rather than make any, he died.

We may rest assured that we fall into a decided trap of Satan's, when we offer to yield even ever so little to the world in order to disarm its malice; we shall, in all probability, be driven from one concession to another, and even if this be not the case, we shall find that, after all, the malice of the world is as strong as it was before. I doubt much whether its malice will not be even stronger, for now it will despise, as well as hate.

The Psalmist took his stand, he said, "as for me," just as Joshua did, who took up his own ground, irrespective of what all others might do, saying, "As for me and my house, we will serve the Lord."

Why need we resort to compromise, to disarm the world of its malice, or rather to neutralize its power, for disarm it we never can. To think of compromise, is as much as to say, "we have not a sufficiency of resource in God, we are driven by hard necessity to these disreputable shifts." If we knew our resources, in prayer, we should never think of compromise for a moment, we should say to ourselves "there is no need for anything of the kind, my God to whom I commit the malice of my enemies in prayer, is able and willing to deal with them, 'as for me, I will call upon God, and the Lord shall save me.'"

Let us further observe, that the Psalmist *does not faint at the isolated position* in which he is placed. His enemies were many, he seemed to stand alone, but instead of succumbing, he flees to God, he says, "I will call," and "the Lord shall save."

Now an isolated position is a very hard and a very depressing one to occupy for any length of time. Men will do and bear in company, what they can neither do nor bear alone; in loneliness there comes the sense of weakness, and oftentimes the temptation to give up.

If any one who reads these lines has to sustain the isolated position, whether it be in his own family or elsewhere, let him remember that in this, as in all other forms of suffering, Christ Jesus has gone before. He was not only the most sad amongst the sad, but He was also the most lonely amongst the lonely. True! multitudes thronged Him, but, as we have often felt ourselves most lonely when in a crowd, because none there sympathized with us or knew us, so Jesus doubtless felt Himself lonely indeed, when crowds pressed upon Him who had no sympathy with Him, and who, in the truest sense of the words, did not know Him.

Oh! there are times of awful loneliness upon the earth; times when, as the sun sinks beneath the horizon, our hearts sink with it, and long deep shadows fall athwart our souls; times when, as the sun rises again in its freshness and its strength, we feel that it brings to us no light, no heat, no healing on its wings. We have now no flowers in our hearts to unfold beneath its beams, our flowers have been plucked, and bloom with us no more; we have no jewels to flash and glitter in its rays, we have had our treasure taken from us, and our heart is like the rifled casket, good for nothing in itself. Have we not been startled by our own foot-falls? have we not been choked by our own breath? have we not looked out into vacancy? have we not dreamed while our eyes were open? have we not felt as though our very selves had been cut in twain, and that we were incomplete, as though a part of our very being had been stolen away? Then, did we not become faint and sick at heart, did we not taste that which he who has once tasted will never forget—the nausea of grief?

Now, be our loneliness what it may, it never can exceed the loneliness of Christ. True! He Himself tells us that He was not alone; for He had the Father with Him: (John xvi, 32) but as far as human feelings and sympathies were concerned Jesus was alone. The *man* Christ Jesus was often lonely; and paint what dreary scene we will, He, from the experience of His earthly sorrows, can sketch us a drearier; heave what deep and exhausting sigh we may, it will be but a faint and feeble echo to those which came from Him in His sorrowing hours.

It is inexpressible comfort to the believer that he can feel Christ's sympathy in seasons such as these; that this his loneliness is known and understood by Jesus; but this loneliness is not the trial upon which we wish now to dwell. The isolated position presented here is one connected with desertion, and bitterness, and opposition, and all which is calculated to appal and unnerve the heart.

Let us observe that there is no fainting under all this; instead of any such yielding, there is a falling back upon God in prayer; a determination to stand upon individual relationship to Him, individual realization of Him; upon the consciousness of His all-sufficiency. *"As for me,* I will call upon God, and the Lord shall save me."

The isolated position may assume many forms; under whichever one it comes to us, may the Lord give us grace to be of good courage, and not to faint. It may be that some reader must stand alone in his own family; that his life must be a protest against theirs in almost every daily act; or perhaps he may be one of a godly family, but is yet, by circumstances, compelled to sojourn amongst the ungodly; obliged to take up the Psalmist's words, "Woe is me that I am constrained to dwell with

Mesech and to have my habitation among the tents of Kedar." Psalm cxx, 5. Or perhaps the reader's isolated position may not be an habitual, but only an accidental one, one which is to last for a few days, or only a few hours; whatever it may be, do not for a moment think of succumbing under it; do not allow your mind for an instant to dwell upon the idea of your being alone; see that you have God on your side; God ready to befriend you, and say, "As for me I will call upon God, and the Lord shall save me."

When we are in the most complete state of isolation so far as man is concerned, we are not, we cannot be, thoroughly alone. It is Satan's policy to direct our attention to ourselves; to shew us that we are by ourselves; to appal us by our isolation; but we must hold our ground under the deep conviction that God is near. When the King of Syria sent horses, and chariots, and a great host, to seize Elisha, and they compassed the city about in which he was, Elisha's servant cried, "Alas, my master! how shall we do?" Then Elisha answered, "Fear not; for they that be with us are more than they that be with them. And Elisha prayed, and said, Lord, I pray Thee, open his eyes, that he may see. And the Lord opened the eyes of the young man; and he saw, and behold, the mountain was full of horses and chariots of fire round about Elisha." 2 Kings vi, 15, &c.

The heart, if left to itself, must sink and fail; flesh and blood, when thrown upon their own simple resources, are not equal to sustaining heavy pressure; they will faint, not only under the pressure, but even at the prospect of it; the one resource is prayer. "As for me, I will call upon God."

When Luther was about to appear before the Emperor Charles, and the assembled princes, at the Diet of Worms, he was troubled and dismayed; the emperor, whose sovereignty extended over great part of the old and new world, his brother the archduke Ferdinand, six electors of the empire, twenty-five dukes, eight margraves, thirty archbishops, bishops, and abbots, seven ambassadors, ten deputies, and a great number of princes, counts, sovereign barons, and papal nuncios, in all two hundred and four persons, had to be faced by the solitary monk; what wonder if he was dismayed? The historian tells us that "his heart had been troubled in the presence of so many great princes, before whom nations humbly bent the knee." The reflection that he was about to refuse to submit to these men, whom God had invested with sovereign power, disturbed his soul, and he felt the necessity of looking for strength from on high. "On the morning of the 18th of April, Luther was not without his moments of trial, in which the face of God seemed hidden from him. His faith grew weak, his enemies multiplied before him, his imagination was overwhelmed at the sight, his soul was as a ship tossed by a violent tempest, which reels and sinks to the bottom of the abyss, and then mounts again to heaven." Never was any man in a greater state of isolation; and what does he do? In this hour of bitter sorrow, in which he drinks the cup of Christ, and which was to him a little garden of Gethsemane, he falls to the earth and utters these broken cries, which we cannot understand unless we can figure to ourselves the depth of the anguish whence they ascend to God.

"O Almighty and everlasting God! how terrible is this

world! Behold it openeth its mouth to swallow me up, and I have so little trust in Thee! .... How weak is the flesh, and how powerful is Satan! If it is in the strength of this world only that I must put my trust, all is over! .... my last hour is come, my condemnation has been pronounced! .... O God! O God! .... O God, do Thou help me against all the wisdom of this world! Do this; Thou shouldest do this......Thou alone......for this is not my work, but Thine. I have nothing to do here; nothing to contend for with these great ones of the world! I should desire to see my days flow on peaceful and happy. But the cause is Thine......and it is a righteous and eternal cause. O Lord! help me! Faithful and unchangeable God! In no man do I place my trust. It would be vain! All that is of man is uncertain; all that cometh of man fails. Oh! God! my God, hearest Thou me not?......My God, art Thou dead?......No, Thou can'st not die! Thou hidest Thyself only! Thou hast chosen me for this work, I know it well!......Act, then, O God! stand at my side, for the sake of Thy well beloved Jesus Christ, who is my defence, my shield, and my strong tower."

After a moment of silent struggle he thus continues, "Lord! where stayest Thou! Oh my God, where art Thou?......Come! come I am ready!......I am ready to lay down my life for Thy truth......patient as a lamb. For it is the cause of justice—it is Thine......I will never separate myself from Thee, neither now, nor through eternity......and though the world should be filled with devils—though my body, which is still the work of Thy hands, should be slain, be stretched upon the pavement, be cut in pieces......reduced to ashes......

my soul is Thine......Yes, I have the assurance of Thy
word. My soul belongs to Thee! it shall abide for ever
with Thee! it shall abide for ever with Thee......Amen!
O God! help me!......Amen!"

And God did help him; for we are told that "after
he had thus prayed, he found that peace of mind, without which, man can effect nothing great. He then read
the word of God; looked over his writings; and sought
to draw up his reply in a suitable form. The thought
that he was about to bear testimony to Jesus Christ and
His word, in the presence of the emperor and of the
empire filled his heart with joy. As the hour of His appearance was not far off, he drew near the holy Scriptures
that lay open on the table and with emotion placed his
left hand on the sacred volume, and raising his right
toward heaven, swore to remain faithful to the gospel;
and freely to confess his faith, even should he seal his
testimony with his blood. After this he felt still more
at peace."

Such was the conduct of a great man in a great trial;
natural boldness he doubtless had, but his trial was too
strong for mere flesh and blood, his resource was in
prayer; there he sought for, and there he found, the
strength that he required. As he did, so may you, dear
reader, do also; and whenever you have to stand alone,
be it in your own families, or in company, or before the
people of the world, for the sake of Jesus, never dream
of getting rid of your isolation by giving up your distinctiveness; hold on, hold out, say "As for me I will
call upon God, and the Lord shall save me."

Let me guard the reader from thinking that I would
not have him *recognize his isolated position* because I

point out to him the need of looking at God's presence with him, instead of his own solitude. When we are in a position of isolation, it is necessary to perceive it; indeed a part of our safety will consist in our full and distinct recognition of it. There is no small amount of power in the words "As for *me*"—these words bring before us at once our separation from the enemies of God, and our being on the Lord's side; they tell us of our resources, of God's regard to us in our distinctive state, of the position we occupy in His sight. In the contemplation of our isolation there may be weakness, in the recognition of it there is strength.

We see then how the Psalmist stood out in strong distinctiveness; let us now see how *he recognises God as a friend in the midst of all this trouble.* "As for me, I will call upon God, and the Lord shall save me." It is very important to observe that the Psalmist did not allow the multitude to hide out God from his view. We see that there were many against him, and the tendency of the natural mind would have been to look at the multitude who were close at hand, and not at God, who might have been considered to be afar of.

This recognition of God the Psalmist made in prayer; he could have made it in no more effectual way, because prayer is a matter immediately between the person praying and the person prayed to, and thus the Psalmist had God steadily before his eyes, no matter what the number of his foes. When we are hard pressed we shall often get a clear view of God in prayer, when we could not in any other way.

Let us, dear readers, take care that in our times of

trial we do not allow the multitude to hide out God; that we do not permit our troubles to assume a prominence which would make them absorb our minds; if we permit this, Satan's purpose is, to a great extent, gained; he will have separated us from our source of strength. We have often met with believers whose troubles had so overwhelmed them that they shut out God; these troubles were like a flight of locusts, whose numbers we are told are sometimes so great as even to obscure the sun. Now we cannot help having troubles, and more than this, we cannot help their coming in multitudes, but the eye of faith can pierce through them all, and herein it has great advantage over the eye of sense. It would be mere affectation to say, "We will ignore the existence of these trials altogether," we cannot do so; trials are hard, solid facts; enemies are substantial realities, as perhaps many of us know to our cost; and when these thicken upon us, we must know and feel the serious nature of our case. It is foolish to hide our eyes from the reality of facts, and, like the ostrich in the desert, to think to escape by shutting our eyes; she supposes, as she hides her head in the sand, that none can see her, because she cannot see them; shall we suppose that our enemies cannot see us, because we do not choose to see them? No, let us give our enemies full credit for their numbers and their might, then let us pass above them all in prayer, and clearly look on God. Satan has continually tried to perplex God's people by *number;* no single foe was particularly strong or unmanageable, but the many were hard to deal with, the multitude could distract the thoughts. Let us be on our guard against this form of spiritual danger, and say, "As for me, I will call upon God, and the Lord shall save me." Zaccheus was very much in earnest in his desire to see Jesus, and so he found means, despite his natural incapacity, of not being thwarted by the crowd; and the woman who had the issue of blood was very earnest in her desire to touch the Lord, and she accomplished her wish, although the multitude thronged and pressed Him; and the friends of the man with the palsy were very intent upon laying their burden at the very feet of Jesus, and so they broke up the roof and let the afflicted one down immediately before the One by whom he could be saved. As they did, so let us do also, and we may rest assured that we shall succeed.

Let us further observe, that the Psalmist did not allow *the closeness of his suffering, which touched him to the very quick, to obscure his vision of God.* Suffering which touches to the quick, has a tendency to make us absorbed in ourselves, or perhaps, to make us dissatisfied with God; we are often so occupied with what we are feeling, so absorbed with our pains and distresses, that we can think of nothing else. Satan has often had great advantage over the saints of God, in their times of deep distress; and the way by which he gained this advantage, was by absorbing the mind on self. In self there was, of course, no resource; self was to be the endurer and sufferer; and by looking at self, and not at God, the picture presented to the mind was " suffering without help." What picture could be darker; what could better suit the purposes of the Evil One? Self without God! Surely this is an equivalent for despair. Many can go through ordinary sufferings without losing sight of God, who yet fail when there comes suffering to the very quick; they are then too hard pressed, even to bethink them of their having a friend.

Let us see how the blessed Lord Jesus Christ acted under such circumstances as these; and let Him be our example. In His agony in Gethsemane, His nature was touched to the very quick; an apostle was then almost in the very act of betraying Him; those who should have watched with Him were sleeping; the cup of extremest anguish was just about to be put into His hand; surely, if ever any one might have been absorbed with his own suffering, that one was Jesus. But God was not hidden out from Him; on the contrary, it was His Father's face He sought; and the appearance of the strengthening angel was a proof that He sought it not in vain. Oh! be His example ours, in the time when we are touched in the very quick and marrow of our natures; then, closeness of suffering will be blessed; the pressure will force us upward, ever higher and higher, until we come with our sorrows before the throne; and perhaps we shall find, that suffering in the very quick, has led to blessing in the very quick also; that blessing has pervaded an inner depth of the soul, of whose very existence we were not aware before.

Observe, also, how the Psalmist did not allow *the discovered hollowness of human friendship to throw a shadow on the divine*. His chief suffering was from his own familiar friend; so also was Jesus'; to which suffering this portion of the psalm prophetically applies. "For it was not an enemy that reproached me, then I could have borne it; neither was it he that hated me, that did magnify himself against me, then I would have hid myself from him; but it was thou, a man mine equal, my guide, and mine acquaintance; we took sweet counsel together, and walked unto the house of God in company."

We are all of us very apt to lean on human friends, and seek in their advice and sympathy, both direction and support. We would raise friendship above the ordinary ebbs and flows of human things, and consider it in a poetical and beautiful light, as able to resist all the fluctuations and changes, which are occurring in the daily wear and tear of life. Nothing shocks our sensibilities more, than a discovery of the hollowness of some friendship on which we built; and the effects of such a discovery, are often very painful indeed. One of these effects is, to throw us in upon ourselves; we have been betrayed, deceived; and we are indignant, and will not subject ourselves to the like again. Satan, ever on the watch to turn each circumstance and feeling to his own purpose, and make something out of it, will now endeavour to throw forward the dark shadow of broken human friendship upon that Divine Friend who " sticketh closer than a brother," and to shake as much as he can our dependence in the friendship of God and Christ. Let us observe where Jesus was found, in the time both of impotent, and of violated friendship. He was in prayer with God, and that Father and truest Friend was unshaken, amid all the shiverings of the potsherds of the earth.

Painful as it is to enunciate such a truth, and treasonable to all sentimentality and poetry, it yet is true that human friendship is not to be relied upon. The friend of to-day will look coldly upon us to-morrow; the man from whom we receive a grasp of the hand now, will perhaps in a little while not even recognise us, should he meet us in the street. Let us be thankful for human friendships such as they are, and while they last; but let us by no means build upon them; they may fail us in the trying hour. But let us be careful to give the Great and True Friend a position in our hearts, and in our judgments, far higher than that occupied by any earthly friend: let us firmly fix the truth in our minds, that He is the friend, "that sticketh closer than a brother;" let us never so much as entertain, for a moment, the thought of its being possible that He can change; let Him be as far removed from all such doubts, as the sun is from the shadows that flit to and fro upon the earth. Thus deeply trusting God, we shall be ready to resort to Him in prayer, in the times when we are thrown off by earthly friends; we shall not have to stop and deliberate, as to whether we have a friend or no; we shall allow no time for a morbid feeling to take possession of our minds; we shall not fall into a state of depression and weakness, which would leave us an easy prey to Satan. We could not sustain ourselves, under the consciousness of being altogether friendless; many of the troubles which we meet are too heavy to be borne alone; henceforth let us go at once to God in prayer, when our trouble comes upon us; let us go in the full conviction that in Him we have a friend, however friendless we might be on earth; let us make the Psalmist's determination ours. "As for me I will call upon God, and the Lord shall save me; evening, morning, and at noon, will I pray and cry aloud: and He shall hear my voice."

There remains yet one more point brought before us here, which is of great importance; *i. e.*, the Psalmist's determination *to continue in prayer;* "evening, morning, and at noon, will I pray and cry aloud."

We have here *continuous prayer under continual pressure.* We find that the natural tendency of continual pressure is to wear us out. Many of us can bear a quick, sharp pain, the very thought of its being soon over helping to carry us through : but prolonged trial, even though in the aggregate it be not so bad as the one quick, sharp pain, we cannot endure. I believe that the only way by which continual pressure can be met, is continuous prayer; when the pressure is actively upon us, prayer in the morning to be kept till noon, and at noon to be kept till night, and at night to be kept until morning dawn again. There is, perhaps, an advantage in thus looking to prayer to carry us on, as it were, fixed stages of our sad and weary way. There is a definiteness in our supplication, which gives it peculiar reality and life; and seeing that the answer, if it come at all, must come at once, we are on the look out for it, and our faith is stirred up to special exercise. Take the case of a person in pain; every hour, even every minute, is a trial of endurance; there is no immediate prospect of release; the very indefiniteness of the time for which the pain may endure, adds to the sufferer's trial; what can uphold like continual prayer, and the strength flowing from it like the supplication, morning, noon, and night? We are sometimes placed under continuous pressure, by the provocations of those with whom we live, or with whom our lot is cast in following the ordinary avocations of life; some persons' circumstances in their trades or professions are such, that they are perpetually harassed to make both ends meet, and many a poor man lives in continual trouble, day by day, to feed and clothe those who are dependent on him; there is nothing like continuous prayer for meeting all this pressure, it will sustain under any amount of burden, and for any length of time.

Some of Satan's temptations might be called " wearing out temptations," the very principle on which they act is the exhaustion of the believer; Satan calculates the limits of man's endurance, then he lays on a pressure which will exceed those limits, and thus act upon the exhausted believer as he will. Continuous prayer will effectually cope with, and foil, such an attempt as this; and the probability is, that when the Evil One sees that the Christian has the secret of success, he will turn to some other method of attack. The believer is now like a garrison in a state of siege; to hold out long enough is to come victorious out of the strife. As long as Abraham continued in prayer, so long God continued to bless, and had the patriarch continued yet further than he did, who can tell what would have been the result?

We have a specimen of the continuance of assault, and the resistance of continuous prayer, in the case of the martyr Glover.

Robert Glover remained in prison eight days, till the bishop's arrival; " in which time," he says, " *I gave myself continually to prayer*, and meditation of the merciful promises of God, made unto all, without exception of person, that call upon the name of His dear son Jesus Christ. I found in myself daily amendment of health of body, increase of peace in conscience, and many consolations from God, by the help of His Holy Spirit; and sometimes, as it were, a taste and glimmering of the life to come, all for His only son Jesus Christ's sake; to Him be all praise, for ever and ever! The enemy ceased not to assault me, often objecting to my conscience, my own unworthiness, through the greatness of the benefit, to be counted among the number of them that suffer for Christ, for His gospel's sake. Against him I replied with the word of God on this sort:—' What were all those whom God hath chosen from the beginning to be His witnesses? Were they not men, even as Paul and Barnabas declared, Acts xiv, 15; subject to wickedness, sin, and imperfection as other men be? They were no bringers of goodness to God, but altogether receivers. They chose not God first, but He chose them. They loved not God first, but He loved them first. Yea, He both loved and chose them when they were his enemies, full of sin and corruption, and void of all goodness. He is, and will be, still the same God; as rich in mercy to forgive sins, without respect of person, to the world's end, to all them that call upon Him. God is near, He is at hand; He is with all, I say, and refuseth none, excepteth none, that faithfully, in true repentance, call upon Him, in what hour, what place, or what time soever it be.' It is not arrogancy nor presumption in any man, to burden God (as it were) with His promise, and to claim and challenge His aid, help, and assistance in all our perils, dangers, and distress; calling upon Him, not in the confidence of our own godliness, but in the trust of His promises, made in Christ. In whom, and by whom, and for whose sake, whosoever boldly approacheth to the mercy-seat of the Father, is sure to receive whatsoever is

expedient or necessary, either for body or soul, in more
ample wise, and large manner, than he can well wish or
dare desire. His word cannot lie; 'call upon Me in the
day of trouble, and I will hear thee, and thou shalt
praise Me.' I answered the enemy also in this manner:—
'I am a sinner, and therefore unworthy to be a witness of
this truth. But what then? Must I deny His word,
because I am unworthy to profess it? As Christ Himself
beareth witness, 'he that is ashamed of Me, or of My
words, of him I will also be ashamed before My Father,
and all His angels.' I might, by like reason, forbear to
do any of God's commandments, because I am not
worthy to do them. These are the delusions of the
devil, and Satan's suggestions; which must be overcome
by continuance of prayer, and with the word of God,
applied, according to the measure of every man's gift,
against all assaults of the devil.'"

These extracts record the patience and faith of the
saint. The conclusion of his history demands attention.
Shortly before his martyrdom he felt his doubts and
apprehensions return; he mentioned the deadness of his
soul, and his want of spiritual comfort, notwithstanding
his earnest prayers night and day, to Augustine Beruher,
one who continually visited the sufferers for Christ whenever he could find opportunity. Beruher earnestly prayed
him to wait the Lord's pleasure, and not to doubt but
that God would visit him in his own good time, and
satisfy him with abundance of consolation. Beruher not
only expressed himself thus confidently upon the subject,
but desired his friend to make some sign, whereby he
might know when this support was vouchsafed.

Glover continued in doubt and gloom, but was still

enabled to hold fast his purpose. *"He had continued all night in prayer,* and was even come in sight of the stake, yet his mind was still weighed down with a burden, almost too heavy to be borne. But though cast down, he was not forsaken. The evening of a dark and stormy day is sometimes illumined by the bright beams of the parting sun; thus the Sun of Righteousness shone upon the last moments of this blessed martyr 'with healing in His wings.' On a sudden he was powerfully filled with God's holy comfort—a foretaste of heavenly joys; clapping his hands together, and turning to his friend, who stood among the crowd, he exclaimed, 'Austen, He is come, He is come!' and that with joy and alacrity, rather as one who had been delivered from the fear of dying, than as one about to suffer the bitter pangs of a cruel death. Surely this was the Lord's doing."

A call for continuance in prayer, in behalf of their children, is often made on parents. They pray, and yet see no result of their prayers; the one they had endeavoured to train up in the nurture and admonition of the Lord, runs riot in sin, goes farther and farther down the road to ruin, plunges deeper and deeper into vice or carelessness; surely it seems almost vain to pray for such an one as this. Even the very ones who would pray for this unhappy creature are spurned and despised by him, he would stop their prayers if he could, but the trial is perhaps one of continuance, and if they continue it may be that they will gain the victory, and this soul will be given to them at last.

St. Augustine has left us, in his Confessions, an affecting account of the perseverance of a mother's love and prayers. True, she had to bear long; rebuff, and scorn, and deceit seemed for many a year to be the only payment of her prayers; but "in due season," says the apostle, "ye shall reap, if ye faint not"—she fainted not, and so she reaped.

"My God," says St. Augustine, "thou spakest to me by her, and warnedst me strongly against the ways of vice. Thy voice in her I despised, and thought it to be only the voice of a woman, which made not the least impression on my mind."

How Augustine's mother prayed for him will best be seen by what he himself says in his Confessions. "In much ignorance, I at that time derided Thy holy servants, and was justly exposed to believe most ridiculous absurdities. And Thou sentest Thy hand from above, and freedst me from this death of evil, *while my mother was praying for me,* more solicitous on account of the death of my soul, than other parents for the death of the body. She was favoured with a dream, by which Thou comfortedst her soul with hope of my recovery. She appeared to herself to be standing on a plank, and a person came to her and asked her the cause of her affliction, and on being answered, that it was on my account, he charged her to be of good cheer, for that where she was there also I should be. On which, she immediately beheld me standing by her on the same plank. Whence was this but from Thee, gracious Omnipotent, who takest care of each and all of us as of single persons? When she related this to me, I endeavoured to evade the force of it, by observing that it might mean to exhort her to be what I was. Without hesitation she replied, 'It was not said, where he is, there thou shalt be; but, where thou art, there he shall be.' Her prompt answer made a stronger impression on my mind than the dream itself. *For nine years, while I was rolling in the filth of sin, often attempting to rise, and still sinking deeper, did she, in vigorous hope, persist in incessant prayer.*"

Augustine had been carried away with the errors of the Manichees, and Monica his mother, in her anxiety for his soul, entreated a certain bishop to undertake to reason him out of his errors. St. Augustine says, " He was a person not backward to attempt this, where he found a docile subject. 'But your son,' says he, 'is too much elated at present, and carried away with the pleasing novelty of his error, to regard any arguments, as appears by the pleasure he takes in puzzling many ignorant persons with his captious questions. Let him alone; only continue praying to the Lord for him; he will, in the course of his study, discover his error. I myself, perverted by my mother, was once a Manichee, and read almost all their books, and yet at length was convinced of my error without the help of any disputant.' All this satisfied not my anxious parent; with floods of tears she persisted in her request; when at last he, a little out of temper, on account of her importunity, said, ' Begone, good woman, it is not possible that the child of such tears should perish.'" For the space of nine years, viz., from the nineteenth to the twenty-eighth year of his age, Augustine lived, as he himself tells us, " deceived and deceiving others, seducing men into various lusts, openly, by what are called the liberal arts, and secretly, by a false religion; in the former, proud, in the latter, superstitious; in all things seeking vain glory, and, to complete the dismal picture, a slave to the lusts of the flesh." In his twenty-ninth year, we find his mother *still praying*, although things seemed as bad or worse than they had been before. God was, however, about to work a great change upon Augustine's heart, and as he begins to trace His dealings with him, he shews us his mother still praying. "Thy hands, my God, (said he in his Confessions) in the secret of Thy providence, forsook not my soul. *Day and night the prayers of my mother came up before Thee*, and Thou wroughtest upon me in ways marvellous indeed, but secret." Augustine sails for Rome, proposing to teach rhetoric in that city; but God had arranged that his going there should be the first step in the immediate chain of providences which were to lead to his salvation. And where was Monica? Following him to the sea-shore, to prevent his going. God's arrangements for the answers of her prayers were about to work the one into the other; but, like many a praying mother, Monica knew not this. "The true cause of this removal was at that time hidden both from me and my mother, who bewailed me going away, and followed me to the sea-side; but I deceived her, though she held me close, with a view either to call me back, or to go along with me. I pretended that I only meant to keep company with a friend, until he set sail; and with difficulty persuaded her to remain that night in a place dedicated to the memory of Cyprian. But that night I departed privily; and she continued weeping and *praying*. Thus did I deceive my mother, and SUCH a mother! Yet was I preserved from the dangers of the sea, foul as I was in all the mire of sin; and a time was coming, when Thou would'st wipe away my mother's tears with which she watered the earth, and even forgive this my base undutifulness. And what did she beg of Thee, my God, at that time, but that I might be hindered from sailing? Thou, in profound wisdom, regarding the HINGE of her desire, neglectedst the particular object of her present prayers, that Thou mightest gratify the general object of her devotions. The wind favoured us, and carried us out of the sight of the shore, when in the morning, she was distracted with grief, and filled Thine ears with groans and complaints; whilst Thou, in contempt of her violent agonies, hurriedst me along by my lusts to complete their desires, and punishedst her carnal desire with the just scourge of immoderate griefs. She loved my presence with her, as is natural to mothers; though in her the affection was uncommonly strong; and she knew not what joy Thou wast preparing for her from my absence. She knew not, therefore she wept and wailed. Yet after she had wearied herself in accusing my perfidy and cruelty, *she returned to her former employment of praying for me*, and went home, while I went to Rome."

At Rome Augustine was seized with illness, and as he himself says, "drew nigh to hell;" and when, after his conversion, he writes the story of his escape from the very jaws of the grave, his mother's prayers are again the prominent features which meet our view. "Morning and evening," he says, "she frequented the church, to hear Thy word, and to pray, *and the salvation of her son was the constant burden of her supplications*. Thou heardedst her, O Lord, and performedst in due season what Thou hadst predestinated. Thou recoveredst me from the fever, that at length I might obtain also a recovery of still greater importance."

From Rome, Augustine went to Milan, and there we

find the praying mother again. Augustine describes her as "courageous through piety, following him by land and sea, and secure of God's favour in all dangers." And there she was, the same praying mother that she had been elsewhere, her son's salvation being her one grand absorbing thought. At length, the long looked, long prayed for time arrived, and Monica's petitions were heard. The teaching of Ambrose, was made, in part, the means of Augustine's conversion; "in part" we say, for there were special interferences of God in its accomplishment; and after a fierce struggle, after the Evil Spirit had rent and torn him, now throwing him into the fire, and now into the water, he was delivered from his power, he arose from the earth a victor in the strife, a converted man! an heir of glory! an answer to a mother's continued prayers!

The closing scene of Monica's life may cheer some sorrowing parent, who has long prayed and apparently prayed in vain. Were not years of prayer well repaid by that one hour by the river side, which almost closed the intercourse of the praying mother and the converted son. "It was through Thy secret appointment," says Augustine, "that she and I stood alone at a window facing the east, in a house at the mouth of the Tiber, where we were preparing ourselves for our voyage. Our discourse was highly agreeable, and forgetting the past, we endeavoured to conceive aright the nature of the eternal life of the saints. It was evident to us, that no carnal delights deserved to be named on this subject; erecting our spirits more ardently, we ascended above the noblest parts of the material creation, to the consideration of our own minds, and passing above them, we attempted to reach heaven itself, to come to Thee, by whom all things were made. There our hearts were enamoured, and there we held fast the first-fruits of the Spirit, and returned to the sound of our own voice, which gave us an emblem of the Divine Word. We said, 'if the flesh, the imagination, and every tongue should be silenced, for they proclaim, 'We made not ourselves, but He who remaineth for ever;' if these things should now hold their peace, and God alone should speak, not by any emblems or created things, but by Himself, so that we could hear His word; should this be continued and other visions be withdrawn, and this alone seize and absorb the spectator for ever, is not this the meaning of 'Enter thou into the joy of thy Lord?' At that moment the world appeared to us of no value: and she said, 'Son, I have now no delight in life. What I should do here, and why I am here, I know not, the hope of this life being quite spent. One thing only, your conversion, was an object for which I wished to live. My God has given me this in larger measure. What do I here?'" Five days after this, this praying mother fell into a fever, and on the ninth day she died; but she being dead yet speaketh, and her voice says, "Christian mothers, continue in prayer."

Yes, Christian parents, continue in prayer on behalf of the apparently lost and ruined one; if he go to the haunt of vice, let your prayers track his footsteps like angels of mercy; if he snatch the intoxicating glass, let your voice still seek for him the water of life; if he gamble away his substance in riotous living, yet pray for him, that even when he has lost all, or, if it must be, yet *through* the loss of all, he may come to himself, and

say, "how many hired servants of my father's have bread
enough and to spare, and I perish with hunger! I will
arise and go to my father, and will say unto him, Father,
I have sinned against heaven, and before thee, and am
no more worthy to be called thy son, make me as one of
thy hired servants." Who can tell at what moment and
in what way, the many prayers of father and mother, of
sisters and brothers, will put forth their wondrous power?
It may be that the prodigal will be arrested in the very
midst of his career of sin, as St. Paul was arrested by
the light from heaven, and suddenly find himself bound,
though not with hempen ropes; struck down, though not
with human hand; arrested, though not by any earthly
writ; at some unexpected time, in some unlikely place,
he may find himself under the influence of a spell which
he can neither fight against nor understand, and turn
homeward, although perhaps he knows not why, yet
never to leave it again. Thus have many wanderers
been reclaimed, and their voices now swell the chorus of
the redeemed; and the praises which they sing, and
which make melody in the ear of God Himself, are the
fruits which have been brought forth by many bitter
prayers! *

* The Rev. Dr. Leland, Professor in the Theological Seminary
at Columbia, S. C. stated in a prayer meeting at Saratoga, that he
had ascertained by personal inquiry that *ninety nine of one
hundred* students in that seminary received their first religious
impressions from pious mothers. At the convention of "Young
Men's Christian Association" at Troy, N. Y. which was attended by about two hundred and fifty young men, those, whose
mothers were praying women were asked to rise, when nearly
all rose, thus testifying to the efficacy of the prayers of godly
mothers.

"A weather-beaten sailor, on making his homeward passage, as he doubled the stormy Cape, encountered a dreadful tempest. The mother had heard of the ship outside the Cape, and was waiting, with the anxiety a mother alone can know, to see her son. But now the storm had arisen, and that, when the ship was in the most dangerous place. Fearing that each blast, as it swept the raging deep, might howl the requiem of her son, with faith strong in God, she commenced praying for his safety. At this moment news came that the vessel was lost.

"The father, an unconverted man, had till this, preserved a sullen silence, but now he wept aloud. The mother observed, 'It is in the hands of Him who does all things well;' and again the soft and softened spirit bowed, commending her son and her partner, in an audible voice, broken only by the bursting of a full heart, to God.

"Darkness had now spread her mantle abroad, and they retired—but not to rest—and anxiously waited for the morning, hoping, at least, that some relic of their lost one might be found.

"The morning came. The winds were hushed and the ocean lay comparatively calm, as though its fury had subsided since its victim was no more. At this moment the little gate in front of the dwelling turned on its hinges, the door opened, and their son, their lost, loved son stood before them. The vessel had been driven into one of the many harbours on the coast, and was safe. The father rushed to meet him. His mother, hanging on his neck, earnestly exclaimed, 'My child, how came you here?' 'Mother,' said he, as the tears coursed

down his sunburnt face, *'I knew you'd pray me home!'*
What a spectacle! A wild, reckless youth acknow-
ledging the efficacy of prayer! It seems he was aware
of his perilous situation, and that he laboured with the
thoughts, 'My mother prays—Christian's prayers are
answered, and I may be saved.' This reflection, when
almost exhausted with fatigue, and ready to give up in
despair, gave him fresh courage, and with renewed effort
he laboured till the harbour was gained. Christian
mother, go thou and do likewise. Pray for that son who
is likely to be wrecked in the storm of life, and his
prospects blasted for ever. He may be saved."

One word I would add of counsel to such as are thus
praying. Do not shut the door against the answers to
your prayers, do not so act as in point of fact to say, "I
will leave no opening by which the wayward one can
return." Many a poor wayward one would have returned,
if only the wanderer's path had been kept clear, if only
the door of home had been kept upon the latch. We
may learn a lesson from the conduct of a poor woman
whose misguided daughter left the paternal roof, and
wandered into the ways of sin. Many were the prayers
which the mother offered for her misguided child; and
when she finished her prayer at night, the last thing she
did was to go and see that the door was left on the latch.
If her child were moved by God to return, she should
always have a shelter to which to come. It was well
that God put this into her heart; for one night the poor
girl turned her steps towards home, and tried the latch,
and came in, and crept upstairs to her accustomed room,
and went out to sin no more again. Keep the heart's
door, keep the house door on the latch, for the answer to

prayer may come in an hour of which you are not aware; that heart, that house, is not degraded, which has written upon its portals, "The wanderer's home."

The subjects of *Intensity in Prayer*, and of *Belief in Prayer*, will meet us in subsequent pages, we need not therefore dwell upon them here, even though they be brought before us by the passage which we have been considering; there is one point, however, to which I wish to draw attention before this chapter comes to a close; *i. e.*, the marvel of our voice being heard at all. "Evening, morning, and at noon, will I pray and cry aloud: and He shall hear my voice."

It is indeed a wonder that our voice is heard at all! So weak, so broken is it at times, that it seems marvellous that it should be heard, even in silence the most intense. But heard it is, not in the midst of silence, but of myriad sounds. The cries of a groaning world are entering the ears of the Lord of Sabaoth; the songs of praising and adoring beings are ascending continually before His throne; the rush of myriad worlds as they whirl through space, is listened to by THE ONE from whose hand they were rolled forth upon their wondrous paths! but despite all these, the mind of the Infinite One is undistracted, and listens in undisturbed calmness to the whisperings of the least among His saints. O my soul, be deep in thy belief of this; and in that belief, even though thou canst pray with but a whispering voice, yet pray; let the belief of the Psalmist be also thine, "Evening, morning, and at noon, will I pray, and cry aloud: *and He shall hear my voice.*"

CHAPTER X.

THE "I WILL" OF PRAYER IN 'OVERWHELMING TROUBLE.'

Psalm lxi, 2. "*From the end of the earth will I cry unto Thee; when my heart is overwhelmed, lead me to the rock that is higher than I.*"

WE are told in the word of God, that "man is born to trouble as the sparks fly upward;" and these troubles, which are the heritage of man as a poor fallen sinner, are not only many, but also various; so that each man has plagues which his own heart knows, and which are, perhaps, unknown to all beside. To this heritage, you and I, dear reader, were born, and into it we have come; the heritages of earthly lands and gold are alienable, but the heritage of sorrow is sure.

These troubles are, as we have just observed, of various kinds; some are *provoking*, some are *gnawing*, some are *perplexing*, and some are *overwhelming*; but whatever form they assume, they are troubles, and are part of the wear and tear of life.

There is a class of troubles which is eminently *provoking*. Perhaps no serious results hang upon them, but they are peculiarly calculated to try and vex our tempers, to stir up our feelings, to disturb the equanimity of our minds, to excite our combative propensities; they are the stones in the shoes of daily life, and as such they are troubles, and it would be foolish to call them by any other name.

There is another class, which might be called *gnawing* troubles. Such eat slowly into the heart's vitals; such fret silently, as the moth does the garment; they destroy life's brightest colourings, and its most beautiful patterns, and leave nothing but wreck and ruin wherever their tooth has come. There are many in the world who have a gnawing at their hearts, which is to them what the canker is to the bud; it eats silently and surely, and leaves a few shrivelled leaves, where there might have been a bunch of full-blown flowers.

Some are afflicted with *perplexing and distracting* troubles. Such troubles do not gnaw the heart, they are too intrusive and pressing for that; they put a person to his wits' ends; they confuse and harass him, and almost wear him out by the anxiety to which they expose him. Such are very often the troubles of trade; of mothers with large families; of persons placed in difficult circumstances in life, and so forth; and many a time they are half driven out of their senses, by the dilemmas in which they are placed. If only they knew what to do, they would do it; but that is the perplexity, and it undeniably brings its trouble with it.

Then, there are *overwhelming* troubles. Troubles which sweep over a man, just as the mighty billows of the ocean sweep over, and submerge the sands. These are troubles which struggle with us, as it were, for life and death; troubles which would leave us helpless wrecks;

troubles which enter into conflict with us in our prime,
which grapple with us in our health and strength, and
threaten to conquer us by sheer force, no matter how
bravely we may contend. Such trouble the Psalmist
knew. "When my heart is overwhelmed, lead me to
the Rock that is higher than I."

It is not, however, in this latter class of trouble alone
that we have need to take up the Psalmist's determination, and say, "I will cry unto Thee." There is but the
one refuge in all trouble, be it great or small, and if we
seek any other, we shall assuredly but increase our
distress. He who is our refuge in the greater, will not
refuse to be our refuge in the lesser also; the same love
which will befriend us in the overwhelmings of trouble,
will not cast us off in the time of perplexities and provocations.

In the present chapter, we have to occupy ourselves in
deep waters, and passing from all minor trials, to consider those overwhelmings, in which we need the Rock
that is higher than ourselves.

Cryings from the ends of the earth,

Cryings in overwhelmings of heart, and

The heart's cry and desire under these circumstances,
are to form the subjects of our consideration now.

And first, a few words are to be said about "*Cryings
from the ends of the earth.*" The centre of all worship
was Jerusalem, "whither the tribes go up, the tribes of
the Lord, unto the testimony of Israel, to give thanks
unto the name of the Lord:" Psalm cxxii, 4. To
be prevented then from coming up to Jerusalem was
a serious trouble to any one who really loved God,

and stood in covenant relationship to Him. "How amiable (says the Psalmist in Psalm lxxxiv) are Thy tabernacles O Lord of Hosts. My soul longeth, yea, even fainteth for the courts of the Lord, my heart, and my flesh crieth out for the Living God, a day in Thy courts is better than a thousand, I had rather be a door-keeper in the house of my God, than to dwell in the tents of wickedness."

The Psalmist here puts himself in the position of one, who is not only prevented for a season from coming up to the holy place, but who is driven as far as possible therefrom—even to the ends of the earth; he is separated from all ordinances, helps, and privileges, but he will not on that account allow himself to be separated from his God; "from the end of the earth will I cry unto Thee."

There are some who seem to be living on ordinances rather than on God, and separation from them seems almost to bring death into their souls; they know much of a God in ordinances, they know comparatively little of a God without ordinances.

Now ordinances are very precious, and so weak are we, that we need all the helps we can get; but what, if we be deprived of them, if we be as it were driven to the ends of the earth?

This may happen to us. Some of God's dear children have been laid for years upon beds of sickness, and some have been located in distant regions, and others have had their lot cast amid unsympathetic and ungodly people, so that they have been constrained to cry, "Woe is me, that I sojourn in Mesech, that I dwell in the tents of Kedar; my soul hath long dwelt with him that hateth peace."

Under these circumstances what is to be done? We

must cry unto God, *from the place and position in which we are,* as Jonah did; and not wait until we are more favourably circumstanced, for thus we might have to wait for ever. God expects us to make the best of the circumstances in which we are placed.

Let us be careful not to allow ourselves to be overcome by the depression which is the natural consequent of a position of isolation, and of deprivation of privilege and help. We are not without privilege even when visible privileges are removed; we have the highest privilege, then, of all; we can cry to God direct; our cry will ascend straight to His throne from the end of the earth.

Here there is assuredly great encouragement for many an unhappily situated child of God; perhaps in his family, father and mother, sisters and brothers, are all against him; perhaps in the lone corner of some far off settlement, he never hears the sound of the sabbath bell, he never sees the face of a minister of God; or it may be, that year after year he lies upon a bed of suffering and pain; oh let him not be downhearted; oh let him not think himself an outcast from the throne of heaven, from the mercy seat, from the altar, from " The Priest!" If Jesus be ours, we may cry from the ends of the earth, as well as from those spots which man has most consecrated to the worship of the Lord; no matter where we are, we come in a moment before the mercy seat, we bring our sacrifice to the altar, we have the services of a priest, the services of Jesus, who knows in His wide-spread power no limit of time, no boundary of space.

We now come to consider *overwhelmings of heart*— times of sad and bitter trial, with which many a tempest-tost child of God is only too familiar, and in which the cry to Him is the only available resource. We have many instances of these overwhelmings in the Psalms. Psalms cii, lxxvii, part of Psalm cvii, and Psalm cxlii, will serve as examples;* and our business now is, to enquire into the condition of the poor heart when thus overwhelmed.

The idea that is brought before us here, is that of a man amid the waters—over whom those waters have the mastery—who would fain buffet with them if he could—but who is conquered by them, so that, unless there be an interference on his behalf, he must die. In such an overwhelming

The natural power of resistance is gone. Man makes a great deal of his natural powers; he will always use them to repel anything which threatens injury to his life; but he may be reduced to such a state, as not to be able to put forth those powers at all. His eagerness to act

* Jonah is a fit representation of a man crying from the ends of the earth, and from amidst overwhelmings of the most terrible kind. "Then Jonah cried unto the Lord his God, out of the fish's belly, and said: 'I cried by reason of mine affliction unto the Lord, and He heard me, out of the belly of hell cried I, and Thou heardest my voice.' For Thou hadst cast me into the deep, in the midst of the seas; and the floods compassed me about; all Thy billows and Thy waves passed over me. Then I said, 'I am cast out of Thy sight; yet I will look again toward Thy holy temple.' The waters compassed me about, even to the soul; the depth closed me round about, the weeds were wrapped about my head. I went down to the bottoms of the mountains; the earth with her bars was about me for ever; yet hast Thou brought up my life from corruption, O Lord my God. When my soul fainted within me I remembered the Lord, and my prayer came in unto Thee, into Thine holy temple." Jonah ii, 1—7.

may be as intense as ever, his dread of injury as acute, but his natural powers of resistance are gone. We can scarcely imagine any circumstances more distressing than these; if the mind were stupified, and the impending danger thus unappreciated, the case would not be half so bad; but to feel the enemy coming upon us, or, it may be, actually upon us, and to have no power of resistance, is terrible indeed. The man overwhelmed by waters, with his strength exhausted, and his limbs powerless to resist, but flung hither and thither by the wild billows at their will, must feel his last few moments of perfect consciousness terrible indeed; and yet this is the condition of children of God at times. Men who have been down in deep waters will tell you that they have been thus tossed to and fro, and that they have had a terrible consciousness of the power of the enemy, and of their own helplessness while they were thus tried. There are many degrees of spiritual trial, which we can resist by the exercise of, what I might be permitted to call, the natural powers of the soul. We can throw off many doubts by *reasoning* against them, and we can overcome many temptations, by a simple *determination* that we will have nothing to do with them; but in circumstances like the present we have lost our old powers, we cannot resist, we are paralyzed for a season. Intense depression generally accompanies such a state as this; we have ceased to be what we used to be formerly, and as we miss the old powers which we once exercised with effect, we feel inclined to say, there remains nothing for us but to die.

At such a season as this, where is our faith? I do not mean any extraordinary faith, but the simple, ordinary faith, wherewith we carried on the ordinary business of our spiritual life. We used to do a good deal through the instrumentality of that faith; it seemed just as natural to us in daily use, as any of the ordinary powers of our bodies; we threw off many Satanic assaults by it; now it can do absolutely nothing: we judge ourselves and say, "we have no faith at all." This is, no doubt, being brought very low; and when we are in this state, there are no fierce strugglings of soul; we are too nearly drowned for them; we are past struggling, and we seem to be almost at the mercy of the Evil One.

As to our love to God, there was a time when we could have done much through that also; that love would have carried us through great trials, it would, by the simple fact of its keeping us close to Christ, have enabled us to defeat many of the temptations which are now almost triumphant: but now that love seems cold, it appears to us to have lost its energies, it certainly does not keep our heart in peace as it used to do. The very consciousness of our dead state as regards love helps to unnerve us, and to make us more helpless amid the waves which buffet and submerge us. Some of our readers have, perhaps, never had any sad experiences like these, but others no doubt have; they have felt themselves helpless amid the billows, their powers were numbed, and their case seemed well nigh as bad as it could be. Oh! what an inexpressible mercy is it, that when we are thus bereft of our ordinary spiritual powers, and apparently at the mercy of every billow that dashes over us, we are not left to "self," or "self's" resources, or anything belonging to "self" at all; that ONE whom the spiritual as well as the natural waves must obey, is ready to put forth His Sovereign power on our behalf! But for this, many a Christian man must have been drowned; but for this, the demons of the storm must have had their own way with him; his limbs were unstrung, his eyes were blinded, his brain was reeling, his heart was chilling; and what hindered their doing with him even as they listed? God gave his poor child, under these circumstances, just strength enough to cry to Him; the cry was perhaps feeble; it was almost drowned by the violence of the storm; it seemed more like the gurgling of a drowning man than anything else, but it was a prayer, and the prayer hearing and prayer honouring God did not despise it; He heard, and when He hears His child is safe.

Let us, when we find our ordinary powers of resistance gone, take care lest we abandon ourselves to despair, as though now, indeed, there is no hope, now we must most surely die. It is true we must abandon all hope in " self;" we must feel ourselves impotent, like Samson, shorn of his locks, but we can utter a cry, be it never so subdued; let us utter it and leave the rest to God.

The heart is here represented to us as being overwhelmed, or, as it is otherwise translated, " covered over;" it is smothered in, unable to perform its functions with proper action, unable to throw out the blood to the extremities, to give them needed vitality, and power for necessary effort. When the action of the heart is paralyzed, even temporally, it will tell upon all the members, a chill there sends its cold vibration through every limb; Satan knows this well, and so all his dealings are heart dealings, efforts to paralyze the very spring of life itself. This is precisely what we ourselves have experienced, we have partially felt death within us, we have felt a gradual numbing of our heart, a gradual diminution in the quickness of its beat, a gradual closing in, and pressure of a weight upon it, and this was the overwhelming process.

Our Lord Jesus Christ had overwhelmings, and it will be worth our while reverentially to consider them for a moment. They were unlike ours, inasmuch as they could not in any wise impair the vitality of His heart; but they were like ours, inasmuch as they were able to inflict upon Him oppression and pain. Jesus' heart was unquestionably overwhelmed in Gethsemane, and still more so upon Calvary; there the heavy waters came in upon His soul, but we know that His vitality, His power of action, was in nowise impaired; in Gethsemane He says, "the cup that My Father hath given Me, shall I not drink it?" and on Calvary, on the cross, He is stronger in action than ever He was elsewhere, He *laid down* His life, no man took it from Him, He laid it down of Himself; He had to die as a deliberate act.*

We must die whether we will or not; He had to will to die: and He did so will, and He carried out that will, by formally giving up His life; and so in the hour when He was most overwhelmed, He put forth the greatest power of action, and proved that no crushing, no overwhelming, could touch for a moment the vitality which dwelt in Him. Does not this speak to us, and say, "If Jesus was so powerful on behalf of His people, in the dark

* Matthew xxvii, 50. Αφηκε το πνευμα, "He gave up the ghost," rather, "He *dismissed* His Spirit." He acted as the priest. He was not only passive as the sacrifice, but active in cutting short His life. None took it from Him.

hour when His heart was overwhelmed, what must He now be, when this pressure is removed, and His heart beats freely in love to them, at the right hand of His Father's throne?"

It was necessary that Jesus should take experience of overwhelmings of heart, as well as of the other temptations and trials, to which poor human nature is subject; "He was tempted in all points like as we are," and this must not be excluded. It is a matter of great moment to us, that we should be enabled to see that Jesus endured overwhelmings; for if we are sustained in other trials by thinking that He had experience of them, how shall we be sustained in this, except in the same way.

Let us now look at some of the overwhelmings which come in upon the believer's soul, in which his only resource is prayer.

There are times when the poor heart is completely overwhelmed, by *visions of sin.* The memory with all its powers, awakes and reproduces, with terrible distinctness, the sounds and sights of, as we thought, *bygone* days. The remembrance of these things is grievous to us, the burden is intolerable; we shrink within ourselves; we wince at the fearful visions which come before our minds. We had no such fearful visions when we were committing sin, sin is sweet at the moment; its bitterness is in its dregs, its memories, its judgment. And now, in the believer's case, the remembrance of sin is made ten-fold worse, from the knowledge which he has acquired of the holiness of God; and the vision of sin comes upon him with that extra power. Perhaps since last he had such a vision, he has increased in knowledge of God's holiness and character; and thus his sin becomes subjected to a stricter test than any by which it had ever been tried before, and so, deeper overwhelmings are his portion now. Such visions of sin are able with great ease, to gain the mastery over any spiritual powers, which the believer may possess; they can soon drown him, there is no use in his attempting to buffet them, they will dash him to and fro, they will numb his vitality, they will break his limbs in pieces; Prayer is the Christian's only resource under these circumstances—the prayer which we find here—that he may be led to the rock that is higher than he.

It may be, that these visions of sin are not the heavy waters in which he is cast; *doubts of Divine love* are, perhaps, his trouble. Not doubts of God's love generally, but of that love as beaming upon himself personally. Hiding of the Father's face is bitterness to the soul; and when doubts come in upon the soul, which hide out the sense of God's love, the overwhelming waters might be said to have begun to break over our heads. Such doubts have come terribly upon many who are plainly marked people of God; they have rolled in one after another upon the heart, until at length they have brought with them actual despair; and all that the poor tempest-tossed believer could do, was just to utter such words as we have here, "Lead me to the rock that is higher than I."

A remarkable instance of a soul under this trouble came under the author's observation some years ago. A Christian man, who had served God for a lifetime, was seized with consumption. The repeated visits of the attending minister seemed to afford no consolation, and, in truth, all the ordinary means of comforting were tried in vain. Thus matters went on for a long time, and at length the invalid went abroad for the winter. At the end of the winter, he returned, and the minister having heard that he continued in the same state of mind as before, held back from visiting him. The invalid, however, desired to partake of the Holy Communion, and so his pastor went to him. It was a very painful scene; the agitation of this poor afflicted Christian was such, that all present were greatly distressed. For many weeks did he linger, the minister now visiting him regularly as before, but the same distressing doubts continued; and to all human appearance, they were likely to shroud him, even in his departure. The mercy of God, however, at length dispelled the gloom. One night the sick man asked for his dressing things, and washed and shaved himself; then he asked for a clean shirt, and when he put it on, and was set up in the bed, he said, "Now I am dressed for my last journey;" thus he remained for a couple of hours, when lo! all clouds and mists rolled from before his eyes; the light of heaven shone in upon him, a ray of brightness streamed through the golden gates upon his soul, and he departed full of joy.

After the death of this worthy man, the author visited his widow, and found from her that one of the strongest characteristics of her departed husband's mind was the doubting of the love of others to him. Satan ever on the watch, to use our own peculiarities of character against ourselves; and ever skilful in working with the tools which he finds ready to his hand; gave this Christian man months, and even two years of grief in this very way. We often supply ourselves the waters for our own overwhelming.

Our very *sense of weakness* has, at times, proved an overwhelming billow. Thrown in upon ourselves, we have been fiercely agitated with thoughts as to what would become of us at last; and Satan pressed us hard; he exercised his pressure upon our very weakest points; and in a short time we felt ourselves amid the waters, with no possibility of escape, unless by the interference of One far stronger than ourselves.

These will serve as specimens of the overwhelmings which come over the people of the Lord; but they are only specimens; Satan's waves and billows are as many as those which break upon the shore, or toss and swell in the open sea. He has the means of overwhelming every heart, and when he makes the attempt, our only refuge is in prayer. Very possibly some of our readers may not be often subjected to such fierce temptations as these; but they may rest assured, that Satan will not allow any soul to gain the haven of everlasting rest, without having first tried upon it his overwhelming powers.

Let us turn for a moment or two, to the overwhelming troubles which come in upon the poor heart, in things pertaining, it is true, only to this life, but still of great importance to us while we are here. Overwhelmings of heart are often the lot of man, as he performs the voyage of life. This man is overwhelmed by the treachery of a friend, whose iniquity has ruined him; and this woman is overwhelmed by the conduct of the child she reared, amid many watchings, and many tears; look on this side, and you will see one, who has his heart overwhelmed by the loss of the one he held most dear; he is choking under the deep waters of bitterest sorrow, and they are howling and dashing over his devoted head; look but a little distance off, and there is another, who to all appearance must drown, suffocating under the prospect of trial which must surely come; (and which is perhaps worse in the anticipation, than in the event.) Let us not make light of any of these things; they are overwhelmings, and in the case of men unhelped of God, they have proved themselves so, by taking away even life itself. Oh! be advised, dear readers, never to face these billows alone; you have no strength in yourselves for bearing up, amid the deep waters of grief; when first they begin to break in upon you, ask to be led to the rock that is higher than you.

Would that we could persuade the Lord's people who read these lines, to believe that the overwhelmings which have reference to this life, are to be brought before God, just as much as those which appertain to another. Would that we could dissuade them from the attempt to buffet the waves by themselves, for this buffeting must end in their being sorely hurt; the longer we buffet by ourselves, the deeper shall we find the water becoming, the stronger the billows, the fiercer their crest, and the more impetuous their rush; yes, and the weaker also our strength. O child of God, when first the waters begin to rise, seek refuge in prayer? and if thou must be tried in the heavy surges of temptation or of sorrow, prepare for them upon thy knees; as the camel kneels to receive its load, so kneel thou to receive thine, say, "when my heart is overwhelmed, lead me to the rock that is higher than I!"

Such, then, are overwhelmings of heart, some of

which are peculiar to the believer, others of which he shares in common with his fellow men.

We now come to *the heart's cry and desire under these circumstances.*

We trace here several points of considerable importance. There is, first of all, *a recognition of a place of safety ;* then we have this place brought before us, as *abundantly sufficient, when personal weakness has been realized ;* we observe further, that this place *cannot be attained, without the helping of another's hand;* and lastly we have *the character of this refuge, and the position of a believer, when availing himself of it ;* the place of refuge is " a rock," and the position of the believer is "upon a rock."

The *bare recognition of a place of safety* is, in itself, a matter of great importance. To know that there is a refuge, that we need not perish, is cheering to the heart; nothing so daunts the spirit, and numbs every energy which otherwise might have been put forth, as the feeling of despair, that, "it is all no use," that we cannot escape. If only we believe in the existence of a place of safety, and that it is possible for us to reach it, we shall feel our spirits revive; hope will enter into, and vivify the heart; and even though desperate struggles must be made, still the heart will rise to the emergency, and success shall crown its efforts, and its prayers.

That, however, with which we now have to do, is not so much personal effort, as prayer made with the recognition of a place of safety. It may be that we feel we cannot by any struggling of ours, attain that place of safety; that it may be like a rock seen by the drowning man, but at too great a distance to be reached by his failing strength; if the recognition of it give us strength to cry, that will be of incalculable worth.

The Psalmist saw the rock; oh! may you, dear reader, ever see safe standing ground, in the worst trial times, May Satan never be able to say to you, "you are hopeless as well as helpless; there is no way of escape for you." Ever let us recognise the place of safety; let us say "it exists; I know where it is; my belief in that point cannot be shaken." It is true this is no very high putting forth of Christian grace, (and yet in overwhelming circumstances, it is perhaps higher than some suppose) but though not a high, it is a most useful, and important one; many a tempest-tossed believer has effectively made his escape, by prayer which was put up under the consciousness of this fact. Should the overwhelming be so terrible, as to make the tried and tempted man say, "I doubt whether Christ *will* save me," oh! may it never pass that boundary, and make him say, "I doubt whether Christ *can* save me."

In the passage which we are now considering, we have the place of safety brought before us, as *abundantly sufficient, when personal weakness has been realized.* Personal weakness had been realized, for the heart had been overwhelmed; now that which alone could avail under the present sad circumstances, is realized also, viz., the high Rock, "Lead me to the Rock that is higher than I." The solidity of the Rock is brought into contrast with the weakness of the believer tossed to and fro; it stands unmoved amid the waves, while he is beaten about amidst them, almost at their will. There is no more apt image of the position which the Lord Jesus occupies towards His people, in the terrible hours of overwhelming temptation, than this of " the Rock." The Rock stands immoveable amid the boiling waters, which at times sweep against it with heavy and unbroken billows, as though they would push it from its base, and at times leap towards it with seething foam, as though they would tear it into pieces, and in their rage sweep in its fragments upon the shore, to add to the water-worn shingle there; now with a deep-toned boom, like the shot of a heavy gun, one mighty broad-backed billow discharges against it all its might; and now, jostling and crowding, a multitude follow quickly in its path, as though they would fling themselves into the breach which this artillery had made; the shriek of the winds is heard in horrid distinctness, as they madden the billows, and lash them onward, with fresh paroxysms of rage; but motionless amid both winds and waves, without the loss of even the smallest fragment, stands the Rock, silent, majestic, and unmoved, the same in storm, as in calm. Such is " the Rock," and such is JESUS; and such He has appeared to His people, ofttimes battered, and almost smothered, amid such waves as these. And it is very important to God's people to remember, that this Rock is always to be found amid these heaving billows, these boiling surges of the devil; let them rage their very worst, there He is, and there, for His people's sake, He ever must be found.

But not only is the Rock recognised, but also *its height*—this is no sunken rock, whose sharp and jagged edges, submerged beneath the waters, amid which the believer is being tossed, must have added fearfully to his distress, lacerating, and bruising him, and conspiring with the waves to take away his life. No, this is a Rock higher than himself, on which he can stand, whose foundation, and whose height, are equally beyond the reach of any power, which the enemy can put forth. This is the recognition of the Psalmist here; he calls it " the Rock that is higher than I."

There is great instruction in these last few words. Self has been seen in all its weakness; it is now proved that it can do nothing; safety must be out of self, it must be in something higher than self, it must be in Christ. And Jesus is abundantly sufficient for us; let us but see this, and laying self aside altogether, seek to stand on Him, and all will be surely well with us. We waste much strength, we incur much peril, in trying to keep our own heads above water; this is a vain attempt; the billows are much higher, and the waves are much stronger than we are; we are not constructed to fight these spiritual billows by ourselves, any more than the body is, to contend with the sweeping billows of the seas. To buffet the waters was not the intent for which the body was made; to buffet the temptations of the Devil was not the purpose for which the soul was created; this has come no doubt to be its lot, but it is not furnished with any powers by which it can do it in itself; that on which we stand must be something higher than ourselves, if we are to stand at all.

In times, then, of fierce overwhelmings, let us look at once for the high Rock; let us seek for nothing from self, let us just cry to have our feet set on Christ; then we shall feel that we have firm ground under us; then we shall see the waves toss themselves, and we shall hear them roar; then we shall look at them as they curl upwards, and at last sink down exhausted, spent by their own fierce throes; and we shall rejoice that all we have to do, is simply to stand on Christ, to be in union with Him, while He bears the storm's brunt, and at once defies and defeats its utmost rage. Stand, beloved Christian upon the Rock; if you ask, but what shall I do? I answer, "only make sure that you are there;" *feel* the Rock under you; then, as when a tempest-tossed mariner has reached a rock, the contest is no longer between the waves and him, but between the waves and the rock; so when you are on Christ, the contest will not be between you and Satan, but between Christ and Him. Unless Satan can vanquish Christ, the Christian must be safe.

There remains one further particular to be looked at, and *i. e.*, the fact that *this place cannot be realized without the helping of another's hand*. The Psalmist here desires to be *led* to the Rock that is higher than he was. In Psalms xxvii and xlii we find him recognising the Lord, as the One who not only provided the shelter, but also who enabled him to reach it. "He shall set me up upon a rock." "He brought me up also out of an horrible pit, out of the miry clay, and set my feet upon a rock, and established my goings."

This helping hand of God we have brought before us in Psalm xviii; here we meet with the floods and deep waters; "the sorrows of death compassed me, and the floods of ungodly men made me afraid, the sorrows of hell compassed me about, the snares of death prevented me;" there were terrible dealings of God also, for "the

channels of waters were seen and the foundations of the
world were discovered at Thy rebuke, O Lord, at the
blast of the breath of Thy nostrils!" then what happened? "He sent from above, He *took* me, He *drew* me
out of many waters."

If we would find ourselves upon the Rock, and enjoy
the realization of being so, we must be dependent upon
another's hand. And that hand can do everything for
us, even in our worst of times. When we are so blinded
by the salt waves that dash into our eyes, so reeling in
brain that we cannot perhaps think, much less make
continuous efforts, there is a hand which can lead us,
which can draw us out of the waters, which can set our
feet upon the Rock. Surely we have already experienced
the power and tenderness of that hand; and it may be
that in the reader's case, the waves, as they made sure
of their prey, found it supernaturally drawn forth from
them, that it might be set upon a Rock, immoveable
amid all waters, and sufficient amid all storms!

CHAPTER XI.

THE "I WILL" OF PRAYER IN TROUBLE.

(Concluded.)

Psalm cxxi, 1. "*I wilt lift up mine eyes unto the hills, from whence cometh my help.*"

THERE is one resource, of which no tyranny of man, no complication of circumstances, can deprive the Christian; *i. e.*, PRAYER.

The limbs may be chained, so that neither hand nor foot can be stirred in self-defence; the view of the natural heavens may be shut out, by the dark dungeon's arching wall; yea, the very eye-sight may be extinguished, so that the dull and heavy balls will reflect no objects in the heavens above, or in the earth beneath; still the man of God can come into the posture of prayer in his soul, can lift up his eyes to the heaven of heavens, can worship, can supplicate, in a word, can pray.

Blessed be God that this is so; for the body is oftentimes so circumstanced that it cannot use hand, or knee, or eye in prayer.

This chapter concludes the portion of our subject which has reference to Prayer in Trouble; and in the passage which it is designed to illustrate, we have these thoughts prominently brought before us :

    I.   *The elevation of the Christian above surrounding circumstances.*

    II.   *The power of spiritual sight in prayer.*

    III.   *The definite point on which the eye is fixed.*

The Psalmist says, " I will lift up mine eyes unto the hills;" his own position, then, appears to be in the valleys in the low ground; and it does not appear that he can extricate himself from them; all that he can do, under present circumstances, is to look unto the hills.

Many of the Lord's people are obliged to walk, for a long and weary while, in the valleys; they have to go from one valley to another; and the atmosphere of these valleys is very damp and chilling to the soul. In some dark places the deadly night-shade grows; from some gloomy caverns ill-omened creatures hoot; the foot-step loses its elasticity, the heart its bound, and the wonder is, how some of these valleys are ever passed safely through. It is true that all valleys are not so bad as this; there are some which are simply dark and cold, some which are rough and lonely, and some which are depressing, because for many a long and weary mile, they shut out the surrounding scenery, with all its variety and life; but whatever the peculiarity of each valley, it is able to act upon the man that travels through it; and who can tell what such places have witnessed, in the way of deep depressions of soul? But why not make our escape out of these valleys ? Simply because we cannot; and because God never intended that we should be able to do so; His design towards us is, that we should be taught to lift up our eyes unto the hills; that we should journey through the valleys, looking to higher ground for all needful help. What God often has in view for His children, is helping them in the valley, rather than helping them out of it.

What long and lonely journeyings have been made, by many a widowed, many an orphaned heart; the rocks which shut in their valley were high; a glimmering light, seldom stronger than the twilight of the evening, was all they had to illumine their weary path; and as day after day passed on, and night after night, these foot-sore travellers said, "Lord, how long?"

What long and stony journeyings have been performed by poverty-stricken men and women, who often tried to scale the precipice sides of the barren valley through which they travelled, but they could not; and faint and cowed, their very heart withering within them, they struggled forward another day's journey, without any motive or any aim.

What dark and dismal journeyings have some Christians performed, in valleys where they seemed to be especially exposed to Satanic temptation, where the Evil One could cause horrid, slimy temptations to cross their path; where poisonous food seemed all that there was to eat; where unearthly sounds whispered, and hooted, and reverberated, and echoed, and re-echoed again; until the poor wayfarer seemed almost driven out of his senses, as though but yet a little more, and he must go mad. Oh! this is a dreadful valley, it is one not travelled by all believers, but it is one only too well known to others. What is there, which the poor believer has not heard in this terrible place? He shudders! he hears a whisper, it says, "There is no God at all."—He shivers with cold!

he has put his foot upon some icy, slimy things, and there runs through his soul a chill shiver of terror; a thought has been infused into his heart that if there be a God He does not care for him. What wild and unearthly hoot is that which now startles him afresh? It is an evil spirit, hooting out that all Christians are fools; and that the wayfarer's Christianity has brought him into this valley; and that he is a fool for having come into it, for that his old neighbours and friends, who troubled not themselves about these things, are in the sunshine, and well off enough. A hissing sound from some reptile now vibrates upon his ear; ah, who can tell what that serpent would have done, had not some unseen influence made it glide harmlessly away? Perhaps that was some evil, which no one in human flesh could have resisted, and which the Lord in mercy, dealt with Himself. Now the Christian hears a whisper, "make away with yourself;" now he hears sounds which have no meaning, but which confuse him, (and that is their design.) Thus it is with some poor souls; oh! wonder of grace, and superhuman power, and love, that they ever reach heaven at all.

Dear reader, to you, if unexercised in such dark valleys as this, all that has now been said, may seem an overcharged account of temptations, which are common to all. This is not so; all men are not tempted to infidelity, to suicide, to despair, and to such like things; there are dark valleys, the inside of which some men never see; why one should see them, and not another, must be left with God; we cannot explain how this comes to pass, but into this very valley, of which I have been speaking now, some of the very holiest of God's people have been cast; and in it, they have performed no inconsiderable part of their journey, towards their present rest.

The point, however, to which our attention is to be especially directed, is, *Elevation above surrounding circumstances, and that elevation, in prayer.* The Psalmist says, "I will lift up mine eyes unto the hills, from whence cometh my help."

The hills towered above the valleys; and all that the Psalmist could do, was to lift up his eyes in prayer, to a height far above the place in which he was. In our times of distress, our valley journeyings, whether the valley be simply a lonely one, or one of stony poverty, or one of darkness, and terrible distress, let us look up, let us fix our eyes on the hills, yea, above the hills; let us say, "my help cometh from the Lord, who made heaven and earth." Looking at surrounding circumstances, has often been the sore hurt of the children of God; we must not venture upon it; we must fix our eyes on the face of God; and He must discern prayer in those eyes, if we are to be safe. Our blessed Redeemer lifted up His eyes to heaven. When He stood by the grave of Lazarus, and the stone was taken away, and He was about to enter into immediate conflict with death, withdrawing from him his prey, He "lifted up His eyes, and said, Father, I thank Thee that Thou hast heard me. And I knew that Thou hearest me always: but because of the people which stand by I said it, that they may believe that Thou hast sent me. And when He thus had spoken, He cried with a loud voice, Lazarus, come forth." John xi, 43. And when the Saviour was about to pass over the brook Cedron, and enter the horrors of Gethsemane, He looked up above all surrounding gloom, and beheld the face of His Father, on behalf of His disciples, yea, and also of Himself. "These words spake Jesus, and lifted up His eyes to heaven, and said, Father, the hour is come; glorify Thy Son, that Thy Son also may glorify Thee." John xvii, 1.

In our trial time we must *lift up* our eyes—we must not try and pierce the far distance; we must not speculate, and derive our comfort from thoughts that matters may turn out in this way or that way; we must look above the valley with its gloom, away from its windings, from the fissures in its rocks, from places which seem likely to afford an outlet, above all, away from all, to God.

We have no natural faculties for piercing the future of our troubles; experience shews us at times that all our speculations, all our calculations are not to be depended on, and that which we thought likely to prove our outlet from the valley, has, in point of fact, but more straitly shut up our path. So long as we endeavour to relieve ourselves, by efforts of human reason, or vision, so long must we remain perplexed, and anxious: the lifting of the eye is, in point of fact, our only true resource.

And how are we to lift up the eye, if it be not in prayer?—Prayer, in which God is distinctly seen, in which His willingness to help is abundantly realised, and acknowledged; one moment's upturning of the eye in this way is of more practical value than the most earnest gaze into the future. Let us look up from the valley to God, and He will look down into the valley on us, and lead us through all its windings, all its gloom, to the point which He can see from His lofty throne, as the only one through which we can make our escape.

Elevation, then, above surrounding circumstances is imperatively called for, from the child of God, when journeying in the valley; at such a season he is to "lift up his eyes."

And this leads us to consider *the Power of Spiritual Sight in prayer*. Spiritual sight is a reality, just as much as the sight of the eye; and in proportion to the keenness of that sight will very often depend a man's power in prayer.

This sight varies in the people of God, just as natural sight varies in power and clearness amongst men. There are some who can see only the dim outlines of things; some who can plainly discern the form, but not the colour of the object in view; and others who, though they can see both form and colour, cannot perceive the details, upon the comprehension of which depends admiration of the object's beauty, or appreciation of its worth. Even thus it is with the children of God; some are dim-sighted, and an indistinct outline of God upon His throne, and of His faithfulness, and love, and power, is all they see; others can clearly perceive all these, but they see them as it were merely in the abstract, colourless, without the warmth and glow imparted to them by personal realization; and there are others yet again, who must have their eyes further opened of the Spirit, ere they can realize in God those details of excellence in which His glory and beauty are most plainly seen.

Let none, however, who read these lines be discouraged, because they feel that in their case all that they have attained to is a perception of the outline of God. All, perhaps, that such can do is to look up unto the hills, to try and see, rather than really to see God in their troublous time. It is no doubt hard work to pray under such circumstances as these—to believe that the One we cannot plainly discern can and will help us out of the valley in which we go heavily, and in which we are almost afraid that we shall die; but God is on high, however small may be our power of realizing Him, and if we lift up our eyes and He sees that we would fain look imploringly and trustingly upon Him, He will surely look down upon us; He will not visit us for our blindness, but will honour our humble effort to lean upon Him; and the bare fact of our having looked *unto* Him, however little we were able really to see Him, will bring us all needful help. What encouragement is here for many who are weak both in faith and prayer! How should such a thought as this lead them just to turn their eyes upward in all their times of difficulty and distress! Satan well knows how bountiful God is, and how He honours even the humblest effort at trusting Him; yea, he knows that just this upward look in prayer, feeble though it be, will surely extricate the believer, at the last, and therefore he would daunt the weak ones of the Lord, by saying to them, "You cannot do well enough in prayer to secure an answer." But do not permit yourself to be deceived; it is not the measure of your power in prayer that is in question, it is the measure of God's faithfulness and love; even looking upward from the valley's depth will be counted by Him as prayer.

Happy, however, is he who can see more than the dim outline of the One to whom he would address himself in his hour of need; who does not merely stand as Moses in the cleft of the rock, to see as it were the back parts, while the face of God is not seen, (Exod. xxxiii, 22,) but who knows what it is to have " the light of the knowledge of the glory of God in the face of Jesus Christ," (2 Cor. iv, 6;) whose outline of God is filled in with the details of His excellence, with attributes, in which he, as a praying man, has especial interest. When such an one lifts up his eyes unto the hills, when he looks upon God, he sees enough in Him for all his wants, no matter how long the journey may prove through the valley, no matter how terrible its horrors, and no matter how accumulated his need. Such an one knows the tenderness of God, and sees that He will not allow the trusting soul to faint for want of a needful supply; he dwells upon the faithfulness of God, and sees that He will not, that He cannot desert him in his trial hour; he sees Him in all His excellencies, all His glorious attributes; he looks closely upon Him, (and he can do so, for these attributes shine upon him with a mellowed light, as existing in, and beaming from his Father in Christ,) and then he is assured of help, he speaks of it as sure, " I will lift up mine eyes unto the hills from whence cometh my help."

Let us seek, ever more and more, for an increase of clearness and power in spiritual vision; that we may see the ONE who is exalted above the hills, caring for us in our travel through the valleys; that we may perceive Him to be a God nigh at hand, and not a God afar off; *no peril, weariness, want, temptation, device of the Devil, or positive assault of his, can do us any hurt while we are in the valley, if only (however feebly) we lift up our eyes unto the hills, from whence cometh our help.*

And here, I would impress upon the reader the importance of the words, " I will." This power of

spiritual sight has *to be exercised by distinct action.*
Just as the man possessed of natural sight has to use the
muscles of the eye to bring it to bear upon the object he
would see, so the man possessed of spiritual vision must
use that spiritual faculty if he would see God. Blessing
is given to distinct action. Distinct action shews
practically the wish of the mind; and that the mind is
willing to make exertion to attain to what it desires, and
this action God will always honour. "Seek and ye
shall find," is as true in this, as in other particulars of
the spiritual life. Have not you, dear reader, come very
short in this exercise of *distinct action* when you were
in the valley? You have walked long and wearily with
the eye downcast, and it may be watering the ground
with your tears; the lid drooped, and it was Satan's
purpose that it should; have not you felt yourself scarce
equal to the exertion of raising the lid and turning the
eye on God? It answers Satan's purpose well enough
that you should be occupied in looking round, and taking
care of yourself, provided that by so doing, you are too
much occupied to look *up;* he does not mind how busy
you are with yourself, provided you be not busy with
God; be encouraged then to bethink yourselves of, and
to exercise distinct action in spiritual sight; the very act
of so doing will make you feel the reality of your connection with Him, will enlarge your expectation from
Him; you cannot reasonably expect to see, unless you
lift up your eyes and look.

And when you thus lift up your eyes, let there be a
definite point on which your sight is fixed. Look straight
to the throne—do not lose time in asking *where* shall I
find help, *who* will sympathize with and succour me?

Let us look to God at once; we have a definite trouble, a definite enemy, let us have a definite resource also in our time of need.

A word or two of caution will conclude this chapter.

Let us not try to manage our *little* troubles by ourselves, lest greater ones spring out of them. Little troubles are like little seeds, they are small enough in themselves, but they are capable of producing great and important results. The oak is the produce of the acorn, the tangled briar comes from a seed on which no thorn is to be seen; the Christian who will manage his little troubles by himself, will soon find that he must manage much greater ones than he bargained for at first.

Let us not allow ourselves to be kept from prayer by the great disproportion between God's resources and our little needs. Satan is able to argue at times apparently on God's behalf; he is all for God's honour, if by magnifying His honour, he can keep the poor sinner away from Him; it is for this purpose, and for this alone, that God's honour is ever magnified by Satan. Let us, however, see through this cheat; let us be thankful, instead of being daunted at the vastness of God's resources, at the great disproportion between them and our wants. By this disproportion, we are all the more secured, and we may rest assured, that however small our troubles or our need, a Father's love will always make God consider them as great.

In all troubles, then, be persuaded, dear reader, to put forth this " I WILL " of prayer. If you can do no more than barely upturn the eye, then say, " I will " do that. Do not undertake the management of even the smallest trouble by yourself; do not shrink from bringing any trouble, no matter how small, to God; around, all may be darkness, perplexity, and doubt; if you would dispel all these, say with the Psalmist of old, "I will lift up mine eyes unto the hills from whence cometh my help."

CHAPTER XII.

THE "I WILL" OF CONTINUANCE IN PRAYER.

Psalm lv, 17. *"Evening, and morning, and at noon, will I pray, and cry aloud: and He shall hear my voice."*

JUST as a scholar may excel in some one branch of learning, or an artizan in some particular department of his trade, so a Christian may pre-eminently excel in some one spiritual grace or power.

And further, as the scholar or artizan may do some one portion of that, their special work, better than another; so the Christian may peculiarly excel, not only in some one grace, but in some particular working of that grace.

Some Christian men are great in one thing, and some in another. Several may be great in the self-same thing, but in different departments of it. Thus is it with prayer. One man may excel in the lightning speed and power of his prayer in sudden emergencies; another may excel in making prayer with the deep and abiding assurance of an answer, and with patient determination to wait for it; while a third has peculiar power of realizing God in prayer; and a fourth is especially able to gather in his thoughts, and concentrate his mind, when he is thus engaged in prayer.

It may be that a Christian is great in all these departments of prayer, and yet that he comes short in *Continuance in Prayer;* which is the subject I am about to consider now. "Continue in prayer, and watch in the same with thanksgiving," says St. Paul in his Epistle to the Colossians. "Evening, and morning, and at noon, will I pray, and cry aloud: and He shall hear my voice," says the Psalmist.

The subject, then, which we are now to consider is CONTINUANCE *in Prayer.*

    I.   *Continuance in Prayer as " a Habit."*

    II.   *Continuance in it "at any one time."*

May grace be given to you, dear reader, to say "I WILL." "Evening, and morning, and at noon, will I pray, and cry aloud."

Let us enquire, first of all, what this continuance in prayer is, looked at as a Habit.

It is the habit of speaking to God *at all times* and *in all places;* when there are *immediate occasions* for prayer, and also when *there are not.**

Yes! speaking to God at *all* times—not merely saying a prayer, or even praying in the morning when we get up, and in the evening when we go to bed; but at many another time of the day; or if we lie wakeful upon our beds, at many a time in the night. Those

---

* St. Augustine's wish was, that Christ when He came might find him "aut precantem, aut prædicantem"—either praying or preaching.

who thus continue in prayer, often put up more than a hundred distinct petitions in the day—it may be that they have only a few minutes leisure between one occupation and another, still in these few minutes how much may be said; or perhaps their occupation is a solitary one, and then, if they so will, they can talk to God nearly all day long. Prayer may be made in one short sentence, yes, in one short word, yes, without even a word at all. There is prayer in the upturning of an eye; there is prayer in the heaving of a breast; and it is often to no more than these, that answers have been sent, the results of which affect the soul, even for eternity itself.

This continuance in prayer, is independent *of place*, as well *as time*. Some people are very dependent upon place, and becoming slavishly so, they are, from this very cause, hindered in continuance in prayer. The old minister's servant maid will teach us how to be independent of time and place in prayer. A number of ministers were assembled for the discussion of difficult questions, and among others it was asked, how the command to "pray without ceasing" could be complied with. Various suppositions were started, and at length one of the number was appointed to write an essay upon it, to be read at the next monthly meeting; which being heard by a plain, sensible servant girl, she exclaimed, "What! a whole month wanted to tell the meaning of that text? It is one of the easiest in the Bible." "Well, well," said an old minister, "Mary, what can you say about it? let us know how you understand it. Can you pray all the time?" "Oh, yes Sir." "What, when you have so many things to do?" "Why, Sir, the more I have to do, the more I can pray." "Indeed! Well, Mary, do let us know how it is, for most people think otherwise." "Well, Sir," said the girl, "when I first open my eyes in the morning, I pray, 'Lord, open the eyes of my understanding;' and while I am dressing I pray that I may be clothed with the robe of righteousness; and when I have washed me, I ask for the washing of regeneration; and as I begin to work, I pray that I may have strength equal to my day. When I begin to kindle up the fire, I pray that God's work may revive in my soul; and as I sweep out the house I pray that my heart may be cleansed from all impurities; and while preparing and partaking of breakfast, I desire to be fed with the hidden manna and the sincere milk of the word; and as I am busy with the little children, I look up to God as *my* Father, and pray for the spirit of adoption, that I may be His child; and so on all day. Everything I do furnishes me with a thought for prayer." "Enough, enough," cried the old divine; "these things are revealed to babes, and often hid from the wise and prudent. Go on, Mary," said he; "pray without ceasing. And as for us, my brethren, let us bless the Lord for this exposition, and remember that He has said, 'The *meek* will He guide in judgment.'" The essay, as a matter of course, was not considered necessary after the occurrence of this little event.

Now, to pass over the ideas which are held by some, as to the extraordinary value of prayer made in certain edifices, set apart for that purpose, let us come to the more domestic life of the Christian, and see how he is affected in this matter.

Some, (and they are often true children of God,)

cannot pray except it be at the bed-side, where they are accustomed morning and evening to kneel, or in some special place in their house, which they have set apart for that purpose.

I say nothing against their having a special place—there are advantages in having such a special place, when practicable; but he who exercises himself in *continuance* in prayer, must be wholly independent of place. He will often have to pray in very strange places indeed. Not long since, I met with a young Christian lady, who was compelled, against her will, to be present at the opera, a place wholly unfit for a child of God, and I suppose in the opinion of most, a very unsuitable one for prayer—but the testimony of that person was, that she never felt herself nearer to God in her life. She was there against her will, and God knew it; and He gave her power wholly to abstract herself from the sights and sounds around, and speak with Him.

A Sunday school teacher, knowing that all the boys in his class were constantly occupied during the week, feared much that prayer was sometimes neglected. He insisted, one Sabbath, on the importance of prayer. At the close, he asked a little boy, of ten years of age, who led a very uncomfortable life in the service of a master sweep, "And do you ever pray?" "Oh, yes! Monsieur." "And when do you do it? You go out early in the morning, do you not?" "Yes, Monsieur; and we are only half awake when we leave the house. I think about God, but cannot say that I pray then." "When then?" "You see, Monsieur, our master orders us to mount the chimney quickly, but does not forbid us to rest a little when we are at the top. Then I sit upon the top of the chimney and pray." "And what do you say?" "Ah! Monsieur, very little! I know no grand words with which to speak to God. Most frequently I only repeat a verse that I have learned at school." "What is that?" The scholar repeated with fervour, "God be merciful to me a sinner."

Here are some instances; and if a man, whose habit is "to continue in prayer," were to note down, for a single week, all the places in which he had prayed during that week, some persons would be very much surprised indeed. The railway carriage, the road, the shop, the garden, would be found to have been places of prayer—and one, just as acceptable as another, before God.

It is a mistake to suppose that it is hard to pray in any of these places. It is the spirit of a man that prays, and the spirit may be quietly before the throne, while the body is whirling along amid the noise and dust of travel. There is many a railway carriage in this kingdom, the corner of which has served as a place of prayer for the child of God—the man that was sitting there was not asleep—behold, he prayed! And many a prayer has gone up from the believer, as he walked along the road. When we are walking alone on the road, or in the fields, is an excellent time for prayer. It is not by any means impossible to pray short prayers, while threading one's way amid the people and carriages which throng the streets of a large town; how much less so to pray, as we walk along in quiet. And thus it will be seen, how entirely vain must be the excuse of those, who say that "they have no time, or no opportunity to pray." If they say, "We have no inclination," will it not be nearer the truth? God will accept real prayer, no matter from what locality it is sent up, no matter at what time. He will listen to the prayer of the poor woman as she bends over her wash tub or ironing board, or plies her needle; and it will be as acceptable to Him, as though it ascended from the fretted aisles of the gorgeous temple, as though it were embodied in the chantings of the minister, and in the responses of a surpliced choir. Pick out the meanest of man's occupations, (provided it be not a sinful one,)—let it be the sweeping of the streets—let it be the gathering, from house to house, of the offal of life's daily supplies; while engaged in such an occupation, prayer, brighter than earth's brightest jewels, prayer, sweeter than earth's daintiest perfume, may be made by the poorest of the sons of men—aye, and while men pass with pity or contempt the man that they think degraded by this miserable occupation, they may, unknown to themselves, have passed a man who, while handling earth's most contemptible things, was moving heaven itself, and holding immediate communion with his God.

Let not this, dear reader, be pointed out to you without some practical result. Something will be gained if you get the well defined idea, that prayer may be made in every time, in every place; that *you* may thus pray; that there need be no formality of posture when you thus, apart from the stated time of prayer, come before your God. The soul may come into a posture of prayer when the body cannot; when we walk, or ride, or sit, our soul may be in reverence before the throne; he who is able to continue in prayer, knows this; he prays at all times, and in all places.

We must observe, further, on this point, that prayer is thus made, not only with some special occasion, but also *without* it.

We have indeed occasions enough continually pressing upon us, and making us, if we be men of God, to engage in prayer. He who knows, and experimentally realizes, that all things must be brought to God in prayer, and that all things *may* be brought to God in prayer, will surely never be at a loss for matter for his prayers; he will never say, " I have nothing particular to pray about, I have nothing particular to say." Scarce a day passes over our heads, without affording special matter for prayer. Dangers are apprehended; some of the wheels of life's daily machinery get out of repair, or need to be oiled with an unction which we cannot give, so that they may run smooth; children or friends are ill; vexations have to be borne; all these, as they arise, either in fact, or in our thoughts, are matter enough for prayer. But let us suppose that everything in life is going on smoothly; God's people have plenty to pray about, nevertheless. They have some temptation to overcome; they have some spiritual comfort and blessing to be obtained, of which they are feeling sore and pressing need; these things are uppermost in their thoughts, and as out of the abundance of the heart the mouth speaketh, so out of the abundance of the heart does the mouth speak in prayer.

Men who are unacquainted with divine things may say, " We never feel these pressing occasions, indeed, very often when we kneel down, we don't know what to pray for next, and, therefore, as we wish to do right, we have bought a book !" Ah, dear reader, was the book ever written that contained all that a Spirit-taught man would say to God? A book is at best a crutch—no doubt it is better to walk with a crutch, than not to walk at all—but surely we ought to have thoughts enough in our hearts, to supply words enough for our lips.

But let us now set the "pressing occasions" entirely aside, and see how God's people find abundance about which to continue in prayer, even without them. Just as a man is full of thoughts and interests in his natural life, so also is he in his spiritual existence; supposing, of course, that he is a real child of God. These give him matter for continuous prayer—some or other of them are continually coming uppermost in his mind, and he speaks about them to the Lord.

Take, first of all, the *thoughts* of a child of God. He longs *to be holy;* he is deeply conscious of how unholy he is; then the thought gives birth to prayer; he may be walking, or travelling, or, perhaps, sitting by his fireside; but his heart goes up to God, he begins to pray. I do not say that he makes a long prayer; but with all his heart he says to God, " O Lord, may the Spirit sanctify me, and make me more like Christ"—the prayer is never breathed in words which fall on human ear, but passes straight upward from his heart of hearts to the throne of the Majesty on high.

Or perhaps his thought is upon *loving Jesus,* (and thoughts upon this subject continually enter and abide in the believer's mind) and this thought soon turns to prayer. Christ's people all deeply feel that they do not love Him more; they are often angry with themselves about this; they often are anxious about it; and soon the thought changes into prayer. They say, "O Lord, how cold, how stony is this poor heart of mine; I cannot love Thee by myself; oh make me love as Thou Thyself wouldest have me love,"—perhaps they repeat the same few words over and over again; yes, twenty times or more—"Lord, make me love." And thus, even so far as thoughts are concerned, the Christian is never at a loss for subject-matter for his prayers.

Now turn for a moment from his thoughts to his *interests*.

We all know what it is to have certain subjects of interest to our minds. We take an interest in, it may be, political, town, or social matters, or in persons or pursuits; all of which are, strictly speaking, outside ourselves. Thus does the child of God—as such; he has an interest in God's cause, perhaps as regards the place in which he is, perhaps in the case of certain individuals; or that interest may take a wider range than either of these. These interests will find their way into the supplications of the man that knows what it is to continue in prayer. He will make such petitions as these—"Lord, awaken such an one to a sense of the ruin which lies before him;" "Lord, deepen the impressions which have been made in the mind of such an one;" "Lord, open Thine hand, and provide the means for carrying on Thy work;" "Lord, prosper Thine own cause in the place in which we live." The man who continues in prayer will say, as he walks to the house where the sick person lives, to whom he would minister in the name of Christ, "Lord, give me access here, make my visit acceptable and useful;" and in all probability he will add another little petition as he goes away. If he hear the funeral bell and knows that at that moment a neighbour is about to be carried to the grave, he will say, " Lord, comfort the bereaved and mourning ones; Lord, bless the solemn season to their souls"—and so on, all days, all weeks, all months, all years, until his own tongue be silent in death ; and he has passed from the place of prayer to that of praise.

May it be given to us to know more and more of this continuance in prayer, for it is not anything high-flown or chimerical in the Christian life, it is solid matter of fact. Some thus pray; so also, by the influence of the Spirit, may many more of us. The Lord pour out that Spirit, and enable us to say with the Psalmist, " Evening, and morning, and at noon, will I pray and cry aloud : and He shall hear my voice !"

CHAPTER XIII.

THE "I WILL" OF CONTINUANCE IN PRAYER.

Psalm lv, 17. *"Evening, and morning, and at noon, will I pray, and cry aloud: and He shall hear my voice."*

WE see from what has been said, what it is to continue in prayer; and that this continuance is a solid practical reality, attainable by ordinary Christians, and, in point of fact, well known to many in the experiences of their daily spiritual life.

We now turn to the consideration of WHAT IS NECESSARY, FOR ENABLING A MAN TO ATTAIN TO THIS CONTINUANCE.

One very important point is, *Realization of privilege*—that a man should feel that he is privileged to take up a higher standing, than that of a mere worshipper, that he may hold communion with God.

It will of course be understood that, no matter how closely a man be drawn to God in sonship, worship is what is due from him as a creature, to God as his Creator. The deepest reverence and awe will ever fill the mind which knows the Holy One aright. Before him even the angels veil their faces, and the heavens are not pure in His sight; this he, who continues in prayer will always keep in mind, and he will never presume to be irreverent, because he has been privileged to hold communion.

There is, unquestionably, a position higher than that of a worshipper. Unconverted men may worship, but higher than that they cannot go. Mere natural religion and education may make a man a worshipper; the first may send a thrill through the mind, as the vastness of creation is thought upon, and the power of the Creator is linked with it; the other may ingraft the idea that God *ought* to be worshipped and honoured, as the Supreme Being in the universe; but here worship ends, and it can never expand into communion. Worship is a duty, communion is a privilege.

He who is enjoying the privilege of communion with God, is in a far higher position than the worshipper; and the realization of this will be a great help to the habit of continuance in prayer. A little consideration will easily shew us how this may be.

If we feel that we have the privilege of sons, we shall act towards our Father as children do towards a parent. A child, from the simple realization of his connection with his parent, comes to him at all times, and asks him about everything. His reverence for his parent is not diminished by the fact, that he may thus come to him; that the father does not require set forms and ceremonies to be gone through, before the child can open his lips. Were this the case, the child would, in all probability, stay away when he had only apparently little things to speak about, or ask for; and would draw near only when

the greatness of the matter in hand would appear to
warrant his approach. It will not be difficult to trace
what serious consequences may result from such a state
as this: great evils often come from very small beginnings, and the little things about which we might
have spoken, had we felt our privilege of doing so, are
perhaps, some of the very beginnings from which evils
are destined to proceed. The buds of evil are nipped, in
the privileged communications which pass between the
believer and his God; when the first pains of a child are
brought before the notice of the tender parent, he takes
measures which avert a grievous illness, and much after
suffering.

Moreover, if we do not feel that we have the privilege
of talking to God, we shall perhaps think we ought not
to commend such things to Him at all, for we may think
that they are not important enough to be made the subjects of set and solemn prayer. This is a mistake, but
our business now is with the results of the error; the
result is simply this, we take the small matter into our
own hands, and do it wrongly, or do it without a blessing,
and thus trouble or loss are sure to attach themselves to
it. A few words of prayer—even a look to God upon
the subject, might have set the whole matter right;
these were not given, not because of any unbelief, but
because of a want of realization of privilege, and the consequences we see.

Let us remember that a man may fail in this point,
even though he may not be unacquainted, and that
practically, with many of the other privileges of sonship.
For example, he may clearly see that God, as a gracious
Father, is educating him when He sends him trials; and

that as a Father, He will, in a general way, make all needful provision for him, and will love him, and eventually secure his eternal happiness; but he fails in this particular point, of realization of privilege.

Let us endeavour ever more and more, to realize the privileges connected with sonship with God; so to realize them, as to use them; let us remember that we have been called to a position far higher than that of a mere worshipper—and not only far higher, but far *closer* also —and that that position confers upon us the privilege of talking to God about everything, and doing so at every time, and in every place.

Some instances of God's answers to prayer will be given in a future chapter; it may be well, however, to impress this subject upon the reader's mind, by some examples; perhaps when these are thought on, they may encourage him to seek God in what may be called the common things of daily life.

Two Christian parents had a little child, whose restlessness at night, accompanied with continual and violent crying, had almost worn out a valuable nurse. At last, in order to give the nurse some rest, the parents determined on taking the little one for a night themselves. At first all was quiet; but in a very little while, the crying commenced, and was carried on until one of the two parents, who was ill, was almost worn out. All efforts to hush the little one were in vain; and at last the parents bethought themselves of doing what they should have done at first. They jointly asked God to still the child's crying for the night; and in answer to that prayer the child then ceased, and went to sleep, and had restless nights no more. Those are true words in the collect,—

"Who art always more ready to hear, than we to pray, and art wont to give more than either we desire or deserve." What could seem more insignificant, as a subject of prayer, than the crying of a child? but God is honoured by the faith that casts little things upon Him, recognising at once the comprehensiveness of His mind, and of His love.

Two Christian persons were about to perform a long and trying journey; one of them was in such a state of health, as to make it likely that the journey would be a very considerable trial to flesh and blood. The mind of one of these travellers was led to commend this matter to the Lord, and to ask Him for such especial travelling mercies, and strength, for his friend, that the journey might not prove wearisome, or too much for the frame which had to sustain it. The hours of night rolled on, and as the morning broke, the one for whom the prayer had been offered, and who had shewn no sign of fatigue, turned to the other and remarked, that, strange to say, no fatigue was being experienced, and that the time seemed flying by rapidly. Then the reason was told, and the secret of the prayer let out; and when the journey was finally accomplished, and rest could easily be had, the traveller did not need it, or take it, but was able to go about, as if the previous night had been spent in bed, and not in a railway train.

A Christian man, a relative of the author, was in great difficulty with reference to a paper of consequence, which was required immediately, but could not be found. Search was made in all parts of the counting house; old drawers and pigeon holes, seldom disturbed, were ransacked, but to no purpose; the document could not be found. When reduced almost to despair, he bethought himself of the power of prayer, and asked the Lord to guide him to the place where the paper was. It now came into his mind to go to a certain spot, and there he found the object of his search.

Somewhat similar to this, is the instance of a worthy man who lost a purse containing a considerable sum of money, as he was returning home. As the money was not his own, he was greatly distressed, for it was not probable that his statement of having lost it would be believed. On reaching a roadside inn he got a lantern and carefully retraced his steps, examining the road as closely as he could, but with no success. At length, well nigh in despair, he went to the roadside, and earnestly besought God to help him in his difficulty, and enable him to find the purse. At that moment he struck his foot against something hard, and on putting down his hand to ascertain what it was, he discovered to his great joy, the purse which he had lost. God had guided him to the very place in which he intended to answer his prayers.

The author remembers a case where it was very necessary that an invalid should take a certain medicine. Three portions had been sent by the surgeon, and the first two were immediately rejected. There remained now but one, and there was every probability that it would share the fate of the previous two. It was a matter of consequence that it should not, and a prayer was offered by a bystander to that effect, and the medicine was taken without any difficulty.

It was necessary that a minister should undertake a journey, for which, however, he had not a sufficiency of

funds. Special prayer was made to the Lord to supply
the means, and on retiring to rest at a friend's house,
which was on the way, the person in question saw an
envelope on his looking glass, which on being opened was
found to contain a ten pound note, and a line saying it
was for "travelling expenses." The minister's hostess
said "she could not go to rest until she put it there; she
felt constrained to do it."

Everything which is not sinful we may bring to God;
the minuteness of His love will always make Him condescend to the minuteness of our need.

That, however, which above all things will enable us
to continue in prayer, is *the Holy Ghost's operation
upon the 'habit' of our minds*.

There are diverse operations of the Spirit, He works
upon the mind's reasoning, and imaginative, and receptive
powers; He works upon its *habit* also. We know, it is
to be hoped from experience, what some of His operations
are in these former particulars. Our reasoning powers
have been rectified, and adjusted, and strengthened, in all
things connected with the spiritual world; our imagination has been cleansed, and sweetened, and our powers
of receiving truth have been deepened and enlarged; but
has the *habit* of our mind been wrought upon by the
Holy Ghost?

If the mind's *bent* has been turned heavenward, the
very fact of its being fixed on God will, in itself, be a
great stimulant to continuous prayer. The mind thus
sanctified will, as it were, naturally fall into holy thought,
and begin to speak with God.

Seek, dear reader, for a sanctified habit of mind, for

it will enable you continually to pray, and will bring down upon you continual blessing. Prayer will thus be not an effort, but an outflowing of the mind. No doubt there will be times when prayer will require intense effort; times of special temptation, special sorrow, or special conflict—then, the occasion being extraordinary, the prayer must be so also; but in all ordinary communings with God, the sanctification of the *habit* of the mind will give us both continuance and power

Let us now enquire into the *results of this continuance in prayer as a habit.*

One result has reference to what we have this moment been speaking about. Continuance in prayer will help to keep up the spirituality of our tone of mind. Do we not find ourselves day by day prone to slip down from any spirituality to which we may have attained? Are we not very like some stringed instrument, the continual tendency of which is to decline from concert pitch? Unless the body be continually refreshed by breathing in pure air, it will droop; the soul is as dependent upon refreshment as the body, and the soul's refreshment is in prayer.

Another most important result is this, we cannot become *strangers* to the throne of grace: nothing pleases Satan more, than to interrupt our appearances before the throne of grace. He will disturb our regular times and opportunities of prayer, if he can; and failing that, he will make us strangers to ejaculatory and continuous prayer.

How often do we find in daily life that we insensibly become almost strangers to those whom once we knew well, but frequent intercourse with whom had become gradually broken! And have we not also found that, as time rolled on, we missed the accustomed intercourse less and less, until at length we found that we could do very well without those in whose society we once found pleasure? Such a thought would at one time have been repudiated, and deemed treasonable against all friendship and fine feeling; but experience shows us that the thought is true.

To make the child of God a *stranger* to the throne of grace, is a continual effort of Satan; he knows that the heart will gradually become less and less willing to talk with God, the confidence of the heart will decrease, its openness and communicativeness will diminish; and as it becomes more and more reserved, it will turn in more upon itself; it will become suspicious and timid, and have the feeling that it has something to *do*, something to *overcome*, before it can speak with God, as it used easily to do in former times. Let us be assured that the feeling of strangeness is one which grows rapidly, and that in an increasing ratio.

Another good result of continuance of prayer is this; we can bring multitudes of things before God as they arise, which otherwise we might have forgotten. Little things are soon forgotten, and yet, as we have already observed, they are often of great importance; being, in fact, but the pivots on which greater things turn. So easily are little things forgotten, that many of them are gone, even before the time for our usual evening prayer. They are gone from our memories, without ever having been committed to God—but though gone from our memories, they have not gone from the field of action;

they have amalgamated with other things, or linked themselves with them, for the production of some result.

There is just one point more which I would notice, and that is, as a result of continuous prayer, we shall have a blessing in *special* acts. When we are about to do a thing, if we ask a blessing upon it, and if that thing be not evil we shall receive the blessing. We should seek for *special* as well as *general* blessings. We often lose the special in the general, and consequently do not receive because we do not ask. Let us have the spirit of continuous prayer, and say, "Lord, help me in *this*, Lord, avert *that*," and the special blessing will surely come.

Thus, dear reader, ever living in supplication, we shall also ever live in giving of thanks; and no matter how varied be our need, we shall ever have a resource; no matter how many our enemies, we shall have a very present help—ours surely, amid all the changes and chances of this mortal life, will be that peace which the world never gave, and which the world can never take away.

CHAPTER XIV.

THE "I WILL" OF EXPECTATION IN PRAYER.

Psalm lv, 16, 17. *"As for me I will call upon God: and the Lord shall save me. Evening, and morning, and at noon, will I pray, and cry aloud: and He shall hear my voice."*

HAPPY is that man who has an expecting heart; who goes upon his knees as a living reality, believing that his words are full of meaning, that God hears them, and that God will certainly answer them; such an one will be great in prayer, and will surely receive signal answers—real answers to real prayers.

The subject of which this chapter proposes to treat, is one of great interest to the believer; it is one to which in all probability the believing reader could add much out of his own experience. Who is there that prays at all, who cannot bring forward some practical proofs from the diary of his own life, that God is a prayer hearing and a prayer answering God?

FAITHFUL EXPECTATION IN PRAYER is the subject which we are to consider now; and here we shall have an opportunity of bringing forward some examples of

God's faithfulness in answering prayers; and very precious such examples are, for the mind loves to dwell on facts, and to argue from them; and with very many, one fact has more weight than a thousand arguments.

Our first enquiry is, *what is it to expect in Prayer ?*

It is to believe that an answer will come, to be looking out for an answer, and to be patient in expecting it.

Vast multitudes of prayers are offered without any positive expectation being connected with them. They are offered up because men think that the proper thing to do under certain circumstances is to say a prayer; or perhaps because men have been used to say prayers, but the living reality of *expectation* is not found in them.

How differently do we act towards God and man. When we go to our fellow man for anything, we are in expectation of receiving it, or we hope so to do; we have some definite idea connected with our words. But when we pray to God, and that, oftentimes for fixed and definite things, we never think about the coming of the answer, we are not really on the look out for it, expecting it, just as we should be on the look out for the post with a letter to us containing money, from a well tried and wealthy friend to whom we had applied in our distress. I can give the reader no better example of such expectation than one which is to be found in Müller's narrative of the orphan houses at Bristol. The account is given in his own words.

"To suppose that we have difficulty only about money would be a mistake; there occur hundreds of other wants and hundreds of other difficulties. It is a rare thing that a day comes without some difficulty or some want; but often there are many difficulties and many wants to be met and overcome the same day. All these are met by prayer and faith, our universal remedy for every difficulty and every want; and I have never been confounded. Patient, persevering, and believing prayer, offered up to God in the name of the Lord Jesus, has always, sooner or later, brought the blessing. I do not despair, by God's grace, concerning the obtaining of any blessing, provided I can be sure my obtaining it would be for my real good, and for the glory of God. I relate here for the benefit of the reader one instance, out of many, to show what are our difficulties under which we give ourselves to prayer, and under which we are helped.

"It was towards the end of November, of 1857, when I was most unexpectedly informed that the boiler of our heating apparatus at the New Orphan House, No. 1, leaked very considerably, so that it was impossible to go through the winter with such a leak. Our heating apparatus consists of a large cylinder boiler, inside of which the fire is kept, and with which boiler the water-pipes which warm the rooms are connected. Hot air is also connected with this apparatus. This now was my position. The boiler had been considered suited for the work of the winter; the having had ground to suspect its being worn out, and not to have done anything towards its being replaced by a new one, and to have said I will trust to God regarding it, would be careless presumption, but not faith in God. It would be the counterfeit of faith.

"The boiler is entirely surrounded by brickwork, its state, therefore, could not be known without taking down the brickwork; this, if needless, would be rather

injurious to the boiler than otherwise; and as year after
year, for eight winters, we had had no difficulty in this
way, we had not anticipated it now. But suddenly, and
most unexpectedly, at the commencement of the winter,
this difficulty occurred. What then was to be done?
For the children, especially the younger infants, I felt
deeply concerned, that they might not suffer through
want of warmth. But how were we to obtain warmth?
The introduction of a *new* boiler would, in all probability,
take many weeks. The *repairing* of the boiler was a
questionable matter, on account of the greatness of the
leak; but, if not, nothing could be said of it, till the brick
chamber, in which the boiler with Hazard's patent heating
apparatus is enclosed, was at least in part removed; but
that would, at least, as far as we could judge, take days,
and what was to be done in the meantime to find warm
rooms for three hundred children? It naturally occurred
to me to introduce temporary gas-stoves, but on further
weighing the matter, it was found that we should be
unable to heat our very large stoves, which we could not
introduce, as we had not a sufficient quantity of gas to
spare from our lighting apparatus. Moreover, for each
of these stoves we needed a small chimney, to carry off
the impure air. This mode of heating, therefore, though
applicable to a hall, a staircase, or a shop, would not
suit our purposes. I also thought of the temporary
introduction of Arnott's stoves; but they would be
unsuitable, as we needed chimneys, long chimneys, for
them, as they would have been of a temporary kind, and
therefore must go out of the windows. On this account,
the uncertainty of its answering in our case, the dis-
figurement of the rooms almost permanently, led me to

see it needful to give up this plan also. But what was to be done? Gladly would I have paid £100, if thereby the difficulty could have been overcome, and the children not be exposed to suffer for many days from being in cold rooms. At last I determined on falling entirely into the hands of God, who is very merciful and of tender compassion, and I decided on having at all events the brick chamber opened, to see the extent of the damage, and to see whether the boiler might be repaired, so as to carry us through the winter. The day was fixed when the workmen were to come, and all the necessary arrangements were made. The fire, of course, had to be let out while the repairs were going on. But now see. After the day was fixed for the repairs, a bleak north wind set in. It began to blow either on Thursday or Friday before the Wednesday afternoon, when the fire was to be let out. Now came the first really cold weather which we had in the beginning of last winter, during the first days of December. What was to be done? The repairs could not be put off. I now asked the Lord for two things, viz., that He would be pleased to change the north wind into a south wind, and that He would give to the workmen 'a mind to work,' for I remembered how much Nehemiah accomplished in fifty-two days, whilst building the walls of Jerusalem, because 'the people had a mind to work.' Well, the memorable day came. The evening before, the bleak north wind blew still, but on the Wednesday the south wind blew, exactly as I prayed. The weather was so mild that no fire was needed. The brickwork is removed, the leak is found out very soon, the boiler makers begin to repair in good earnest. About half-past eight in the evening, when I was going to leave the New Orphan House for my home, I was informed at the lodge, that the acting principal of the firm whence the boiler makers came was arrived, to see how the work was going on, and whether he could in any way speed the matter. I went immediately, therefore, into the cellar, to see him with the men, to seek to expedite the business. In speaking to the principal of this, he said, in their hearing, 'the men will work late this evening, and come very early again to-morrow.' 'We would rather, sir,' said the leader 'work all night.' Then remembered I the second part of my prayer, that God would give the men 'a mind to work.' Thus it was; by the morning, the repair of the boiler was accomplished, the leak was stopped, though with great difficulty, and within about thirty hours, the brickwork was up again, and the fire in the boiler; and all the time the south wind blew so mildly that there was not the least need of a fire."

Here, then, is a plain instance of expectation in prayer, a definite blessing was sought, and a definite blessing was obtained.

A tradesman was about to return to London from a watering-place, where he had been staying for a few weeks; his presence was necessary at his place of business, where a number of hands were employed, and where everything was not going on very smoothly. This tradesman was to have started in the afternoon, and in the morning he went to take a last plunge in the sea. In plunging, he struck his head against the bottom, and injured the vertebræ of the back; for weeks afterwards he lay dead from his neck downward, but perfectly alive and sensible, so far as his head was concerned.

The great earthly trouble pressing upon this man's mind, was the state of affairs in his office in London; this he told the minister who attended him. The minister said, "Let us commit the matter to God;" so he knelt down and prayed that God would be graciously pleased to operate on the minds of all the workmen, to make them attentive and diligent, to make them feel that God's eye was upon them, and His hand over them, to keep them from bad conduct of every kind, and to make things run smoothly. It was also humbly submitted to God that this business was this poor man's means of livelihood for himself and a large family. Two or three days afterwards, some of the chief hands in the business came to see their sick master, and told him that "there was a wonderful change in the office, that something had come over them, and that they all felt they could not do enough for him!"

Or take the case of the worthy people mentioned in the following occurrence; what could be more definite than their petition, or what more definite than the answer they received.

"Considerable difficulty and annoyance having arisen in the affairs of a certain religious community, owing to the perverse and contentious spirit of one of its members, it became necessary that steps should be taken to prevent his doing mischief. This could only be accomplished by obtaining the signature of a gentleman who lived at some distance. Two members of the church were deputed to obtain the needful signature, and before they started on their journey they knelt down and prayed that God would further them in the work they had in hand. On arriving at this gentleman's house and stating their business, he informed them that he never did anything of that kind without the advice of a friend, who lived at a considerable distance. In vain they urged him, he absolutely refused. At length they rose to take their departure, but on being pressed to remain to dinner, stayed. While at dinner a horseman rode up to the door—it was the very person whose advice was required, and who said that he had been several miles on his way in another direction, but had felt constrained to turn and come and see his friend. The case was immediately laid before him, his consent obtained, and the document signed, just in time to disappoint the contentious man, who arrived immediately after."

Or take the case of the Cree Indian in Rupert's land, who told his story to one of our native catechists. The man and his family were in their wanderings exposed on one occasion to a fearful fire, which was running across the dry prairie with great violence and speed; it was burning all around fearfully, and there appeared no way of escape. Suddenly he remembered what Pratt had told him, of the one great God over all: and while his family were crying, and clinging to him, he fell upon his knees and said, "O Thou great One, who art above all, whoever Thou art, save me from this fire;" and ere the fire touched him, or any one of them, there fell upon it such a heavy shower of rain as totally extinguished it. In consequence of this, that individual now denies the Indians' gods, and acknowledges none but One.

One of the missionary periodicals furnishes us with the following simple story of a definite request and a definite answer, and though the request was small it was definite, and its apparent unimportance adds to its value, for if we may be definite in that which is least, how much more in that which is greatest.

"A poor servant girl was very anxious to do something for the missionary cause. She gave what she could herself, but that did not satisfy her. She was living in a rich family, who she knew could give plenty if they chose. So she got a missionary box, and placed it on the kitchen dresser, and then prayed to God to bring it about so that it should find its way upstairs. She asked advice of the living Lord of the mine. One day, the pet of the house, little Amy, happened to come into the kitchen with a message, and she saw the box and begged to have it to play with. Poor Peggy had her thoughts; but she did not say anything except 'O yes, Miss Amy, to be sure you may, and keep it as long as you like.' Half an hour after the bell rang, and Peggy was called upstairs; and there she found her master and mistress, and the young gentlemen, and the young ladies, crowding around the box, and she was asked what it was. She told them, with many blushes and curtsies, that it was for 'the missionaries who taught the blacks,' and that she put her spare money into it. They all seemed pleased, and begged to be allowed to put their spare money into it too. So the little green box was promoted from the kitchen dresser to the white marble mantlepiece in the drawing room; and it was not long before it was sent down to Peggy with a thick penny sticking out of its mouth—it was so brim full.

There is a very interesting instance of this definiteness both in the petition and the answer given us in a work entitled, "The Ladies of the Covenant." We are told that, "On the forenoon of the day on which he (the

Marquis of Argyll) was to be executed, she (the Marchioness) and Mr. John Carstairs were employed in wrestling with God, in his behalf, in a chamber in the Canongate, earnestly pleading that the Lord would now seal his charter by saying to him, 'Son, be of good cheer, thy sins are forgiven thee!' It is a striking circumstance that, at the very time of their being thus employed, the Marquis, while engaged in settling some worldly affairs, a number of persons of quality being present with him, was visited in his soul with such a sense of the divine favour, as almost overpowered him; and, after in vain attempting to conceal his emotions by going to the fire and beginning to stir it with the tongs, he turned about, and melting into tears exclaimed, 'I see this will not do; I must now declare what the Lord has done for my soul! He has just now, at this very instant of time, sealed my charter in these words, 'Son, be of good cheer, thy sins are forgiven thee!' This comfortable state of mind he retained to the last, and to this scene he alluded in his dying speech on the scaffold. Can it be doubted that the bestowment of the very blessing, prayed for by this devout lady and that godly minister, to the dying martyr, at the very instant in which it was sought, was a signal answer to their believing prayers?"

A lady lay upon her bed suffering violent pain in the head, and while thus suffering, she said to a friend, who was watching by her side, "if I only could get ten minutes sleep I should feel better." The friend said nothing, but offered up a silent prayer to God to grant the ten minutes sleep. True! the petition was feeble and the faith feeble, but the Lord, who is very tender, did not despise either the feebleness of the faith, or the smallness of the subject of the request. The patient immediately slept, and described her sleep as most delicious, that she had "the sensation of having been fanned off to sleep."

Simeon gives us an account of a definite answer which he received to a definite prayer, when he was in great trial.

"Many years ago," says he, "when I was an object of much contempt and derision in this university, I strolled forth one day, buffeted and afflicted, with my little Testament in my hand; I prayed earnestly to my God, that He would comfort me with some cordial from His word, and that on opening the book I might find some text which should sustain me. It was not for direction that I was looking, for I am no friend to such superstitions as the *sortes virgilianæ*, but only for support. I thought I would turn to the epistles, where I should most easily find some precious promise; but my book was upside down, so without intending it I opened on the gospels. The first text which caught my eye was this, 'They found a man of Cyrene, Simon by name; him they compelled to bear His cross.' You know Simon is the same name as Simeon. What a word of instruction was here, what a blessed hint for my encouragement! To have the cross laid upon me, that I might bear it after Jesus! what a privilege! It was enough. Now I could leap and sing for joy, as one whom Jesus was honouring with a participation in His sufferings." Relating this on another occasion, Mr. Simeon added:— "And when I read *that*, I said, 'Lord, lay it on me; I will gladly bear the cross for Thy sake.' And I henceforth bound persecution as a wreath of glory round my brow!"

A friend some time since furnished me with the following instance from his own knowledge. He gives two instances in his letter, one of which will here suffice.

"The first occurred to a person now living, with whom I was formerly intimately acquainted. He was from early life a sedulous reader of the Bible, and having married a person of similar religious feeling, their store of biblical information became considerable, and the husband, to whom I allude, subsequently became a writer on prophecy, and published a work, called '————.' In his career of mercantile life, his whole property was involved in the speculations of his partner, and he was reduced at once to very severe want, and his wife not choosing to deprive the creditors of anything which they mutually possessed, determined to submit her marriage jointure, (which was considerable,) to the general wreck. In the midst of their distressing indigence, they still spent many hours in reading their Bible and in prayer, both by day and night. During this period of gloom, which would have thrown many into despair, he still entertained views of hope, that God would open to him a way of escape. His main anxiety was the immediate necessities of a young family, whom he sustained, as well as he could, by depriving himself. His clothes became bad, and his shoes were so worn, that his feet were exposed to the ground. He was desirous to supply himself with a single pair, and had enquired their price, which was stated to be nine shillings and sixpence. *This he made the subject of special prayer,* but determined not to buy them till he had the money in his possession. But whence it was to come, he had no idea. In due time, he was walking along the streets in Leeds, where he was then living, and finding that he struck something with his foot which bounded before him, he was induced to pick it up. It was a small cotton bag, like a child's purse, which he opened, and found in it the precise sum, which for some time had been the subject of his special petitions. He was greatly struck with the coincidence. But thinking an owner might be found for it, he employed the crier, and went and reported the circumstance at the police station. But no one coming forward as a claimant, after waiting some time, he devoted his God-send, as he considered it, to the purchase of his much needed shoes."

A converted Jew who had suffered fearfully for conscience sake, narrates the following instance of special help vouchsafed to him after special prayer. "Here again," he says, "we were met by the goodness of God, exercised to us through your instrumentality. Permit me to call to your remembrance your having forwarded to us at this time a hamper, containing the contributions of your household, thus supplying us with the food needed, in a way which we had not anticipated. I must also mention another fact connected with this circumstance, which much affected me. Although you had kindly supplied us with provisions, still we were without money, and we were in great want of a small sum, which we did not possess, and the next day being Sunday, we had neither means nor opportunity to seek for it. In this extremity we applied to Him who had so frequently helped us through the wilderness, and never shall the needy apply to Him in vain. In a singular way relief came to our hands. As it was Saturday, my wife was putting our house in order, cleaning every part, and whilst so doing, she thought she discovered amidst the sweepings of the room something folded up in a piece of paper. She picked it up and opened it, and what was her surprise when she found it contained the exact sum we needed. We immediately concluded that in unpacking your hamper we had overlooked this little paper, which had dropped out of one of the parcels in which you had enclosed it. Joy and gratitude filled our hearts. We could not but observe how remarkably the Lord had timed this relief. Had we discovered it before, we should not have felt half so thankful, but having been made to feel our necessity, and then having gone to the Lord to ask for help, we received it more immediately as a gift from Him. In a few moments it might have been swept away in the dust."*

Let us now turn to *the grounds and Scripture warrants for Expectation in Prayer.*

We have many *statements in Holy Scripture* which

---

* "Who else was it but the God of Elijah, who, only a short time ago, so kindly delivered a poor man out of his distress, not indeed by a raven, but by a poor singing bird? The man was sitting early in the morning at his house door. His eyes were red with weeping, and his heart cried to heaven, for he was expecting an officer to come and distrain him for a small debt. Whilst sitting thus with a heavy heart, a little bird flew over his head into the cottage, and perched itself within an empty cupboard. The poor man closed the door, caught the bird, and placed it in a cage, where it soon began to sing very sweetly, and it seemed to the man as if it were the tune of a favorite hymn, 'Fear thou not

afford good ground for Expectation in Prayer. The following will suffice for our present purpose.

"What things soever ye desire, when ye pray, believe that ye receive them, and ye shall have them." Mark xi, 24.

"Ask, and it shall be given you." Matt. vii, 7.

"Whatsoever ye shall ask in My name, that will I do." John xiv, 13.

"If ye abide in Me, and My words abide in you, ye shall ask what ye will, and it shall be done unto you." John xv, 7.

"If any of you lack wisdom, let him ask of God, that giveth to all men liberally and upbraideth not; and it shall be given him. But let him ask in faith, nothing wavering." James i, 5, 6.

"If ye have faith, and doubt not, ye shall not only do this which is done to the fig-tree, but also, if ye shall say unto this mountain, Be thou removed, and be thou cast into the sea; it shall be done. And all things, whatsoever ye shall ask in prayer believing, ye shall receive." Matt. xxi, 21, 22.

when darkness reigns;' and as he listened to it, he found it soothe and comfort his mind. Suddenly some one knocked at the door; but instead of the officer, whom the poor man so much dreaded, it was the servant of a respectable lady, who said that the neighbours had seen a bird fly into his house, and wished to know if he had caught it. 'Oh, yes,' replied the man, 'here it is;' and the bird was carried away. A few minutes after, she came back and said, 'you have done my mistress a great service; she sets a high value upon the bird that had escaped. She is much obliged to you, and requests you to accept this trifle, with her thanks.' The poor man received it thankfully, and it proved to be neither more nor less than the sum he owed!"—*From Krummacher's Elijah.*

All these give us warrant for strong expectation; so also does *sanctified reasoning upon the character and attributes of God.*

If we reason on God's character, how can we but trust that He will answer our prayer? We know He is *true;* we have read His promises; we believe that He will be as good as His word; His very character is a guarantee on which we can rest.

Is He not also *loving;* does He not care for the true interests of His children; does He not wish them to have everything that is good for them; is not His heart's affection set upon them; if so, have they not a warrant for expectation from the existence of this feeling in God? The consciousness of another's love emboldens us to ask from those on earth; how much more should it from the One in heaven! Never was love so true, so steady, so large and ungrudging as His; He is our Father, and we, if in Christ, are His children; and we should expect from His love, just as a child expects from its parent's love.

Is He not also *omnipotent;* has He not all resources at His command; are not all the beasts of the forest His, and the cattle upon a thousand hills; can He not "make all things work together for good to them that love Him," and should not all these considerations strengthen our expectations in prayer? We have to limit our expectations from our fellow-men by their resources; they may be willing, and yet not be able to help us; they may be able to do a part of what we want, but not the whole; there should however be no limit in our expectations from God; we should look at Him in prayer as able to do all we want, and to do it with the greatest ease.   If I want money for His cause,* or my own need, I think " He owns every guinea in the world." As I walk along the road, I say " He can turn the very stones into gold, if he will, He can make the dust on the road side gold dust; " I look up at the sky, and there I

* It is a matter of great importance that we should simply look to God as the great and original proprietor of all wealth, without allowing ourselves to be influenced by the possibilities of things. The author had need of £10 for a specific work which he proposed to undertake for God; he committed the matter to God in prayer, and said that he would consider the Lord's sending the money as the token that the enterprize was to be undertaken. Unless the money came within a limited time, the occasion for its expenditure would have passed away. Day after day the matter was laid before God, but the money did not come. At last, one Saturday, a stranger called, and took five sovereigns out of his pocket, and gave it to the author to spend in charity. The latter asked him " to what he wished it applied?" He answered, " to anything you like:" " have you no object particularly in view to which you wish it given?" " No, you are to spend it any way you like." He was then told of the enterprize in hand, and how the Lord had been asked to put money at the minister's own disposal, with a view to its being spent in that particular way. " Well," said he, " I have just come from your church, and I was about to drop these five sovereigns into the boxes at the doors, for the new schools; but something said to me, " Don't do it, perhaps the minister will want them more for something else, and if you don't get the other £5 anywhere else, I'll give it to you." The author was now anxious that it would please God to send him the £5 from some other quarter, so that the giver of the first £5 should feel that he was not as it were come down upon for the whole sum, and that he might not think that the Most High was limited in His resources; and it was put before the Lord in this way— " Lord, is it not more for Thy honour and glory that this other £5 should come from some other person?" The second £5 also, was sent by post, a few days after, from a very unexpected quarter.

see white fleecy clouds, or clouds like heaps of glowing gold, and I say, "if He willed, He could turn that fleecy cloud into bank notes, and tear from it a thousand for me; He could turn that glowing mass of vapour, into solid metal, and break off a piece for me, which would be a thousand-fold more than I require."

He has a great treasury; and with my mind's eye I contemplate that treasury, and I say to Him, "Put thine hand into Thy treasury, O Lord; take from it what I need; give it unto me," and then expectation rises under such considerations as these.

Is not God *generous;* does not He love to give; is He not always giving; did He not give up His only Son to die for us, and "how shall He not with Him also freely give us all things?" Hear what He says to the Jews by the mouth of His prophet Malachi, (iii, 10,) "Bring ye all the tithes into the store-house that there may be meat in mine house, and prove me now herewith, saith the Lord of hosts, if I will not open you the windows of heaven, and pour you out a blessing, that there shall not be room enough to receive it." When Jesus fed the thousands, the fragments exceeded the original provision; when bread was rained from heaven upon the multitudes in the wilderness, it fell in profusion, so that there was abundance for all; when Hannah asked for one son, she received four sons and two daughters. The epistles are full of the generosity of God; we read of " the exceeding and eternal weight of glory,"* and of " the exceeding greatness of His power,"† and of " the exceeding riches of His grace,"‡ and of "the grace of the Lord exceeding

---

* 2 Cor. iv, 17   † Eph. i, 19.   ‡ Eph. ii, 7.

abundant,"* and of "exceeding great promises."†
"Now," says the apostle, after he had spoken of the
wondrous extent of the love of Christ, "unto Him that
is able to do exceeding abundantly above all that we ask
or think, according to the power that worketh in us,
unto Him be glory in the church, by Christ Jesus,
throughout all ages, world without end. Amen." Eph.
iii, 20, 21.

It would greatly help our expectation in prayer, if we
called all these attributes of God to mind, and meditated
on His character in connection with our need; if, when
we were engaged in any hard matter, or when our faith
began to stagger, we exercised ourselves for a few minutes
in such thoughts as a preliminary to prayer. If we did
this, in all probability our faith would rise, our expectation would strengthen, and an earnestness and reality
which otherwise might have been wanting, would enter
into our prayer. Try this, dear reader; it will not be
without good effect.

Let us now consider, *The Results of Expectation in
Prayer.*

One result will be, *more precision of meaning in our
prayers.* Many prayers are offered, with, it is to be feared,
but little precision of meaning; in fact with so little
meaning, that the petitioner would be in no small degree
astonished, if he were taken at his word in prayer; perhaps, if God were to say to him, "I will grant that fully,"
he would be inclined to start back, and not repeat the
prayer again.

There are many things which we think we *ought* to

* 1 Tim. i, 14. † 2 Peter i, 4.

pray for, which our spiritual knowledge tells us a Christian should desire; but do we really desire them, are we really anxious to get them, when we ask for them in prayer? For example, we pray that God would by His Spirit reveal more and more to us the naughtiness of our own hearts and evil natures; is the petitioner really desirous of an answer; is he ready for disquieted hours, for humbling experiences, for deep depressions, for more self-loathing than he has ever experienced as yet? Or, he may ask for higher exaltation above the world, and its pursuits, and aims, and interests; he knows that that is a very fitting prayer for a true hearted Christian man to make; but is he really anxious that God should in His own way grant the thing that He desires? It is useless to pray with the expectation of being answered in the way, or by the process we desire; if we pray, we must leave the method of the answer entirely with God; and when we offer a prayer like this, do we really mean that God should answer it, and do what we have asked?

If we have learned *to expect in prayer*, to believe that an answer will really come in the very point in which supplication has been made, we shall surely be precise in what we say to God. If I have learned from experience to expect an answer to prayer, then if I want money for the Lord's cause, or even for my own necessities, what I am to ask for is *money*; if I am going a journey and ask for divine protection, then what I am to expect is, that God will give His angels charge over me, and that they will take care of my body, and that accidents which were perhaps imminent will be averted, and obstacles cleared out of my path; these will serve as examples of precision and meaning in prayer.

And why should we not be precise in prayer? We are precise in our dealings with our fellow men; no one thinks of going to another with merely a vague petition to give him something; or with a string of meaningless petitions, to give him things which he does not want, or which he does not care to have; this want of precision would destroy all reality in the petitioner's supplications, and would pretty surely be the means of sending him empty away; oh, let us not deal with God with less earnestness, and reality, than we employ with our fellow man; when we pray to Him let us at least mean what we say. And we shall thus mean, if we expect; and thus meaning, and expecting, our prayers will be real, and solid, and precise; they will be divested of many unmeaning words, and their very plainness will add to their intensity, and plain answers will be sure to come to such plain prayers. Dear reader, if you have not hitherto been precise in your prayer, begin to be so now; you will find incalculable advantage from being so; offer no prayer, in which you are not both willing and desirous that God should take you at your word.

Another good result of this expectation in prayer, will be a *greater readiness to pray*. If we think that God will grant our petitions, we shall assuredly be all the more ready to come and make them. We are very loth to go and ask a favour, where we think we are likely to be denied; we have not the heart to go and make our petition; but if we really expect from God, we shall be very ready to come, and ask for what we want. Prayer, when thus looked at, is too productive to be allowed to remain unused; we shall be quick to ask, when we are sure to get. One cause of backwardness in prayer is our doubt and uncertainty, if not our actual unbelief, about getting an answer; these take away our cheerfulness and readiness in prayer, and make it hard labour instead of blessed privilege.

A further good result will be *less expectation from, and leaning on man, seeing we have the Everlasting God Himself to go to.* Man has always been a snare to his fellow man, leading him to trust in human flesh, instead of in the living God. Israel leaning upon Egypt is a picture that is reproduced every day. We have a beautiful instance of simple leaning upon God and turning away from man, together with expectation from God in prayer, in the book of Ezra. " Then I proclaimed a fast there, at the river Ahava, that we might afflict ourselves before our God, to seek of Him a right way for us, and for our little ones, and for all our substance. For I was ashamed to require of the king a band of soldiers and horsemen to help us against the enemy in the way, because we had spoken unto the king, saying, ' the hand of our God is upon all them for good that seek Him, but His power and His wrath is against all them that forsake Him.' So we fasted and besought our God for this, and He was intreated of us." An immense treasure was now put into the hands of a helpless company of priests to convey to Jerusalem, their only protection being the prayer offered on their behalf; but that prayer was sufficient safeguard, not an ounce of gold or silver was lost. " Then we departed from the river of Ahava, on the twelfth day of the first month, to go unto Jerusalem; and the hand of our God was upon us, and He delivered us from the hand of the enemy, and of such as lay in wait by the way." Ezra viii, 21, 22, 23, 31.

To lean on man is to lean upon a broken reed it is to throw ourselves in the way of disappointment and in most instances it is to dishonour God.   Why need we thus lean, if we be really expecting what we want from God; why should we subject ourselves to vexations and distress; why should we consider our circumstances bad when men fail us; why should we be *dependent* upon them at all?   One of the best cures that we can possibly have for all this, is *to expect answers* to our prayers to God, to tell Him of our need, and then to expect from Him, as one both able and willing to supply our wants.

A spirit of expectation in prayer would further *make our minds much more cheerful after our prayer has been offered up.*   We should then have rolled off our pressing care on God, and be proportionately unburdened in our own minds.

The very fact of having committed a trouble to God ought to give us cheerfulness and peace; we may now, if we have an expecting spirit, say, "my God will take this matter in hand, and arrange everything for me for the best; He will bring His resources and His wisdom to bear on my behalf; my care is cast on Him."   How often, however, are we as sad after prayer as we were before we went to commit our troubles to the Lord; we took our burden to the throne, and brought it away with us again; if we laid any, we laid only a part on God.   A certain man carrying a burden on his back was met by a rich man as he drove along, and invited to get up behind the carriage, which offer was thankfully accepted.   After a while the rich man turned round, and saw the burden still strapped to the traveller's back; he asked him why he did not lay down his pack on the seat beside him? but he answered, "he could not think of doing that; it was quite enough that he himself should be allowed to sit behind the carriage, without putting his burden on the seat also." This is what many amongst us are doing; we keep our burden strapped tightly to us; we expect at the best but some relief; we think it too much to expect God to bear it all.

A certain man with small means, and a large family, struggled on year after year; and as each child was born, he felt a fresh load of care come upon his shoulders. At length when the eighth was born, he felt that the weight of their provision was a burden heavier than he could bear, let him toil never so hard; so he deliberately handed them all over to God, and henceforth became a cheerful and prosperous man.

Surely if we rise from our knees without some sense of relief, and some lightening of heart, we cannot have had an expecting spirit in prayer.

Go up, then, Christian reader, to your closet, with tears in your eyes, but come forth from it without them, having wiped them away as you rose from your knees; go up with a heavy tread, bearing almost a mountain of care upon your heart, but come down with a lighter, if not with an elastic step, expecting that God has heard your prayer, and will answer it without fail; you may not be able to feel joyous, but surely you may feel cheerful, and you *will* be cheerful, if you practically expect an answer, if you believe that one will come.

It may, perhaps, be thought by some, Will not such feelings as these take away a man's energy in the use of means? Far from it. We note as a further result of expectation in prayer, that *it will give more energy in the use of means*. The Christian is no wild enthusiast; he knows that while God can work without means, He yet in almost all instances works by them. It is very seldom also that the means are not plainly indicated; we may pray that they should be so, and when we have thus prayed, and they are opened out, then in the expectation of a blessing we shall work with redoubled energy and zeal. The probability is, that our very expectation will give us such a spring of energy, as will produce with God's blessing the desired result. We know that there is great difference in the work of a spirited and a spiritless man. A man who feels that he has no chance of success, or that the chances are largely against him, has little heart for his work; difficulties easily daunt him; opportunities which open out before him, he does not avail himself of; the very elements of success are wanting. But let the same man, and in the very same position, have a fair prospect of success; let him feel that he can succeed; let him have a still stronger feeling that he is destined to succeed, and he now appears a very different man from what he was before; he is alive in his work, he is hearty in it, and that very life and heartiness go far towards securing success. When Alexander was giving away estates and domains with lavish prodigality, before setting forth on his eastward march, Perdiccas asked him what he reserved for himself. Hope—was the sole reply. And the whole secret of his wondrous career of insatiable conquest, fearless intrepidity, and boundless aspiration, lies wrapped up in that sublime answer.

Dear Christian reader, not only pray, but also expect

an answer to your prayer; take up the Psalmist's " I
will," and say, " As for me I will call upon God, and the
Lord shall save me. Evening, and morning, and at
noon, will I pray, and cry aloud: and He shall hear my
voice."

He, however, who says with the Psalmist, " I will call
upon God, and the Lord shall save me," must not only
believe that an answer will come, but must further
be on the look out for that answer. It might be truly
said, that many a Chistian is taken unawares by the
answers to his prayers. Is it not a fact that we often
send forth our petitions, and think no more about them,
as though it were a matter of indifference whether an
answer came or not, or as though it were a matter for
speculation whether our prayers were heard? So much is
this the case, that there is little doubt but that we have
had many things in answer to prayer, which we have never
recognised at all as having come in that way, and for
which we have never thanked God. If we write to a
rich and kind friend to help us in some hour of need, we
watch the post for an answer; if we invest money in any
enterprize, we look for a return; we will not believe our
petitions or our hopes to be in vain, until they are proved
to be so; in prayer alone do we act as though from the
very commencement we took it for granted that they
must be so. " The Rev. Joseph Alleine, writing from
Ilchester prison to his flock at Taunton, says, ' Let
prayer never be a form; always realize it as an approach
to the living God for *some specific purpose*, and learn
to watch for the returns of prayer.' A Sabbath
school teacher, in the village of Brading, in the Isle of
Wight, said to another teacher, ' W——, I am quite

sure I shall be made useful to-day, in the conversion of some of my boys.' 'Why?' was the reply. 'Because,' said he, 'I have had such nearness to God, and have been enabled to exercise faith in His promises.' That praying Sabbath school teacher came expecting an answer to his prayers, and was not disappointed. Four of the boys were that day converted to God through his instrumentality; and for twenty years, those boys have evidenced that it was the work of the Holy Spirit upon their hearts. Three of them became preachers of the gospel, and the fourth lived a very consistent private Christian." *

It is not honouring God, to pray, and yet not look out for the answer to our prayers; what could we expect from our fellow man if we showed such carelessness as this? God is greatly robbed of His glory, when He gives, and when we do not recognise what we receive as His gift; the display of His attributes which unfolded themselves in His answer to our prayer is thrown away on us; and can God be robbed of His glory without our having to suffer chastisement in one form or another?

But we must be *Patient in Expectation*. This subject of "Patience in Expectation" is one of the utmost importance. God's ways are not as our ways, nor His thoughts as our thoughts, and some answers to prayer have to be brought about by the working of complicated machinery, event fitting into event, and influence working with influence for many days.

If we be men of prayer, we must expect our patience to be tried by many temptations; God is honoured when His people *wait* upon Him, and Satan will not see them

* Phillips's Remarkable Answers.

waiting upon Him without endeavouring to shake their faith. All attempts to hurry God's dealings are sure to be productive of bad results; even when we are most sure of having asked according to God's mind, and of receiving an answer, we must leave the time unresevedly to Him.

It is no doubt very hard to expect in patience, when all things seem to be going against us; when week after week, and it may be year after year pass by, and the answer appears no nearer at hand than it was before; but let us remember that God gives liberal interest for every year that He keeps our prayers unanswered; and that what becomes us, is to wait at His footstool, and not to hurry His arrangements. The most luscious fruits are often those which are longest in maturing, the richest blessings are often those which take longest in coming; an unripe blessing may prove sour to the teeth, and unhealthful when partaken of; impatience is almost always accompanied by loss.

We add two or three instances of answers given to prayer, after apparently long delay; how full, how rich are they—how well worth waiting for—how gradual in their incoming—how grand their results—verily there are great answers for patient prayers.

"A mother had been for years the only Christian in the family. Her husband and nine children were not immoral, but none of them gave evidence of piety. Had this mother been less firm in character and faith, and less resolute of purpose, she might have yielded to the current, pleading that resistance was unavailing. But she was qualified to meet the responsibility of her position. She felt that God had committed to her trust ten unconverted souls, dear as her own life, and that she must so fulfil the obligations resting on her, that if any were lost, it should not be through her neglect of duty. She carefully endeavoured, first of all, that her own life should be consistent with her profession, and she also improved every propitious season in giving judicious instruction and warning. She used all appropriate means, and in her various efforts, love was the dominant power exhibited in those acts of kindness which is 'a potent winner of the heart.' But her great reliance was upon fervent, unceasing prayer, sent upward to the mercy-seat, with unwavering faith in the Divine promises. In the many supplications offered in secret, the strength of maternal love added fervour to devotion. She used to say that her thoughts were diverted, and the ardour of intercession damped by passing over different topics; and therefore, although she prayed for all her family at once, yet so she could not 'pour out her heart like water before the Lord.' She presented each child separately before the throne of grace. In this individual supplication she formed the habit of what might be called *concentrated* prayer. The power of supplication was expended upon one child, as if it had been an only one; and intense became the earnestness thus fixed and kindling upon a single object. This was indeed prayer, and in His own time it prevailed with God.

"But long had this mother seemed to pray in vain, and her faith was sorely tried through years of 'hope deferred.' Yet now the reaping time was near. She who had gone forth weeping, sowing the precious seed, was to return again, bringing her sheaves with her.

"The first convert was the eldest daughter; the two

eldest sons soon after obtained the good hope through grace. And successively, at intervals, the whole of the nine children made a profession of faith. Unbounded thankfulness and joy filled the mother's heart, but one sorrow remained, the husband and father was still impenitent. There was great despondency on his account, for he was now advancing in years, and he had begun to form the habit of intemperance. For him, the many prayers remained unanswered. Had the supplicating wife, in the abundance of her blessings, received all that God was willing to grant? Must the father see all his family in the kingdom of heaven, and he himself 'thrust out?' This thought was a burden too heavy to be borne, and yet she who by 'the fervent effectual prayer of the righteous' had availed so much, feared that her last desire, the salvation of her husband, might not be granted. All her tears, entreaties, and prayers, had not prevailed; and might not the harvest be past? After much painful reflection, the faithful wife resolved to make one final effort, and then leave the case with God. She spent a night of anguish, with a fervour of supplication she had never before experienced; and in the morning she thus addressed her husband: 'I have offered for you many prayers; have often entreated you to attend to your salvation; but it has been all in vain. God has given me my children, but you are without hope. I can do no more. We have lived happily together in time, but I fear we must be separated in eternity; I have but one more request to make, and then I must leave you with God. *Do this moment seek the salvation of your soul.*'

"This message, brought down from the 'mount of

God,' was irresistible. The husband seemed for a moment paralysed and speechless. Finding utterance, he simply replied, with significant emphasis, 'I will.' He immediately left his work and retired to the field, resolving, as he afterwards said, never to return till he had become a Christian. The whole long summer day down to the deep shades of night was he absent, to the alarm of his family, who sought but found him not.

"Thinking himself that they would be distressed at his absence, he returned, not a Christian, but deeply laden with the burden of sin. Some days passed away, and then he experienced a change from death unto life. He dare not at first trust the evidences of conversion, but the light increased as he 'followed on to know the Lord,' and fear was overpowered by joy.

"A revival of religion had commenced at the time, and the aged convert attended the evening meeting. He supposed that none had heard of the change in his character, but there was joy on earth as well as 'among the angels,' for the tidings had spread abroad. When the meeting was dismissed, the young converts and members of the church gathered around the new disciple, taking him by surprise as they rejoiced over his salvation. It was a moving scene. As he described it, 'the young people wept and I wept, we were all children together, and I as much a child as any of them.' The cup of the praying mother could hold no more. God had granted all that she asked, and she could now hope to sit down at last with all her family in heaven. Oh, infinite reward of faith and prayer! What glory of earth can be named with this?

"The praying mother still lives, extremely aged, blind,

infirm, but retaining remarkably her mental faculties and her spiritual vigour. She has seen her children connected with pious families, and listened to some of them as preachers of the gospel. Most of her grandchildren are also members of the church, one a missionary to a foreign land, and for each of the unconverted she continues the daily prayer. The aged disciple patiently waits, but longs to depart. She often turns her sightless orbs up towards heaven as if asking 'How long, Lord, how long?' But, long as her life has been protracted, she has not lived in vain. Christian mothers, see in this example what power God has granted you. Use it faithfully and well, for great is 'the recompense of reward.'"

It is told in the "Life of Mrs. Winslow," that she determined, with God's blessing, that every member of her family should appear with her at God's right hand.

She wrestled long in prayer, and she had the happiness of seeing, one after another, her children brought to God, until not one was left " without God in the world." She ascribes this to no miracle, except the miracle of grace that is wrought in every soul brought home, but she does recognise answer to prayer in her having lived to *see* this wondrous sight.

For many a long year did the seaman's prayer lie in the old oak chest, but at length, like the chrysalis, it burst its shell and came forth to life and light. Captain Mitchell R—— was from early life accustomed to the sea. He commanded a merchant's ship that sailed from Philadelphia. After his marriage, he again went to sea, and committed to writing, while in a highly devotional frame of mind, a prayer for the temporal and eternal happiness of his beloved wife and unborn babe.

This prayer, nearly filling a sheet of paper, was deposited, with his other writings, at the bottom of an old oak chest. The captain died before the completion of the voyage, in the year 1757, and his instruments, papers, &c., were returned to his wife. Finding they were generally what she could not understand, she locked up the chest for her babe, (who proved to be a son,) at some future time. At eighteen this son entered the army, and in 1775 marched for Boston. He gave the reins to his lusts, and for many years yielded to almost every temptation to sin. At length, he was called to the death-bed of his mother, who gave him the key of his father's chest, which, however, he did not open, lest he should meet with something of a religious kind that should reprove his sins and harass his feelings. At length, in 1814, when in his fifty-sixth year, he determined to examine its whole contents. When he reached the bottom, he discovered a paper, neatly folded, and endorsed, "The prayer of Mitchell R—— for blessings on his wife and child, August 23, 1757." He read it; the scene, the time, the place, and circumstances under which it was written and put there, all rushed upon his mind, and overwhelmed him, for often had his widowed mother led him to the beach, and pointed to him the direction on the horizon where she had traced the last glimpse of flowing canvas that bore his father from her, never to return. He threw the contents back into the chest, folded up the prayer, and put it into the case with his father's quadrant, locked up the chest, and determined never again to unlock it. But his father's prayer still haunted his imagination, and he could not forget it. At length his distress became extreme, and a person with whom he lived entreated to know the cause. He looked on her with mildness, and replied, "I cannot tell you." This only increased her solicitude; he entreated her to withdraw; as she left the room, she cast an anxious and expressive look upon him, and he instantly called her back. He then, with all the feelings which an awakened guilty conscience could endure, told the cause of his agonies—his father's prayer in the old chest. She thought him deranged, his neighbours were called in to comfort him, but in vain. The prayer had inflicted a wound which the Great Physician of souls only could heal. From that period he became an altered man, forsook every way of sin, united himself to the Church of Christ, set his slaves at liberty, and lived and died a humble, exemplary Christian.

Let the parent, then, who prays for the conversion of a child, or the husband or wife who prays for the conversion the one of the other; let the man who prays for some spiritual blessing, it may be perhaps for that of deep assurance, or the perfect victory over some besetting sin, let such, and all who are praying according to the mind and will of God, be patient, "In due season they shall reap if they faint not." "Behold, the husbandman waiteth for the precious fruit of the earth, and hath long patience for it, until he receive the early and latter rain, be ye also patient," the answer is on its way, hail even a little sign of it; it was from a cloud no bigger than a man's hand, that the heavens became overcast, and then there fell, in answer to the prophet's prayer, abundance of rain.

CHAPTER XV.

THE "I WILL" OF INTENSE PRAYER.

Psalm xxviii, 1. "*Unto Thee will I cry, O Lord my rock: be not silent to me: lest, if Thou be silent to me, I become like them that go down into the pit.*"

Psalm lv, 17. "*Evening, and morning, and at noon, will I pray, and cry aloud: and He shall hear my voice.*"

Psalm lxiii, 1. "*O God, Thou art my God; early will I seek Thee: my soul thirsteth for Thee, my flesh longeth for Thee in a dry and thirsty land, where no water is.*"

HOW shall we undertake to speak of this subject? What do we know of it? Where is the pen that can write worthily of it? When we see a specimen of it in Jesu's prayer in Gethsemane, when we think of the agony of supplication there, we are ashamed to take up the subject of Intensity in Prayer; none could speak worthily of it, save He, who realized it in His own tears, and woe, and bloody sweat.

And yet this subject must not be passed by, for it is one of great importance to the Christian; the higher we rise in our spiritual life, the more shall we know practically of Intensity in Prayer.

We are to consider here,

THE SEASONS OF INTENSE PRAYER.

There are two distinct seasons of intense prayer; (1) those with which circumstances have to do; and (2) those in which man is being wrought upon by immediate and independent operations of the Spirit.

We are sometimes brought into such circumstances, that *a fixed and speedy time must settle a question.** Perhaps the life or death of a beloved relative is in jeopardy; a decision in some important question has to be made; relief is required for pain which must be borne within the next hour; strength is needed to carry us through an interview, which must come off within the next few minutes; grace and wisdom are needed for our lips in dealing with some one whom we love, and whose soul is in jeopardy, and now an opportunity is afforded of speaking to him; these are some examples of circumstances, in which time becomes an element of intensity

---

* "When the Rev. Mr. Clarke and Dr. Prince were in Western Africa, they penetrated a part of the interior, where a warlike tribe resided, which they had never before seen. It being a perilous undertaking, they offered special prayer for the Divine protection and blessing. At length, on the top of a hill, the tribe appeared, with their weapons of war. At the command of their chief, they rushed down the hill with their pointed lances, as if intent on the destruction of the two strangers. The missionaries again earnestly prayed that the Lord would manifest His protecting power and give them an opportunity of proclaiming Christ to these savages. They encouraged each other to exercise confidence in God, with the words, 'Stand still and see the salvation of the Lord.' They therefore stood still and prayed. The tribe soon encircled them; and when death seemed most imminent, the warriors threw down their weapons to the ground, and the missionaries at once made known to them the glorious gospel."—*Phillips's Remarkable Answers.*

in prayer. But they are only examples, for such circumstances are continually occurring; if an answer is to be given at all, it must be within a certain time.

God has often taught His people the meaning of intensity in prayer, by bringing them thus decidedly to a point; they now find with how little intensity they had often prayed before; they seem to themselves never to have prayed at all; they feel what a strong reality prayer is. Many a mother has thus learned Intensity of Prayer, by the bed-side of a fevered child; many a father by the bed-side of an almost dying wife; into a few moments, they seem then to compress all the prayers of former years. Call not, dear reader, upon God, to teach you how to pray intensely by such experiences as these: if you be a child of God, you must be taught "Intensity in Prayer," but you *need* not learn it thus; you may obtain it by direct influences of the SPIRIT: and then, when the time of need has come, you will be called upon to *use*, not to *learn* intensity of prayer.

Another season of intensity in prayer, is when *sudden calamity comes upon us*. There are occasions in life, when we feel ourselves in a moment plunged into trouble, bereft of our usual resources, and friends, and left solitary to get out of our affliction as best we can; we awake as in a moment to find ourselves in circumstances of great distress, from whatever cause that distress may come. At such seasons, we find ourselves brought into the immediate presence of God; we feel that we must have more than human support, or we shall be unable to bear up under the sudden pressure that has come upon us; we are driven by our sharp distress to intense prayer.

And it is thus that sudden calamity should indeed be met. Nothing will so calm the mind, and fit it for deliberation, as a few moments of intense prayer; in that intense prayer, we may rest assured, God will be found by His children; and having secured Him on their side, they will be able steadily to meet that, with Him, which it would have been ill meeting indeed, without Him.

When we have had *special realizations of the magnitude or importance of the thing to be prayed for,* is another season of intense prayer. The true proportions of things are not always seen; we often pray, little knowing the greatness of that which we are praying for.* We pray, for example, that God would graciously preserve us in health, and strength, continuing to us the use of our faculties, and various blessings, and we prav languidly enough : but let us be threatened with the speedy loss of some of these blessings, or say, of *one* of them, of our sight,—let us shut our eyes, and picture to ourselves a state of darkness continued as long as we live; let us feel ourselves about to be shut out from the loving faces of our friends, from the flowers, and trees, and fields : let us think that soon every step must be taken with uncertainty—that we are destined, it may be, to be a burden on those around us; now we have special realizations of the magnitude of that for which we are about to pray, when we ask, it may be, that something troubling the eye may be removed; the meaning of which now is, that we may not be left to spend our days in blindness; and we shall pray with intensity when we bring this matter before God.

We shall presently meet with these realizations of

* " Ye know not what ye ask." Matthew xx, 22.

magnitude in spiritual things; the above will serve as an example of what we mean with regard to such realizations generally.

We little know, how great are the blessings for which we are often praying, and on this account our prayers are dull; God sometimes sets them before us in their true light, and quickens us into intensity of prayer.

When we have been completely shut up in our own resources, and there is heavy pressure upon us, we often learn the meaning of Intensity in Prayer. It often happens that, without our knowing or intending it, we permit the possession of even one slender resource to affect our intensity in prayer. We honestly do not wish this to be the case; we wish to cast ourselves on God alone; we wish to look to Him alone, but poor weak human nature makes us squint out of the corner of our eye at some means which seem at hand, or from which we should hope much, if only we could get them within our reach. Ask men who have been really "shut up," and that "under pressure," and they will tell you the meaning of Intensity in Prayer.

Let us turn, however, to those seasons of intense prayer which are experienced, owing to *immediate and independent operations of the Spirit.* We have now to consider times, when no particular circumstances are working upon the mind, to wind it up to such a pitch of earnestness as might fitly be described by the word "intense"—times unknown to the people of the world —times well known to the people of God.

These workings of the Spirit may have reference to man in a struggling state, or to man in a state of attainment. Take man in a struggling state; he has perhaps *just failed in some point in which he earnestly desired, and in which he had determined, to do well,* or it may be that he *is brooding over such past failures, and is half maddened at them;* the Spirit of God is now working upon him, He is shewing him his weakness, He is proving to him what flesh and blood really are, what man is in himself, even though he be honest, and well intentioned, and active in making effort. Full of shame and self reproach, and it may be of fear with reference to the future, the soul now becomes quickened into intensity of prayer, it looks to God, it enlists His strength, it seeks to Him as a refuge from its own demerits and shortcomings, it sees Him in Christ, and puts intensity into some such words as these—" Unto Thee do I cry, O Lord, my Rock, be not silent to me, lest, if Thou be silent to me, I become like them that go down into the pit."

Or it may be that the *pressure, and burden, and evil of sin are now being peculiarly felt.* There are times when the Spirit of God deals especially with a believer in this matter; when the Lord reveals to a man more than he ever knew before of his position before Him as a sinner; when he feels sin to be exceeding sinful. Then comes the cry, " O wretched man that I am," then comes the deep consciousness of individual vileness and baseness, then the heart groans, being burdened. There is now no taste of sweetness about sin, but all is unmingled gall and bitterness; there is now playing around it not a sparkle or gleam of light, but all is thick and oppressive darkness; there is now no joy or gladness connected with it, but it is like Ezekiel's roll, written both within and without with woe. Oh! when the Holy Ghost is dealing with a man with reference to sin, sin wears an aspect far more awful than that which it wears simply under the reproaches of conscience. Conscience can tell the difference between good and evil, right and wrong, it can tell what is sin, but it cannot tell the exceeding evil of sin. To know this, there must be a revelation of the holiness of God; there must be a revelation of the intrinsic evil and corruption of sin; there must be certain teachings with reference to our own nature; there must be certain *feelings,* not one of which is it the immediate office of conscience to bestow, but which, one and all, come from the operation of the Holy Ghost.

When a man is under these operations of the Spirit, he knows what it is to be intense in prayer—to pray as a pressed and burdened sinner who sees sin to be exceeding sinful. Jesus, though sinless, put himself in the position of a sinner, and having done so, He had to feel realizations of what sin was. Although sin was not in Him, and had never been committed by Him, all its anguish, all its horror came upon Him; these were, doubtless, some of the ingredients of that cup of gall and wormwood which He drank of in Gethsemane, and drained even to the last of its dregs upon the cross. We need scarcely point out that these experiences of sin, and intense prayer in connection with them, are unknown to the people of the world. Very superficial indeed are their views of sin, very superficial their prayers about it; but God's people know something of all this; even though such seasons as these of which we have been speaking are short, mercifully short, and the prayer connected with them be but one agonized look to heaven, or one abashed and broken-hearted look upon the ground.

Hard following upon this season comes that, in which *man longs intently for inward comfort and peace.* He wants the peace of God which passeth all understanding; he wants rest in the Lord. There is a state of rest for the soul, and that is what he craves. At this time what might be called a vision of peace comes over him; he sees much of its blessedness, though he feels that he possesses it not; and this drives him to intense prayer. It is God's intention that this peace should be given, but it is His intention also that it should be earnestly sought; and He stirs up the soul to such prayer as has power with Him and will prevail.

There are, however, other immediate and independent operations of the Spirit, which have reference to man, not so much in a struggling state as in one of attainment.

The Spirit is ever working, ever teaching, ever leading; and these workings, and teachings, often have reference to prayer. Let us take the case of a man who has made attainment in divine things; there are seasons when such an one's heart is under the special influences of the SPIRIT for *elevation.* The Holy Ghost is raising the man, is upheaving his nature, is kindling within Him great desires, is gifting him with larger power of prayer. That gift is working, and the man thus favoured is enabled to pray under immediate influences from above. These seasons are gifts from God; may they be bestowed upon us more and more; they are sure to produce great results, and they are manifest tokens of divine favour.

Then, there are times when there is kindled in the

soul *earnest desire for some spiritual blessing*. This
desire is kindled by the Holy Ghost. At such a time
the exceeding preciousness of this particular blessing is
brought vividly before us; the want of it is made more
keenly felt; the heart's eager and earnest desire is set
on the possession of it; it becomes, perhaps, the one
leading thought of life, and we wrestle with God in
prayer, and say " I will not let Thee go, until Thou bless
me." Thus many such blessings have been obtained;
happy is he whose earnest longing for spiritual blessing
has taken such a development as this; in intensity of
prayer the blessing has been won.

And who is there at all accustomed to exercise himself
in prayer, who has not experienced apparent denials;
denials which required faith to be borne with, denials
which seemed at the time to be harsh and rough? At
times it appeared as though God had forgotten to be
gracious, as though He had shut up His ear, as
though He would not listen to our request; and faint
hearts have sunk so low, that they restrained prayer,
until by some special dealing of the Spirit they were
roused to it again. Now in all *purely spiritual blessings*
we may, as it were, say, that we will take no final
denial from God. He has been graciously pleased to put
Himself in all such things within our power, so that He
cannot go away from us, leaving us without the spiritual
good, for which He Himself has given us the grace to
long. The history of Jacob's successful wrestling with
the angel is a palpable proof of this; and we may be
sure, that what took place with the patriarch actually, has
taken place with many a man symbolically, and God has
graciously yielded, when He found Himself with one who

by the power of His own Spirit could say, "I will not let Thee go, except Thou bless me."

Again we would repeat, that men may come to the throne of grace for *purely spiritual* blessings, with a determination to receive no final denial from God—but let it be understood, that this refers to spiritual blessings alone. All else we must leave unreservedly to God; and even in the matter of purely spiritual blessings, how, and when, and through what instrumentality they are to be vouchsafed, must be left wholly in God's hands. It would be most sinful to kneel down and pray, that without any special reference to God's wisdom and will, we should receive such and such a blessing—that a child should recover—that a husband or a wife should be spared—that a speculation in business should succeed—that failing health should be restored— or the anguish and debility of illness be taken away.

To be answered in many such desires, might be the means of eventually excluding us from the kingdom of heaven—in anger God has answered such prayers as these; He has given men their heart's desires, and "withal sent leanness into their souls." All such things must be left entirely to God's judgment and will; and not only these, but a large class of spiritual blessings also. You might come, and kneel down, and ask for immediate peace of mind, or for immediate knowledge of the deep things of God, or for deliverance from some Satanic pressure upon your soul, or for a variety of blessings of this class, each one of which is undoubtedly most excellent and desirable in itself, and not only excellent and desirable, but also a fit subject for prayer; and yet the amount of the answer, and the time when that amount shall be vouchsafed, must be entirely left in the hands of God. A spiritual blessing, by coming at an improper time, might prove a spiritual curse; and the peace which we desire so much, if given at once, might, for all we know, but provide the elements of some future snare, or keep us back from a future high position which otherwise might have been attained. For some blessings, however, we may ask, without any reservation or any limit. The inestimable blessings of love, of grace, of faith, of humility, of patience, and all such, may be sought for with such eagerness, that he who seeks for them might be said to appear determined to take no denial; and such a feeling is acceptable to God; it is not presumption, it is faith; it is not audacity, it is boldness; it is not desperation, it is energy; such a feeling shall assuredly gain the blessing, and the perseverance which it exercises shall be crowned abundantly with success.

But while denials of whatever is for our good, are only apparent, delays are real, and often most distressing to the soul. Promises have been so long delayed, as to have been to all human appearances lost, and the exercise of the spirit has been carried on, through great disquietude of the flesh. Amid all delays, however, the promises of God are sure; though they tarry, they will not tarry beyond the appointed time. And whilst we are now waiting and watching for promised blessings, the command comes to us to ask, to seek, to knock; silence on God's part, is not to be met by silence on ours; His delays must not destroy our hopes.* There is not a child

* See the case of the Syro-phenician woman in Matthew xv, 21, &c.—first, " He answered her not a word;" then He said, " I am not sent but unto the lost sheep of the house of Israel;" and lastly, "It is not meet to take the children's bread and to cast it to dogs."

of God on earth, who has not from time to time been exercised by delays; under the trials of delay, some of their finest graces have come forth, and the highest lustre been conferred upon the jewels of their heavenly crowns. Little did men know, what God was doing for them, when He kept them a long time waiting, even for that which He had positively assured them that He would give; little did they know, as they looked forward in patience, and humble trust, that each day thus spent, had appended to it its own reward—but thus it has ever been—God's promises bear an interest, which accumulates every day, and in full tale both principal and interest shall be paid.

To us, then, dear reader, may it be given to pray—to pray in trouble—to pray continuously—to pray expectingly—to pray intensely—to pray in the Holy Ghost. Let us tread our pilgrimage's rough road with prayer; let us face our fierce enemies in prayer; let us be prepared to meet, alike the perils of life's lonely places, and its thoroughfares in prayer; the prayers of this life shall soon be needed no more; then shall our voices mingle in the praises of the life that is to come.

CHAPTER XVI.

Action.

Psalm lxxi, 16. *"I will go in the strength of the Lord God."*

Psalm lxxxvi, 11. *"Teach me Thy way, O Lord, I will walk in Thy truth."*

Psalm cxvi, 9. *"I will walk before the Lord in the land of the living."*

Psalm cxix, 32. *"I will run the way of Thy commandments, when Thou shalt enlarge my heart."*

THE men of the world are steeped in ignorance as regards all things belonging to God, and the spiritual life. The world lies in darkness; it loves darkness; it cannot comprehend any other conditions save that of darkness; and it will not come to the light because its deeds are evil. Nor was the condition of the world changed by the coming of our Lord; it rolls on in darkness now, just as it did when He was upon the earth; and so it will roll, until He appear again in light and glory, when the light shall overcome the darkness, and that, when it is thicker and denser than ever it was before.

It is true, we have daily displayed before us the increasing knowledge of man: but knowledge is one thing, and *true* wisdom is another, and the world by its wisdom knows not God.

With all man's increase in knowledge, it is really wonderful how little he has increased in practical wisdom. The pages of history seem to have taught him but little; the experiences of others seem to be thrown away on him; and in kingdoms, societies, and the individual circles of men's daily life, we see the same old faults and follies renewed again and again. If we strip these of the adventitious circumstances connected with them, we shall find how little variety there is in sin. If the people of the world continue thus ignorant in those things which come so easily within their comprehension, which come so frequently under their observation, and in which their own visible interests are concerned, is it any wonder that they are ignorant of the things of God, of His ways, of His laws, of His mind, of the fact that God seeth not as man seeth, that His ways are not as our ways, nor His thoughts as our thoughts?

The wonder is, not that we were ignorant, but that we were ever made wise; and the wonder is dispelled, only by our seeing that this was done by the immediate working of the Spirit.

There is no point on which the world is more dark than that of its own ignorance—we might truly say, "it is ignorant of its ignorance"—it knows enough when it learns by rote a few first principles of religion; it comforts itself that it is not atheistical because it believes that there is a God; but as to knowing His ways, laws, mind, or any such things, with them it has nothing at all to do.

The people of the world do not care for enlightenment;

they feel no pressing need for it; in all probability they
have an instinctive feeling that if enlightened they would
know a little more than they wish to know; that their
newly acquired knowledge would interfere with their old
habits and ways, and this is one reason why all spiritual
teaching which goes beneath the surface is distasteful to
the majority of men. They cannot bear to be brought
into contact with God, in anything but a general way;
the particulars of His character may not agree over well
with the particulars of their lives!

It is the fashion in the present day to talk of man's
enlightenment, and to represent human nature as upheaving under its load, as straining towards a knowledge
of truth; such is not in reality the case, and wherever
there is an effort in the mind untaught of the Spirit,
it is directed towards God as the great *moral,* and not as
the great *spiritual* Being. A man untaught of the Holy
Ghost may long to know a *moral,* he never can desire to
know a *spiritual* Being.

Dear reader, cease to wonder that spiritual truth has
made so little progress in the world, rather wonder that
it has made so much; marvel not that so few know
anything of God, rather marvel that even so many
are found, who say, "Teach me Thy way, O Lord."

The idea, then, of those whom we are accustomed to
call "good people" in the world, is that when they
recognise the existence of God, they do enough; when
they acknowledge His moral government, no more can
be required; the ideas of God's people on these points
are, however, very different. In the first place, they feel
that they can neither know nor desire God's way by
themselves. This they have been taught by the Holy

Ghost. The Spirit has made them *feel* that the natural
bent of their minds was away from God; they have even
detected their minds in the very act of loathing divine
things; they have felt themselves vile and wicked, in
their distaste to all that is spiritual; but with all this
knowledge they could make no advance, the truth being,
that they had still the carnal heart, which, no matter
what it knows or feels, is, and must be, " enmity against
God."

Dear reader, your own experience may doubtless be
appealed to on this subject. Was there not a time when
you felt no desire to know more of God, of His laws,
and ways, than you had learned in the ordinary teaching,
which you received perhaps as a child? That sufficed
for you ; and if from time to time you saw some
glimmering of light, it was just enough to make your
darkness visible, but you did not care to come to the
light, nor that that light should grow stronger, revealing
more and more of God. The retrospect of such a season
as this makes the believer see distinctly how completely
he is a debtor to grace; he says, " had I been left to
myself, I should never have sought the Lord; never
could I have had a yearning of heart for spiritual views
of God; I remember my distaste to divine things too
well, to deceive myself by supposing that I have *grown
into* spiritual desires, or that I have *struggled* into them,
or *worked myself up to them*, or have *had the smallest
part in procuring them for myself.*" Every man that is
born of the Spirit knows that he was ignorant, and that
he loved to continue ignorant, and that he felt a natural
aversion to be taken out of his ignorance, and that he
struggled against the workings and strivings of the Spirit,.

be it more or less, when that Spirit came into his heart,
to enlighten him about the ways of God.

Such, then, were the thoughts of God's people in former times; very different are they now. They say with
the Psalmist, "Teach me Thy way, O Lord." The
Spirit of God has taught them that "there is a way
which seemeth right unto a man, but the end thereof are
the ways of death;" and that there is another way of
which it is written, "in the way of righteousness is life,
and in the pathway thereof there is no death."

Now, it sometimes happens that the process of *discovery*
is going on for a considerable time, before the process of
desire is wrought out in the heart. Many a man is
having the excellence of God's ways set before him, and
conviction of their excellence forced upon his conscience,
before his heart is being wrought upon to respond to his
judgment. While a man is in this condition, he must
be very unsettled, in all probability he is very unhappy;
he is losing, if he have not already lost, the measure of
satisfaction which he experienced in the old ways, he has
not attained to that which is to be found in "the more
excellent way;" the old food is nauseous; the new he has
not power to eat. And here we see how a true work upon
the soul must be begun, continued, and ended in the
Spirit; He must not only give the power of leaving the
old way, but also that of entering on the new; and when
He is carrying on this latter part of the work, He teaches
the soul to cry in earnest, such words as those before us
now, "Teach me Thy way, O Lord, I will walk in Thy
truth."

The ideas, then, of those who are under the teaching
of the Spirit, are, in this matter of "the ways of God,"

entirely distinct from those of such as remain in ignorance of divine things; let us further enquire, *with what sentiments of mind do such persons desire to be taught?* The answer to this question will entirely depend upon what their exact state is, when the question is asked.

Some, who are under the early stages of the Spirit's work, simply desire to have an end put to their perplexity and discomfort; they do not know as yet, that no matter what they learn, they will be ever prompted, under the living influences of the Spirit, to desire to learn yet more and more; they think that they can get some one teaching, which will put them in the same road as that which is being travelled by the children of God. There is ignorance in their wish; yet would to God, that such as it is, it were shared by more. When they have attained their desire, and feel that they are indeed upon the heavenly road, they will surely pass on to a higher stage of spiritual life, and desire to know more of God's way, because they want to know more of Himself. Progression is the law of life.

Those, however, who are advanced beyond this low point, say, "Teach me Thy way, O Lord," with a higher aim. They desire *entire conformity of mind* with God, and as a consequent, *entire conformity of life.* They know that their own ways, even when most clear, and apparently unblameable, may be very far from the ways of God; and they would no more grieve Him by an ignorant, than by a wilful act. A wilful act of sin is far more wicked than an ignorant one; it will be visited with far severer punishment; he who knew his Lord's will and did it not, shall be beaten with many stripes, while he who knew it not shall be beaten with but few; but the difference in the amount of *guilt* does not set the mind of the child of God at ease. No! the Spirit-taught man has spiritual sensibilities; he feels a wound if he feel that he has broken God's law, or departed from His way, or left a portion of that way untrodden through ignorance, or if he have come short of the glory of God. Sensitiveness on these points is the consequent of the new life, and it makes men not only quick to do what they know should be done, but further, desirous of being taught wherever they are ignorant. The child of God aims at nothing short of perfect conformity to the mind of God; he wants not only that his life should be brought into exact obedience to all declared laws, but that his mind should by God's Spirit be brought into harmony with God's rules of action. He knows that God seeth and judgeth, not as man seeth and judgeth, that He has principles of action of a standard infinitely higher than any which exists in man's highest code of morality, and so he says, "Teach me Thy way."

Dear reader, what do you know of this in your own practical experience? Have you been content with *your own* way, or with the laws of morality, or with what you could pick up for yourself out of the recorded laws of God; or have you gone further, and feeling that much more could be attained to, asked God by the Spirit to teach you, "His own way?"

It will, doubtless, be one of the delights of heaven, that there the saint shall have his mind in perfect conformity with the mind of God, but need we wait for heaven to have at least a longing for this? Oh surely not; we may say, "O teach me Thy way," now while we are upon earth. This request is ever according to the mind of God; it is one, we may rest assured, that He will be pleased to grant.

It may be practically useful to enquire, for a few moments, *What it is that God's people desire to know, when they say, " Teach me Thy way."* We may make the prayer in the passage before us either generally cr particularly; no doubt the people of God do both continually.

There are seasons when we feel ourselves peculiarly drawn out in desires after holiness and conformity to God, seasons of high aspirations, and would to God that we had them oftener and that they lasted longer. At such times no special difficulty is before the mind, we are simply absorbed in the longing to be like God, and our thoughts are expressed in the Psalmist's words, "Teach me Thy way." The meaning of the prayer under such circumstances is this, "O Lord, I want to be like Thee; I want to know all that will be pleasing to Thee for me to do; I would understand Thy principles of action; I would see more plainly the boundary lines of the path which Thou markest out for Thy people; yea, I would see the lines of the path on which Thou walkest Thine own self; I have no spiritual eyesight of mine own with which to discern all this, Thy way must be revealed by Thyself, oh, teach it now to me."

We may rest well assured, that whenever we feel within us a spiritual aspiration, it is capable of being productive of a spiritual result, and moreover it is intended so to be. Spiritual aspirations come from the Holy Ghost, and He bestows no gift which is not capable of putting forth vital energy, and producing its own peculiar fruits. The aspiration of which we have now been speaking is no exception to the rule; longing for more knowledge of God, and conformity to Him in His mind and ways, will be sure to make us cry to Him to reveal Himself to us, for how can we know Him unless He manifest Himself to us? "No man knoweth the Father but the Son, and he to whom the Son will reveal Him." If, under such feelings as these, we cry, "Teach me Thy way, O Lord," we shall be sure to have an answer. God will, in all probability, reveal Himself more and more to us in His holy character; He will honour us by letting us more and more into the secrets of His mind; and when He reveals to us His mind, we shall the more easily trace His way. When we say, "Teach me Thy way," not under the pressure of any present doubt or difficulty, we may be sure that God will recognise the desire to know Himself.

But who is there that does not know, only, alas! too well, the need of being taught what is God's way when placed in difficult circumstances, and when difficult questions arise? It is very true, that if our *principles of action* are taught us of God, they will carry us through innumerable difficulties, solving hard questions, pointing out the one right way where many roads appear to meet, but there are occasions when such principles of action do not carry us through our need. The fault may be in ourselves, but at such a time we need teaching as to which is the way of God. We are now so circumstanced that we must act one way or another; we are pressed upon from without, so that we must decide, and that perhaps at once; we may fail to trace any *external* indications of the Divine will; what remains for us but the Psalmist's prayer, "Teach me Thy way?" We may confidently assert that wherever this prayer is made in an earnest and honest mind, it will be respected and answered by God; none can seek His glory in carrying out His mind and will without being helped to act for it by Him. We may be prepared for action; to do whatever is to be done, or to do the very reverse may be easy; the question is, "what, or which is to be done?" God will shew, if we say in truth "Teach me Thy way."

God has many ways of giving guidance in action, when the direction is thus left to Him. Sometimes He will close up all avenues except the right one; at times He will so strongly impress the mind, that there can be no doubt but that He is speaking to it; or He will, perhaps, give a wonderful unanimity of judgment to those who are consulted about the matter, so that looking at the question even from different points of view they still come to the same conclusion; it may be that He will not use any of these means, but will so order incidental circumstances, that they may gently and almost imperceptibly put us into such a position, that we *can* act in but one way; he who says "what or which is the way of God?" shall never be left unguided.

If we turn to Psalm xxxii, 8, we have a beautiful promise of guidance, which is well worth our consideration, from the way in which that guidance is to be given; "I will guide thee with mine eye." What is the promise here? That of guidance. How is this guidance to be given? By the eye.

By some no doubt it will be said, "Guidance! well, after all that is not much; we have sufficient sense to guide ourselves; we have the Scripture, that is guide enough; we do not want a religion that deals in specialities; we understand no such peculiarities as 'guidance with the eye.'" This is no uncommon language from the world, and very often when men shrink from saying this, they by no means shrink from acting it out. But God's people recognise in the promise of guidance a most valuable blessing. They know their position here, that they are strangers and pilgrims; they know how many roads cross, or for a time run parallel with, the way of life; they are not ignorant of the existence of myriads of evil spirits, whose sole aim is to seduce them from the narrow path, who spend every energy in trying to ruin their souls; all this they know; and they know moreover that if left to themselves they must be seduced and finally fall away. The people of God know their need of continual guidance, and that, in every day life, as well as in their purely spiritual things, in little matters as well as great. But this is not always known at once. Some of the Lord's dear people have thought that they could guide themselves; they were well-intentioned; they really wished to do what was right; they were possessed of excellent natural abilities, but with all these advantages they have gone deplorably wrong. God let them go their own way for a while, just to teach them that their way was not His, and that it was only so far as they were under guidance that they were safe.

There are some who it seems must be taught in this manner, or else they will not learn at all, no doubt such are saved, but no doubt also such are sorely bruised.

In what position are you, dear reader, standing now; have you learned your need of guidance; does this appeal to your experience; are these matters well known to you; or do you think they are things with which ordinary people have nothing at all to do? The Lord's people know well that this guidance is a matter of positive necessity. It is not more necessary that a little child of two or three years of age should be guided in the crowded street, than that they should. It does not matter how old or how wise we are, or how good our natural abilities, or how often we have guided others, and advised them well in their temporal affairs; we need guidance in everything, in every place, and every day.

Let us enquire what is our present standing? Have we entered God's family, and learned to look into the Father's face; have we been espoused to Christ, and learned to read His looks; do we feel that we cannot do what is right, unless we be specifically taught of God?

The phrase "doing what is right," must not now be taken in the low sense which is generally given to it by many in the world. They mean by it, coming to church, and giving subscriptions (generally the stereotyped "guinea") to charities, and having family prayers, and paying their debts, and keeping good company, and being in the ordinary acceptation of the words "good living people." But God's guidance leads a man far beyond all these. All these can be done without any guidance from heaven at all. What is now meant by "doing right," is acting consistently as a member of the family of God. When we are placed in delicate and difficult circumstances, when all ordinary landmarks are removed, when our usual counsellors are silent, when even outward providential circumstances are withheld, are there such communications passing between God's mind and ours, that we can feel that we are under His guidance? Can we hear God speaking to us when there is not a sound? can we see Him when there is not a sign? can we read where nothing is written? have we the intelligence of love?

Say, in what does the perfection of home relationship consist? is it in the fact that meals are spread at proper hours, that cleanliness is the characteristic of the house, that there is no open jarring or quarrelling, no gross violation of well known rules, and such like things? All these have their value in the happiness of home; but the perfection of happiness requires something more. The gross, or to use a gentler term, the unrefined mind will be content with such things as are catalogued above; but there are other minds too highly polished, too finely strung for this; their estimate of what the happiness of home should be, is pitched too high to be reached by what might be called the common decencies and civilities of life.

No! the perfection of home relationship consists in the intuitive understanding of each other's heart, in the mutual possession of that secret, which makes one look stand for many words, yea, for feelings, which the great Creator never intended to be expressed in words at all; such an instrumentality as this, stands in the place of a thousand rules; and gives guidance, and direction, in countless emergencies, and difficulties, and apparently little things. This is what makes brethren dwell together in unity; what anoints the wheels of life, so that they never creak and jar; no, not when they have to bear the heaviest load, or have to go over the roughest road; this is like the ointment which flowed down upon the skirts of the High Priest's robe; who can tell what springs up beneath it, for it is as the dew of Hermon, and as the dew that descended upon the mountains of Zion? And now, come back from all earthly homes, to the matter which they have been illustrating, and remember that as in them, so also in the family of God, much is required, for which there is no rule, no guide, but the intuition of love; no remembrancer but (not the declaration, but) the expression of God's mind; and is it not an inestimable blessing to all who wish to be one with God, that they have given to them the promise which we have been considering now? Oh, that we so continually fixed our minds upon our Father's face, that we so daily gazed upon His looks, and that we were filled, yea, so fully, with His love, that we needed neither bit nor bridle, neither goad nor rod, nothing but a look, nothing but the fulfilment of the promise, "I will guide thee with mine eye."

May God give to all who read these lines, that delicate organization of heart, by which they shall have intuitive understanding of His look, and mind, and will. Oh may He separate us more and more from the grossness of mind, which requires the bridle or the goad; oh may He refine us by the mysterious processes of His unearthly love; then, in the midst of all perplexity, we shall not be confused; in the midst of all failure we shall not be cast down; but calmly and peacefully shall we pass onward to our rest, as safe in the darkness as in the light, by the precipice as in the plain, in the crowd as when alone; each child of God a traveller through a strange land to his own bright home, wayfaring, it is true, yet wayfaring in the security of a promise from above, hearing at every hard pass of his onward path, the promise we have here, a promise from the eternal God Himself, "I will guide thee with mine eye."

Thus, then, the people of the Lord desire teaching, and that from Him, preparatory to action. They want to know God's will, in order that they may do it, "Teach me Thy way, O Lord, I will walk in Thy truth."

Honesty of mind is a characteristic of every man really born again of the Holy Ghost. The Spirit-taught man is led to say, without any reserve or limitation, "I will walk." There are many who are prepared to go so far, but no further. They will carry out God's teaching, provided it does not make too great demands upon them. Perhaps such persons are not themselves conscious of the state of mind in which they are. They think that they are prepared for everything; and so they are "for everything they know;" but what if God set before them something much harder than anything that had ever entered even into their imagination? We have such a case as this brought before us in Matthew xix, 16. A young man comes to Jesus and says, "Good Master, what good thing shall I do that I may have eternal life?" Jesus puts forth the moral law, as a simple answer to his question, for no doubt if he kept that, without a single flaw, he could be saved by it; "if he did," but who ever did? who ever could, save Jesus? and then proceeding yet further, He says to Him, "if thou wilt be perfect, go and sell that thou hast, and give to the poor, and thou shalt have treasure in heaven, and come and follow Me. But when the young man heard that saying, he went away sorrowful; for he had great possessions."

Here was indeed a hard trial, an opening up of a path far more difficult than had ever entered into this young man's mind; and the hard trial discovers limitations, and reservations, which otherwise might never have been perceived. Would a like trial discover like imperfections in ourselves?

If indeed we know ourselves, we shall almost tremble at this thought; we shall feel the awful solemnity of saying such words as these, "Teach me Thy way, O Lord, I will walk in Thy truth;" and yet we shall not dare to hold back from making them our own.

How can we be true-hearted, and yet hold back! What then shall we do? Let us prepare to pray the Psalmist's words, from the bottom of our hearts; let us also prepare to make his determination, in deep reality of soul. True! there is something awful in this; but if we know our weakness, and simply rely upon Divine strength, we shall be carried through; God Himself will undergird us for the storm-tossed waters, through which we may be called upon to sail; by Him shall we be shod for the rough road on which we may be called upon to tread; and we shall be enabled to carry out, as well as make the determination of the Psalmist, which is before us now. Who can tell whither such a walk will lead him upon earth; whither, when he has done with earth for ever?

CHAPTER XVII.

THE "I WILL" OF HEARTINESS IN ACTION.

Psalm cxix, 32. "*I will run the way of Thy commandments when Thou shalt enlarge my heart.*"

THE great Physician knows at once where to look for the cause, when He sees anything amiss in the outward life of His people. He well knows that all spiritual disease is heart disease, and it is heart remedies that He must apply. At one time, our Physician sees symptoms which are violent in their nature; at another, He sees symptoms of languor and debility; but He knows that both come from the heart; and so, it is upon the heart that He operates, when He is about to perform a cure.

The strong action of the heart in all holy things comes from the blessed operation of the Spirit upon it; then only can we *run* the way of God's commandments, when He has enlarged our heart.

HEARTINESS IN ACTION is the subject to which the reader's attention is here directed, and it is one of considerable importance.

There are many believers, who for want of enlargement

of heart are occupying a poor position in the church of
God. They are trusting to Jesus for life eternal, and
He will doubtless not disappoint them; He will be true
to His word, that "he that believeth shall be saved;"
but they are still, alas! to a deplorable degree, shut up
in self; they have contracted hearts; still do they take
narrow views of God's claims, and their own privileges,
and the position in which they are set in the world; and
however much they might be said to stand, or sit, or
walk in the way of God's commandments, they cannot
be said to "run" in it. Running is a strong and healthy
action of the body; it requires energy, it is an exercise
that needs a sound heart; none can run in the way of
God's commandments, except in strength and vigour
imparted by Him. The running Christians are comparatively few; walking and sitting Christians are
comparatively common; but the running Christian is so
uncommon, as often to be thought almost mad.

Let us, for the sake of order, classify our observations
on this subject, under the following heads:—

    I. *What Heartiness is.*

   II. *What Heartiness does.*

  III. *Whence Heartiness comes.*

The Heartiness spoken of here under the term "enlargement of the heart," is cheerfulness in doing God's
will—love for that will—a drawing out of the affections
towards it—an interest in it; all this it is, and a great
deal more, which it is not easy to describe or define.

A good deal may be done by a man in the way of
keeping God's commandments, especially His prohibitive
ones, without his possessing anything worthy of being
called enlargement of heart. A man need not have an

enlarged heart, to enable him to keep his hands from
picking and stealing, and his tongue from evil speaking,
lying, and slandering; nor to enable him to perform any
specified acts of duty which come before him with all
the force and authority of law; his affections have
nothing to say to this obedience; he obeys because he
thinks he ought to obey; he might be fitly described, as
keeping within the bound of a commandment, (so far as
man can do) but not as running in the way of it.

We are very ready to admit that true religion has to
do with man's judgment, and his conscience; would that
it were readily and practically admitted, that it has to
do with the affections also. Alas! how much coldness
may there be in a man, whose judgment is sound upon
the question of the excellence of God's commandments.
Such an one may approve them, may see that they are
pre-eminently suited for the governance of man, may
believe that he will best consult his happiness by
observing them, and that he can never violate them
without entailing upon himself both misery and loss; he
may be a philosopher in holy things, and yet have no
heartiness for God's commandments, have no insight
into their principles, which have their foundation in the
very nature of God. Our judgment may be well
informed, and we may act upon it in all we do, and all
we abstain from, as regards the commandments of God;
but let us be assured, that our judgment never can make
us *hearty*, in running the way of His commandments.

Nor can our conscience. Conscience can make us do
things because we ought to do them, and leave them
undone because we ought not to do them, but it cannot
make us *hearty* in our obedience. It is highly possible

to perform a duty, and in a certain sense to do it well, and yet not to have our heart in it at all.

Where there is enlargement of the heart by God, there is an outgoing beyond all the limits which fallen selfishness assigns. The heart contracted at the fall; it shrank when sin entered into it; it became unequal to containing great and generous thoughts; it became a bondaged heart. True! the responsibilities of duty could not be escaped, nor could the directions of conscience, but the affections are voluntary, and the fallen heart drew in its affections from God; it felt that it had the power of withholding them from Him and His commandments, and it rejoiced to shew its enmity, in withholding its sympathy, where it could not withhold its obedience. There is sin, there is the development of fallen nature at the root of all want of Heartiness in action for God. What an aspect, then, will many of the performances of duty wear in the day when all things are revealed in their real light; how will it be found, that man had withheld from them all he had to give, *i. e.*, his heart. There is no thank to him for not withholding the assent of his conscience, and the opinion of his judgment; what he had to give is wanting; it was the heart that Christ wanted, what good are those works in which it is not found?

Now, as we have already said, where the heart is operated on by the Spirit, and all its natural evil overruled, it has outgoings which are entirely beyond the limits that fallen selfishness assigns. Love is inwrought with it, the union of sentiment, the identity of interest which love inspires, pervade it, in all belonging to God, for it has received these from God; the heart becomes unbondaged from mere rules, or perhaps to speak more correctly, it rises above them, and it feels—not merely it *knows*, but it *feels*—so much of the beauty of God's commandments, that it delights to *run* in them; it loves to be hearty in them; its interests, its affections are in them.

It is very possible that both writer and reader feel ashamed, and ready to judge themselves when they look at much past, or perhaps present service in this light. How often have we done just as much as we felt ourselves obliged to do, and no more; how often have we done a good deal, and yet had no heart *for* doing, or *in* doing it? Much of our work has been a labour to us, and some of God's commandments have been grievous to us, for want of this heartiness which would have made all joyous and pleasant; let us seek, dear reader to have our hearts opened out to God—to have them enlarged to take in great thoughts about Him, and His work—to have them ennobled to make great plans and efforts for Him—to have them capable of energy, even the energy of love, in all they do for Him. It makes all the difference whether we run, or walk, in the way of God's commandments. The word "walk," is used to denote the habitual obedience of divine life; but the word to "run," signifies its energy : "I will run the way of Thy commandments, when Thou shalt enlarge my heart."

Let us now see what Heartiness does.

Heartiness in action has *a good effect on others*. Even in ordinary society we see how much effect one gloomy, unwilling, or desponding nature can have on others. Even without any active opposition, such an one is able to damp the energies, or enjoyments, of those around; and on the other hand, we see how one who is hearty, and joyous, and goes about whatever is to be done with a will, is able to infuse spirit into those, who otherwise would have dragged heavily through their work. The presence of a hearty Christian seems to infuse oxygen into the very atmosphere around; there is something effervescing, and sparkling in such an one, which drives away surrounding heaviness and gloom; and often those, with whom such an one comes into contact, find out for the first time, from what another is doing, what they themselves can do.

Try, dear reader, to be a living energy, and not a dead weight in the spiritual world; to be a sunbeam, and not a murky cloud; to be an electric spark kindling fire in others' hearts, and not a wet blanket putting out and smothering the smoking flax. There are such things as sympathy and influence in man's contact with his fellow man; what influence have we exercised; what sympathy have we drawn others into with ourselves; what have we been to them in the congregation of which we are mutual members—in the family—in any enterprize in which they and we were associated—in fact, in all the relationships and events of life, in which we came in contact with each other? We have, perhaps, often been hinderers and impeders, and our want of heartiness has damped the ardour of others. On the other hand, if we have been really alive in the cause of the Lord, have we not helped on others; have not they commenced to act when they saw us in action; have not they found out, that they also could do good, and that it was pleasant to do good, when they were led on to try, by the kindling effect of our life in action for God?

This Heartiness in Action *embraces a large circle.* The circle in which a man hearty for God moves, and acts, is one ever widening and increasing; a man that runs in the way of God's commandments does not keep running round and round, always within the same circumference, but in one that increases continually. It may be that when the spiritual power was small, the sphere of action was small also, but as the spiritual power increases, so does the sphere also. This must be so; for Heartiness in the divine life is incompressible, and it must find a vent, it must find a sphere in which to act. This is true even under the most untoward circumstances. Take the case of a Christian, strong and vigorous in spiritual life, but reduced so low in the body that he cannot leave his bed; his means are small, his contact with his fellow creatures is limited; he surely has no circle in which his heart can throb with living energies, each pulsation being followed by some positive result;— so we should think—but let us remember that the body does not chain the mind, and that that sick man's interests and prayers may pervade a circle which embraces every church of God, and every believer upon earth! What wider sphere of action can any man desire than this? And this is open to the bed-ridden and the maimed; by prayer the lever can be moved which moves the world, and the sick man can pray, and if he be hearty in the action, he can move, and act, in a circle too large for any bodily energy to pervade. It is true, we have taken an extreme case: but what, if one thus circumstanced be proved to have exercised more real spiritual power than many of us whose every faculty is perfect, whose bodily energies are unimpaired?

Let the reader search himself as to how large a circle he is pervading—as to whether he be pervading any circle at all. The merchant who is hearty in his desires for wealth, and in his action in the mercantile world, pervades a large circle; he has to do with persons and things almost at the ends of the earth; his energies have driven him out into this great circumference of action; and whither, dear reader, have your energies, your heartiness, driven you forth? Have you had living impulses, which forbade you to be centred, to tarry in self?

Remember that where the heart is strong in its action, *it drives the blood to the extremities*. If the blood be not well driven into the limbs, they are weak in action, and unless it be driven to the extremities, the very parts which have to act grow cold. Our most distant point in action, our most remote means of operating therein, should be under the influence of the strong vitality of the heart. Ours is a centralized system, and the centre is the heart; and one reason why interest so often flags in the outer verge of our circle, and why our action there is weak, is, because we have not strength to drive out our energies and sympathies beyond those inner circles which are closest to our heart. For example, here is a man who can act within the circle of his own family, but he is not hearty enough to fill a circle which would embrace in its action for God, neighbours and friends; here is another who can not only act in his own family, but also amongst neighbours and friends, but he cannot go forth to those who are without, and who are unconnected with him by any visible responsibility or ties. Nothing but an enlargement of the heart by the Holy Spirit will send him forth; and make him to understand the meaning of the apostle's words, "Look not every man on his own things, but every man also on the things of others;" and make him copy the example of the One of whom it is written, "But God commendeth His love toward us, in that while we were yet sinners Christ died for us."

Let us also notice that this Heartiness *honours our profession*. We cannot but perceive how much the religion of Christ suffers in the world from the want of Heartiness in action shewn by its professors. One half the zeal shewn by the heathen in their false religion, would soon startle the world, if it were shewn in the disciples of Christ; but it is not shewn; and it is impossible to read of the liberality of the heathen to their false gods, and their self-sacrifices, and pains, without asking "Where amongst any of the churches shall we find in the mass of their members, a heartiness of action similar to this?"* One

* The Hindoos when gathering in their harvest, before it is removed from the threshing floor, take out the portion for their god. However poor, or however small their crops may be, their god's portion is given first.

The Rev. J. J. Weitbrecht says, in his "Protestant Missions in Bengal, illustrated," "My readers will be surprised to hear how much wealthy natives spend upon their idols. I once visited the Rajah of Burdwan, and found him sitting in his treasury. Fifty bags of money, containing 1000 rupees (£100) in each, were placed before him. 'What,' said I, 'are you doing with all this money?' He replied, 'it is for my gods.' 'How do you mean that?' I rejoined. 'One part is sent to Benares, where I have two fine temples on the river side, and many priests who pray for me; another part goes to Juggernaut; and a third to Gaya.' And thus one native is spending £25,000 annually from his princely income upon idle Brahmins."

would think, that "rest," not "action," was the rule and privilege of a Christian's life; but it is neither the one nor the other; his privilege is rest for his soul; his rule must be action for the energies—rest in justification in Christ's blood—action in sanctification of the Holy Ghost. The religion of Christ suffers more harm from the inaction of its professors, than from the action of its enemies; and be it observed, it suffers not only from their inaction, from their not doing anything, but also very often from the way in which they do that to which they put their hand. The half-heartedness of God's people in action goes far towards persuading the people of the world that their religion is no better than a form; they are keen observers, not only of what we do, but of how we do it, and they will often judge of Christ's religion, not by its abstract principles, but by the way in which we carry them out.

Let us take the one instance of *Giving;* "Giving" is one form of action for God; and what is the aspect which in this particular many of the Lord's people present to the world? Where is their heartiness in it? Can they say that their profession, or their position in the church of God is honoured by the way in which they do it? In how many instances is this only the giving of form, and not the giving of decided action. "Honour the Lord with thy substance, and with the first-fruits of all thine increase," is surely as much binding upon the Christian as the Jew; let us be assured, that a great sympathetic nerve runs between the heart and the pocket; a large heart and a large hand befit each other. Why should £1 1s. be the stereotyped form of expressing the state of a Christian's heart?

There are some, however, who while reading this, may

sigh, and say, "Such a sum would be beyond my reach to give." Let such remember that there are many who are steeped in poverty, who yet are rich indeed in action, according to their opportunity, and who are accepted "according to what they have, and not according to what they have not." How much do we learn from the case of the poor widow, and her two mites! we may be permitted to digress for a moment to consider it.

Look at the position of this widow in life, and in the temple; neither in life, nor in the temple, was she anybody in the world's estimation. She was so very poor, that when she threw in the two mites, our Lord describes her as having cast in "all that she had, even all her living." No doubt she fared hard in worldly sustenance; her lodging was the meanest, her food the scantiest, her raiment the coarsest, and she had all the accompaniments of poverty, bitterness, and reproach, and neglect, and want. And what she was in the outer world, that also, as far as man was concerned, was she in the temple of the Lord. We can imagine, how the servants of the man clothed with purple and fine linen thrust her out of the way; how the Pharisee, with his broad fringed garment, swept by her in all the pomp and circumstance of religious state; how the wives and daughters of the rich gathered in their ample robes, lest they should be soiled by contact with such beggarly attire; no one thought it worth his while to notice her, unless it were to despise; and yet she, and she alone, receives the commendation of the Lord.

Now what is this widow, as she appears in this scene, but a very type or picture of the general condition of the true church of God? That church is for the most

part hidden, as regards the attainment in the world's eye
of any position, either in temporal or spiritual things.
There are but few of the Lord's true people who make
much figure in the world: and the general opinion
entertained of them is very mean and low. There is
nothing more common than to find men dwelling upon
the miserable poverty of the saints, and thinking them
absolutely poor. But poor as they doubtless are, they
are the possessors of title deeds of exceeding wealth.
This poor widow had no doubt engraven upon her heart
the choice promises of God, which made over heavenly
estates to such as made over their hearts to Him. And
I would that the children of the kingdom dwelt more
upon the actual possessions which are to be theirs!
They are too dim and shadowy, too misty and undefined
in their hopes; they are to have what is substantial,
what is actual, and real, and in their depths of earthly
poverty they ought to think of this. A realization of
the substantial nature of this future property will make
them feel the value of the position which now they
hold, as children of God—the position, to which this property is attached; though all that appear on earth be the
two mites, in heaven there is a possession for each saint,
which the offer of even the universe itself could not buy.
In spiritual things also the condition of the saint is
hidden from the eyes of men. It appears that none save
Christ valued this poor widow's offering and piety at
their real worth, because Jesus alone could search her
heart and try her reins. To outward eye, the Scribes
and Pharisees were far more holy than she; but to that
eye which seeth not as man seeth, she was immeasurably
above them all. We need not be surprised at this, and

the children of God will do well to remember, that the
world will not always let them hold that position, even
though it be in spiritual things, which they have a right
to claim. He, who in humble earnestness, belongs to
God, must make up his mind to be very often despised,
even by apparently religious people, and be content to
hold his rank in the estimation of Christ alone. No
doubt to many who are truly the children of God, this
seems very hard; if they have no reputation in the
world, the least they may have is some position in the
church; but like the widow in the text, they are known
to but One, and that One is God, who approves their
deeds, and treasures up their names against His own
great day.

Let us contemplate this widow as *under the observation
of God.* We are told that in the crowd of worshippers,
there were rich men who offered much, but not one word
of commendation do we find vouchsafed to them. And
this was not because their good deeds were done without
having been seen by God—far from it; He noted the
amount of every gift, and in His own mind compared it
with the circumstances under which He knew each one
to be placed; and forming His estimate upon these
grounds, the widow alone was praised. The gold and
silver of the rich had no attractions for God; His
admiration was riveted on the widow's mites alone, for
they only came from a heart, which poured itself out
unreservedly to God. And let this teach us, how that
when we think we are unobserved, we are nevertheless
doing all under the immediate eye of God. Oh! we
forget too much, that we are the servants of One, who is
ever looking at us, and ever taking note of what we

think, and speak, and do. Content to be amongst the crowd, we think ourselves then best off, when no special notice is taken of us at all; but it ought not to be thus; it should be the greatest sorrow and disappointment, if God did not vouchsafe to fix a special look on us; we should be able to say " Look, Lord, and see if this be done according to Thy will." In all our givings, how-ever the amount be hidden from the eyes of man, we should so perform these acts that we do not desire them to be hidden from the eyes of God; we should be able to open our hand before the One, to whom we are about to offer, and say, " Look, Lord, this is for Thee—this is not the mere cold offering of duty, but it is that of love; Thou knowest my circumstances, and knowing them, with this I trust that Thou wilt be pleased." The reason why we do so little, and that so badly, is, that we are ever sinking our individuality in the crowd; ever for-getting, that we stand each one as it were alone before his God. So long as we go on thus, we shall never do well; and even though, if we be rich, we cast in much, we shall never attain to the testimony which was the portion of the widow.

And if it be the shame and loss of many, that Christ looks upon them as they perhaps cast in much, and bestows no word of commendation upon their gift, is it not the blessing and the gain of others, that His eye is upon them, though they can give but very little; and that little wins from him words of approval and of praise? He who is like this poor widow will delight in the thought, that his Lord knows all; he will say, "Thou knowest all things, Thou knowest that I love Thee;" " Thou knowest that this is the offering of love;"

and the heart shall have its own sensations of joy, as it feels that God has seen, and that God has been well pleased.

Thus Jesus notes the earnestness of all earnest-minded men, and shall we believe, that with that notice, the whole matter ends? Not so! He passes an opinion upon the conduct of such as have given evidence that their hearts are His, and that opinion is recorded in the books of life and death; "She hath done what she could," found an entrance not only into the gospels of the Evangelists, but also into the judgment books of heaven. Christ's observations are all chronicled against the day of trial, when He, as the One to whom all judgment is committed, shall reward every man "according to his deeds." And let this encourage such of you, as are earnestly endeavouring to do all you can for Him. No effort is lost: if there be *two* mites in your hand God knows it; perhaps He says, "Why are there *two* mites there? dull formality required but one; surely inasmuch as there are *two*, this second comes from love." And in the great day, when the true hearted people of the Lord shall be set in glory on His right hand, how blessed will it be, to find ourselves there, as men long since known and observed by Him; to feel with humble pleasure that we are no strangers to Him, for that he often watched our deeds of love; to think that there are hard solid facts which are valuable as proofs; and after all do not facts speak an hundred fold more than words? Deeds of love are good for nothing in the way of procuring salvation, but they are very precious as tokens that love was true. Act then, on all occasions as though you wished Jesus to look on. Remember whenever you approach the treasury, that Jesus is in the temple, and opposite you, as you make your offering to the Lord; so give, so do, as that you shall be able to say, "I am thankful that Jesus saw!"

We are furnished in Holy Scripture with many examples of "Heartiness in Action." Jesus is the great example in whom we find all excellence, and He was hearty indeed, in running the way of God's commandments; His ear was opened, His heart was enlarged for service. What were His words? "I delight to do Thy will, O my God; yea, Thy law is within my heart." * "Not my will but thine be done." † See how hearty Jesus was in His journeyings, in His preachings, in all words and errands of mercy; how earnest were His exhortations, how ready were His deeds. He toiled from morning to night; and oftentimes He prayed from night to morning; and when His short life was ended, so many were His wondrous deeds, that the Apostle John winds up his gospel with saying, "And there are also many other things which Jesus did, the which, if they should be written every one, I suppose that even the world itself could not contain the books that should be written." ‡

Such was Jesus on earth; and it is a blessed thought for His people that such also is He now in the presence of God. He carried all His excellencies with Him, when He ascended up on high; and amongst them His "Heartiness in Action." Yes! it is with an earnest heart that He makes intercession for His people, that He loves them, that He interferes and acts for them; in a word, that He does everything for them; He is full of life on behalf of His people; oftentimes when we are

* Psalm xl, 8.   † Luke xxii, 42.   ‡ John xxi, 25.

only languid for ourselves, He is hearty for us, and we receive according to His earnestness, and not according to our own.   This is a blessed truth, and as we realize it, may it be given to us more unreservedly and devotedly to give our heart to Him, whose service is so hearty for us!

Or, let us take Paul, the great Apostle of the Gentiles: he was hearty for his Lord; he was "in labours more abundant, in stripes above measure, in prisons more frequent, in deaths oft;" of the Jews five times received he forty stripes save one; thrice was he beaten with rods, once was he stoned; thrice he suffered shipwreck; a night and a day he was in the deep; he was in journeyings often, in perils of waters, in perils of robbers, in perils by his own countrymen, in perils by the heathen, in perils in the city, in perils in the wilderness, in perils in the sea, in perils among false brethren; in weariness and painfulness, in watchings often, in hunger and thirst, in fastings often, in cold and nakedness; in addition to which there came upon him daily the care of all the churches.*   He counted not his life dear unto himself so that he might finish his course with joy, and the ministry which he had received of the Lord Jesus.†   He gloried in tribulations.‡   "What mean ye," said he to the disciples at Cæsarea, "to weep and to break mine heart? for I am ready not to be bound only, but also to die at Jerusalem for the name of the Lord Jesus." § Paul was a living example of the precepts which he gave, "fervent in Spirit, serving the Lord." || "And whatsoever ye do, do it *heartily*, as to the Lord, and not unto men." ¶   And let us remember that Paul was not

---

* 2 Cor. xi, 28.   † Acts xx, 24.   ‡ Romans v, 3.
§ Acts xxi, 13. || Romans xii, 11.   ¶ Col. iii, 23.

called to "Heartiness in Action" one whit more than we are! The same Christ who appeared to him, and gave him life in the midst of his career of death, appears to our souls, and gives us life also; the same grace is vouchsafed to both, if so be that we have received the Lord at all. Instead then of thinking, that because Paul was an Apostle, more was required from him, than there is from us; or that he was possessed of any extraordinary energies, which are above the ordinary lot of man, let us see in him a man with an enlarged heart, and in his life, with all its labours, nothing more than what we ourselves are called upon to exhibit *in our own spheres*—"Enlargement of heart in action." Our sphere may not be that of an Apostle, but our heart may be like his; and we may fill our sphere as acceptably as he filled his; it is not at *spheres*, but at *hearts* that God will look; and however small the circle in which we move, if only we be hearty in it for the Lord, ours also may be the Apostle's words in our departing hour; "I have fought a good fight, I have finished my course, I have kept the faith; henceforth there is laid up for me a crown of righteousness, which the Lord, the righteous judge, shall give me at that day; and not to me only. but unto all them also that love His appearing." *

See how large-hearted the Macedonians were, "their deep poverty abounded unto the riches of their liberality; for to their power (says the Apostle) I bear record, yea and beyond their power, they were willing of themselves." †
Look at the Israelites, how they offered for their tabernacle; "they came, every one whose heart stirred him up, and every one whom his spirit made willing, and

* 2 Tim. iv, 7, 8. † 2 Cor. viii, 2, 3.

they brought the Lord's offering to the work of the
tabernacle of the congregation, and for all His service,
and for the holy garments; and they came, both men
and women, as many as were willing-hearted, and brought
bracelets, and earrings, and rings, and tablets, all jewels
of gold, and every man that offered, offered an offering
of gold unto the Lord." * With them it was not how
little but how much they could give. "And they
brought yet unto him (Moses) free offerings every
morning."† At last " the wise men that wrought all the
work of the sanctuary, came every man from his work
which they made, and they spake unto Moses saying,
'The people bring much more than enough for the
service of the work, which the Lord commanded to
make.' And Moses gave commandment, and they caused
it to be proclaimed throughout the camp, saying, 'let
neither man nor woman make any more work for the
offering of the sanctuary.' So the people were restrained
from bringing. For the stuff they had, was sufficient for
all the work to make it, and too much." ‡ David was
large-hearted, and would have built a house for God;
and when he was directed not to carry out his intention,
because he had shed blood, he shewed that he had
enlargement of heart toward God, by the preparation
which he made for the accomplishment of his design by
his son; he prepared iron in abundance, and brass in
abundance without weight; also in his trouble he
prepared for the house of the Lord an hundred thousand
talents of gold, and a thousand thousand talents of
silver.§ The heartiness of the king made him do what

* Exodus xxxv, 21, 22.   † Exodus xxxvi, 3.   ‡ Verses 4—8.
§ 1 Chronicles xxii.

he could, as he could not do what he would. Let us look on a little farther, and we find this heartiness again in Nehemiah, and those who were joined with him in the work of the Lord. Each man's work is chronicled in chapter iii. "So built we the wall:" (said he in chapter iv.) "And all the wall was joined together unto the half thereof, *for the people had a mind to work!*" How active, how energetic, they were, we see from chapter iii, 12. "And next unto him repaired Shallum the son of Halohesh, the ruler of the half part of Jerusalem, he *and his daughters.*" Here was Heartiness in action; the heart constrained the hand, and rough as the work was for women to engage in, it was willingly undertaken. Of you, dear reader, may it be also said, that you had "a mind to work." As every man is to give as he is disposed in his heart, not grudgingly or of necessity, for God loveth a cheerful giver, so is every man to work as he is disposed in his heart, for God loveth a hearty worker. The work of each of the restorers of Jerusalem is chronicled in Nehemiah; there is another book in which is chronicled the work of each of us—our work—its motives—its intensity—not only the fact that we worked, but also why, and how!

The readiness of the daughters of Shallum is recorded, so also is the backwardness of the nobles of the Tekoites; "but their nobles put not their necks to the work of their Lord." No position excuses man from work for the Lord in the sphere appointed to him; a record of shortcoming as well as of diligence is kept; many a feeble woman will hereafter be honoured for her rough work for God, when the nobles are reprobated, who put not their necks to the work of their Lord.

Let us now turn to the very important and practical enquiry, *Whence does this Heartiness come ?* Like every other good and perfect gift, it comes from the Father of lights, "with whom is no variableness nor shadow of turning ;" it is wrought in us by the Holy Ghost. The Lord's people are "made willing in the day of His power."* " It is God that worketh in them, both to will and to do of His good pleasure."† The Spirit of God in man's sanctification comes in contact, not only with the heart as warped, but with it as contracted also ; He finds in it not only a bias towards what is evil, but an inaptitude to what is good ; its only dealings with holy things will be in the way of duty ; it knows nothing of the law of love. The Spirit of God creates love, and in so doing opens out the heart, and quickens its pulsations, and puts its actions under a new and impulsive law ; the heart will do, under the impulsive law of love, what it could not be induced to do by any other power. If you, then, feel the backwardness of your natural heart ; if you have tried, and tried in vain, to warm it up to energy, and power, and what we commonly call "heartiness," in the cause of God ; and if you have found yourself, however active in duty, still wanting in heart, I beseech you to apply to the Holy Spirit to supply your need. In vain will you turn to any other source ; in vain will you devise methods or expedients of your own ; the living principle will be wanting, and therewith life itself. Heartiness must be inwrought, or we shall never be able to abound in the work of the Lord ; we may commence enterprises with zeal, fascinated by their novelty ; or we may continue in them, for in various ways they may

* Psa. cx, 3.   † Phil. ii, 13.

suit our natural taste; but heartiness, embracing all service, and continuing *in* all service, must be the gift of the Holy Ghost

In working within us this spiritual power, the Spirit may have to contend with our natural temperament; to overcome sloth, timidity, indifference, and much of a similar kind; but if we yield ourselves to Him, He will not allow us to be like the Laodicean church, "neither cold nor hot," and fit only to be "spued out of the mouth."— Rev. iii, 16. He will prevent our hiding our talent in a napkin; He will make us the good ground bringing forth fruit abundantly, an hundred and a thousand fold; and to us shall be spoken those most blessed words: "Well done, good and faithful servant, enter thou into the joy of thy Lord!" The utmost heartiness in service is compatible with the closest walk with God; and we need not fear our summons coming, when engaged in action for Him. A lady once asked Mr. Wesley, "Supposing that you *knew* you were to die at twelve o'clock to-morrow night, how would you spend the intervening time?" "How, madam,?" he replied, "why just as I intend to spend it now. I should preach this evening at Gloucester, and again at five to-morrow morning; after that I should ride to Tewkesbury, preach in the afternoon, and meet the societies in the evening. I should then repair to friend Martin's house, who expects to entertain me, converse and pray with the family, as usual, retire to my room at ten o'clock, commend myself to my heavenly Father, lie down to rest, and wake up in glory." Blessed exchange! the heartiness of service on earth, for the heartiness of service in glory!

CHAPTER XVIII.

THE "I WILL" OF DETERMINATION IN ACTION.

Psalm lxxi, 16. *"I will go in the strength of the Lord God."*

HEARTINESS will be sure to bring out the weakness of the *individual;* the enlarged heart will not only propose, but will actually make us embark in enterprises for God, which will severely try the other parts of our spiritual constitution. We may have the heart for such and such a thing, whether it be a sacrifice or an action; but have we the faith, the energy, the perseverance, and such other Christian graces as are necessary to carry us through? Better for us to be hearty, though we be weak, than to be strong, and indifferent withal.

When a man's heart is enlarged for action for God, to run the way of His commandments, his heartiness will be tried. There will come temptations to desist; Satan will endeavour to neutralize that heartiness by every means in his power. He will represent to us our own weakness, and the enemy's strength, just as he did to David, by the mouth of Saul, when he was about to attack the Philistine, "Thou art not able to go against this Philistine to fight with him, for thou are but a

youth, and he a man of war from his youth."* Peter was
hearty in his desire to go to Christ, but when the waves
were looked at, they brought out the smallness of his
faith. He was hearty also when he said, "though all
men shall be offended because of Thee, yet will I never
be offended; though I should die with Thee, yet will I
not deny Thee."† In the first of these cases there was
no failure, in the second there was; although, in all
probability, the heartiness in Peter's case was as much
as that in David's, if not more. Let us seek for grace
to have our powers equal to our heartiness for action,
then we shall be able to produce great results. And
further, let us never draw back because we discover
weakness in ourselves; our duty is to go forward "in
the name of the Lord;" the remedy for our weakness is
to be found in the verse which is under consideration
now, "I will go in the strength of the Lord God."

We find in Holy Scripture many examples of DETER-
MINATION IN ACTION. Moses was pre-eminently called to
action for God, and the position in which he was placed
required great determination; he had to face a monarch
exasperated by repeated chastisements which had nearly
ruined his kingdom; he had, humanly speaking, every
reason to be willing to make a compromise, and draw
off his people from the land of Egypt; but he was
determined in the work of the Lord, and would hear of
nothing of the kind. "And Pharaoh called unto Moses,
and said, Go ye and serve the Lord, only let your flocks
and your herds be stayed, let your little ones also go
with you;" but Moses would not yield, even in the
matter of the meanest animal belonging to an Israelite,

* 1 Sam. xvii, 33. † Matt. xxvi, 33, 35.

"Our cattle also shall go with us, there shall not an hoof be left behind."* David, as we have already seen, was called to decided action for God, and he did not flinch, even though his brethren taunted him, and Saul would have discouraged him, and Goliath did all he could to affright him.† Elijah was pre-eminently called to action for God, and although he knew that Ahab sought his life, he sends a message to him by Obadiah, "Behold Elijah is here. As the Lord of hosts liveth, before whom I stand, I will surely shew myself unto him to-day!"‡ His attitude on Carmel was one of determined action. "And Elijah said unto them, take the prophets of Baal, let not one of them escape; and they took them; and Elijah brought them down to the brook Kishon and slew them there." It was necessary for Shadrach, Meshach, and Abednego, to take up a decided position, and they did so; they said, "O Nebuchadnezzar, we are not careful to answer thee in this matter; if it be so, our God whom we serve is able to deliver us from the burning fiery furnace, and He will deliver us out of thine hand, O king. But if not, be it known unto thee, O king, that we will not serve thy gods, nor worship the golden image which thou has set up."§ "When Daniel knew that the writing was signed, he went into his house, and his window being open in his chamber toward Jerusalem, he kneeled upon his knees three times a day, and gave thanks before his God, as he did aforetime."‖ Nehemiah said, "Should such a man as I flee? and who is there that, being as I am, would go into the temple to save his life? I will not go

---

* Exodus x, 24, 26.   † 1 Sam. xvii.   ‡ 1 Kings xviii.
§ Daniel iii, 16—18.   ‖ Chap. vi, 10.

in."* When Peter and John were brought before the High Priest and his kindred they shewed their Heartiness in Action. "And they called them, and commanded them not to speak at all nor teach in the name of Jesus. But Peter and John answered and said unto them, Whether it be right in the sight of God to hearken unto you more than unto God, judge ye. For we cannot but speak the things which we have seen and heard."† When Paul appeared before Nero, at his first answer no man stood with him, but all men forsook him; notwithstanding the Lord stood with him, and he was delivered out of the mouth of the lion.‡ But of all the examples of holy "Determination in Action" the brightest is furnished by our blessed Lord Himself; His life was determined action from beginning to end. We read of Him, that "He steadfastly set His face to go to Jerusalem," although He knew that there He was to meet His death; all His life, from the day that He entered upon His public ministry, was a progress to Jerusalem; it was a fulfilment of certain requirements which lay between Him and the cross, so that the cross could not be reached until they had been met. In meeting all these, we can well believe that the Lord Jesus had to exercise "Determination in Action," that He had to keep His human flesh steadily to the point, from which as mere human flesh it would have doubtless shrunk; in Gethsemane He is determined; even though flesh and blood be weak; He says, "'not my will but Thine be done,' and there appeared an angel unto Him from heaven strengthening Him."§

* Neh. vi, 11.   † Acts iv, 18—20.   ‡ 2 Tim. iv, 16, 17.
§ Luke xxii, 42, 43.

These then are a few of the Scripture examples of
Determination in Action; let me now direct the reader's
attention to some particulars connected with this determination to do, or to go; "I will go in the strength of
the Lord God."

He who is determined to do, or to go, in the service
of God, will often have to be very determined with himself. He will find many opponents of his will in the
actings of his own flesh and blood; he will find the law
of the flesh struggling against the law of the mind; he
will have to put down Self before he can act. Self-ease,
self-interest, self-indulgence, together with a whole tribe
of arguments, and opinions belonging to the flesh, must
be dealt with, and that, with a stern and uncompromising
hand. Few, save such as have had actual experience of
this conflict, can have any idea of the force which a man
has to exercise upon himself; many, however, of the
children of God know this, and they shall hereafter receive glory for these very victories which they won over
themselves. No eye saw them, no ear listened to them,
they were not sustained by the sympathy of masses
engaged in a like conflict to their own, but God was
looking, hearing, feeling for them, and His book of
remembrance was open, and in it an account was entered
of all this determined strife. The harmony of our whole
being in thought and action for God, will form a part of
the blessedness of heaven, but we must expect the want
of harmony to form a part of the strife and warfare of
earth.

It might be asked, however, "In what sort of things
have God's people to put in force this determined 'I
will' over themselves?" Sometimes in very important

ones, and sometimes in what would appear to common observation to be merely trifles. We sometimes require to be more determined with ourselves about trifles, than more apparently important things. A victory gained in a conflict, where the point in question is a trifle, is often a victory which helps *to determine character*, and is thus of immense importance. We have many a time to put great constraint upon ourselves to keep silence, and put a bridle on our lips, when we are provoked to answer again: we have to be determined with ourselves when we want to show kindness to those, who for a long time have been recipients of our acts of kindness, giving us in return nothing but unkindness, and thanklessness, if not opposition and hate; we have to be determined in carrying out rules of Christian life—things to be done— and things to be left undone—which are mixed up in the whirl of our daily calls, employments, and duties; in many such things we have, by the help and teaching of the Spirit, to lay down as it were the law to ourselves, and to see that it is carried out.

There are also many other striking points in which we have to exercise determination over ourselves. We may be called upon to take some part in the Lord's work, which can only be done at considerable sacrifice or cost; we may hear the Lord plainly saying to us, "Take up that position, lift up that burden," and flesh and blood decline; then comes the need for pressure; then we must be determined with self, and by God's blessing we shall prevail. Many a man has had to exercise this determination, before he could make up his mind to bring down upon himself the enmity or ridicule of some he respected, or loved; before he could bring himself to undertake something, which could be done only at considerable cost; it needed determination to carry him through, but he sought and received it from the Holy Ghost.

Nor let us suppose that the bare fact of making a determination will be sufficient to carry us through; the determination itself will be assailed. Let us be on our guard in this particular; the first attempt of Satan will be to prevent our making up our mind; the next, to prevent our good determination taking effect. Hence we must be on our guard against making excuses, and being ready continually to say that 'circumstances are altered,' and that 'we have been compelled by circumstances,' and the like. In many cases, we can master circumstances, alas! in how many do we let them master us! "In the matters of God," said Luther, "I assume this title, ' cedo nulli,' ' I yield to none;'" happy should we be, if, in all spiritual determination, a like motto were ours.

Determination in Action is then the duty of the Lord's people; blessed be God that in it they have not to depend upon themselves, but are privileged to have a Realization of external power. "I will go in the *strength of the Lord God.*" We may be determined, and yet wholly fail, owing to a want of God's presence with us. Thus was it with the Israelites, as we read in Numbers xiv; they would go against their enemies in spite of the commandment of the Lord, "They rose up early in the morning, and gat them up into the top of the mountain, saying, lo, we be here, and will go up into the place which the Lord hath promised, for we have sinned. And Moses said, wherefore now do ye transgress

the commandment of the Lord? but it shall not prosper.
Go not up, for the Lord is not among you, that ye be
not smitten before your enemies. For the Amalekites
and the Canaanites are there before you, and ye shall
fall by the sword; because ye are turned away from the
Lord, therefore the Lord will not be with you. But
they presumed to go up on to the hill top, nevertheless
the ark of the covenant of the Lord and Moses departed
not out of the camp. Then the Amalekites came down,
and the Canaanites, and discomfited them even unto
Hormah." Here we have an example of Determination
in Action, in which man goes forth, relying on his own
strength; and, as he thinks, on his own good intentions :
divine strength however was withheld, and miserable
failure is the consequence.

When we are about to come forth in determined
action, let us beware of the danger of ' looking too much
at what our own resources are for accomplishing the end
in view.' We are to go in the strength of the Lord God, and
if we parade our own resources, and say, "I will go in the
strength of this or that," failure most assuredly lies
before us. There are temptations connected even with
our growth in grace; we never attain to any spiritual
acquisition, but that Satan is on the watch to ensnare us
in it, yes, and perhaps to ensnare us *by* it, saying to us,
" Now you have faith, venture on such and such a thing."
Woe be to us, if, depending upon our faith, we determine
to do anything of the kind : our faith, our spiritual
power, whatever it be, will no doubt come out well in
action when it has to work, but we must distinctly go " in
the strength of the Lord God," and in that only.

There is another danger, but it is of an opposite

character; 'if, instead of keeping steadily before us the strength of the Lord God, we muster our own spiritual resources, then, seeing their insufficiency, we may be deterred from determined action at all.' We might well take up the words which David used of Saul's armour, and say "I cannot go with these." Some, perhaps, will be inclined to discover in this an excuse for refraining from action for God altogether; they might say, "I am not equal to what is required of me; I feel I have no spiritual ability for occupying such and such a position;" but then, dear friend, what about "the strength of the Lord God?" The Psalmist's "I will go," was a determination made with reference to His strength; oh! let yours be the same, and there is little doubt that you shall be upheld and strengthened in the might that cometh from above. "I can do all things," said the Apostle, "through Christ which strengtheneth me."

Let us observe, further, that "realization of external power will keep us close to such power;" one of our great dangers being to get independent of it, or to forget it. "Realization!"—but then it must be realization indeed; not merely a correct theory about divine power, but an actual realization of it. All the theorizing in the world could never make a man practically say, "I will go in the strength of the Lord God." We never can separate ourselves from divine strength, without coming under the depressing influences of human weakness.

The realization of this external power—even the strength of the Lord God—will have this further benefit; "We shall be more contented and peaceful in the failure of customary, expected, and it may be, humanly speaking, useful, and all but necessary supplies." All these are liable to failure; there is not a human spring, but that may run dry—not an earthly friend, but that may prove false—not a finely tempered weapon, but that may snap—not a single appliance, but that may prove out of order, when we want it most for use. The ordinary course which man pursues, under circumstances such as these, is to retire from action, no matter how determined he may have been, for he has no longer the means at hand, on which he relied. In man's judgment there would be no disgrace in this; circumstances have altered; and the man has been controlled by, or been the victim of, circumstances. If we, however, be what we ought to be, if we have made our determinations with reference to the strength of the Lord God, the failure of all these things need not affect us violently; the strength of the Lord God is wholly unimpaired. "Although the fig tree shall not blossom, neither shall fruit be in the vines; the labour of the olive shall fail, and the fields shall yield no meat; the flock shall be cut off from the fold, and there shall be no herd in the stalls; yet I will rejoice in the Lord, I will joy in the God of my salvation. The Lord God is my strength, and He will make my feet like hinds' feet, and He will make me to walk upon mine high places." Habakkuk iii, 17, &c. Resources will dry up like Elijah's brook; but the Lord's hand is not shortened that it cannot save; and amid ever-varying*

---

* In Gideon's case we have a notable instance of the altering of circumstances; his army of thirty-two thousand, is brought down to 300, but the word of the Lord concerning them was, " By the 300 men that lapped will I save you, and deliver the Midianites into thine hand. Arise, get thee down unto the host, for I have delivered it into thy hand." Judges vii, 7, &c.

circumstances, amid defections, disappointments, external fightings, and internal fears, the man of God, realizing that his strength comes from a source external to himself—from God—may carry out his determination into action, until it be brought successfully to a close.

Let us now, for a few moments, glance at *the consequences of the realization of external and Divine power in action.*

That will be attempted, under the influence of this realization, which otherwise would never have been thought of. The larger a man's resources become, the more important become his plans, and the wider becomes the range of his thoughts, and aspirations, and aims. If then a man have the strength of the Lord God in which to go, whither may he not determine to go, what may he not determine to do? No marvel if we be slow to undertake, when we see nothing but our own strength; an equal marvel is it that we are so unwilling to go forward, when we may say, "I will go in the strength of the Lord God."

Another consequence will be, that *appearances will not retard action.* "He that observeth the wind shall not sow; and he that regardeth the clouds shall not reap." Eccl. xi, 4. Appearances are often dead against the proposed action of the people of God; it is God's intention that we should start upon our day's journey, or set about our day's work with a cloudy morning, but the sun will break out as the day advances. If we see our way clear as to the duty of acting, let us determine to advance in the strength of the Lord God, and difficulties will gradually disappear.

There will also be *humility in success.* We are naturally inclined to be proud of our success, and Satan is ever on the watch to make us take the glory to ourselves, as though by our own might and power we had accomplished whatever has been done; the safest remedy for this, is just to bear in mind in whose name and strength we originally set out; that we said "I will go in the strength of the Lord God."

We shall thus *ascribe all the praise where it is due.* We shall say, "He hath done marvellous things: His right hand and His holy arm hath gotten Him the victory." Psalm xcviii, 1. It is dangerous to rob God of His honour; to withhold it from Him, even though we do not try to steal it for ourselves; an effectual preservative from this will be to remember what His strength has done. "Be strong" then, dear reader, "in the Lord, and in the power of His might;"* like the apostle of old you also may say, "I can do all things through Christ which strengtheneth me."† If you feel yourself weak, do not on that account shrink from action, but rather seek strength from above; an answer shall be given; you shall hear some such words as these, "Fear thou not; for I am with thee: be not dismayed; for I am thy God: I will strengthen thee; yea, I will help thee; yea, I will uphold thee with the right hand of My righteousness. For I the Lord thy God will hold thy right hand, saying unto thee, fear not; I will help thee."‡ If we feel daunted at the prospect that lies before us, though our course of action be clear, let us cry as Asa did, when he set the battle in array against Zerah, whose host was a thousand thousand, and three hundred

* Ephesians vi, 10. † Philippians iv, 13. ‡ Isaiah xli, 10, 13.

chariots; he said, "Lord it is nothing with Thee to help, whether with many, or with them that have no power; help us, O Lord our God; for we rest on Thee, and in Thy name we go against this multitude. O Lord, Thou art our God; let not man prevail against Thee."* Thus let us cry, and in due season we shall take up the Psalmist's words and say, "In the day when I cried Thou answeredst me, and strengthenedst me with strength in my soul."† Be wise, be determined in the work of the Lord; the Psalmist has given you the formula in which your determination is to be expressed, "I will go in the strength of the Lord God."

---

* 2 Chronicles xiv. 11.   † Psalm cxxxviii, 3.

CHAPTER XIX.

Praise.

Psalm vii, 17. "*I will praise the Lord according to His righteousness, and will sing praise to the name of the Lord Most High.*"

Psalm ix, 1. "*I will praise Thee, O Lord, with my whole heart, I will shew forth all Thy marvellous works.*"

———— 2. "*I will be glad and rejoice in Thee, I will sing praise to Thy name, O Thou Most High.*"

Psalm xiii, 6. "*I will sing unto the Lord, because he hath dealt bountifully with me.*"

Psalm xvi, 7. "*I will bless the Lord, who hath given me counsel, my reins also instruct me in the night seasons.*"

Psalm xxviii, 7. "*The Lord is my strength and my shield, my heart trusted in Him, and I am helped, therefore my heart greatly rejoiceth, and with my song will I praise Him.*"

Psalm xxx, 1. "*I will extol Thee, O Lord, for Thou hast lifted me up, and hast not made my foes to rejoice over me.*"

Psalm xxxiv, 1. "*I will bless the Lord at all times, His praise shall continually be in my mouth.*"

Psalm xxxv, 18. "*I will give Thee thanks in the great congregation, I will praise Thee among much people.*"

Psalm lxxi, 14. "*But I will hope continually, and will yet praise Thee more and more.*"

Psalm civ, 33. "*I will sing unto the Lord as long as I live, I will sing praise to my God while I have my being.*"

———— 34. "*My meditation of Him shall be sweet: I will be glad in the Lord.*"

Psalm cviii, 1. " *O God, my heart is fixed; I will sing and give praise even with my glory.*"

Psalm cix, 30. " *I will greatly praise the Lord with my mouth, yea, I will praise Him among the multitude.*"

Psalm cxi, 1. " *Praise ye the Lord, I will praise the Lord with my whole heart, in the assembly of the upright, and in the congregation.*"

Psalm cxviii, 19. " *Open to me the gates of righteousness, I will go into them, and I will praise the Lord.*"

———— 21. " *I will praise Thee, for Thou hast heard me, and art become my salvation.*"

———— 28. " *Thou art my God, and I will praise Thee; Thou art my God, I will exalt Thee.*"

Psalm cxix, 7. " *I will praise Thee with uprightness of heart, when I shall have learned Thy righteous judgments.*"

Psalm cxxxviii, 1. " *I will praise Thee with my whole heart; before the gods will I sing praise unto Thee.*"

———— 2. " *I will praise Thy name for Thy loving-kindness, and for Thy truth, for Thou hast magnified Thy word above all Thy name.*"

Psalm cxxxix, 14. " *I will praise Thee, for I am fearfully and wonderfully made, marvellous are Thy works, and that my soul knoweth right well.*"

Psalm cxliv, 9. " *I will sing a new song unto Thee, O God; upon a psaltery and an instrument of ten strings will I sing praises unto Thee.*"

Psalm cxlv, 1. " *I will extol Thee, my God, O King; and I will bless Thy name for ever and ever.*"

Psalm cxlvi, 2. " *While I live will I praise the Lord, I will sing praises unto my God while I have any being.*"

THE Christian's life may be compared to the mountain stream, whose rise is always small, and often shrouded in remoteness, whose progress is varied, but whose destination is ever to the open sea.

Here and there you find in such streams the deep and shaded pool, where all is silent, and where, as we look

into it, a dreamy sense of mystery comes over the soul.
And on a little further, all is changed; in swift and
narrow current the water seems hurrying in earnest to
some distant goal, and though there is so much motion
there is no sound; all is motion, but all is silence too.
On yet a little further, and the same waters have changed
their character, and they ripple with murmuring music
over the smooth pebbles which break them into tiny
waves, and make them dance like sunbeams in the
brilliant light of the summer day. But that which,
perhaps beyond all other features of the stream, attracts
our attention most, is the bright cascade. Full of
exhilaration and life, the stream bounds over the precipice
of stone, and every drop becomes a diamond, and the
sunshine crowns it with a rainbow, spanning the wreathing
mist with its many-colored arch; and we almost feel our
own hearts leap with the leaping waters, as they sparkle
and effervesce, and boil, and weave veils of watery
vapour, and form rings of seething foam, and then haste
away, laden with bubbles all tinted with the brightest
hues, as though they had real youth and life, and were
off to some wedding feast.

Such is the mountain stream; such I might also add,
often is the child of God. His life is varied indeed; he
has seasons of deep, and silent, and mysterious experiences; he has times of rapid, silent, earnest action; he
has days of softly murmuring happiness; why should he
not also have times of praise—joyous, joyous times—
effervescing times, when all the heart rushes forth to
God, in brightness, and energy, and joy? Daily praise
should ascend from each of us to God, as the perfume of
the daily sacrifice ascended in olden times; there must

not be fewer sacrifices under the new dispensation than
there were under the old; we are priests to offer unto
God the sacrifice of praise and thanksgiving. (Hebrews
xiii, 15.) Alas! the dull and monotonous canal, with
its muddy banks, is more like many a Christian than
this dazzling, leaping, living mountain stream! Praising
Christians are very few in number, and very faint in
their work; they bear scarce any proportion to praying
Christians; we shall not be far astray if we say that
God hears a hundred prayers for every song of praise.

How shall we account for this? One reason of this
sad shortcoming is to be found in *the natural ingratitude
of the human heart*. The heart of poor fallen man is
ungrateful by nature; and that ingratitude is especially
shewn towards God; it is harder for man to acknowledge
a favour from God than from his fellow man. We act
as though we had a right to expect from God, and unless
grace come in and sanctify our souls, bringing with it
gratitude as well as other good things, we shall not give
God such praise as he desires to hear; praise which
comes from the heart and the heart's feelings, and is not
a mere acknowledgment of mercy received, as cold and
business like a thing as a common stamped receipt.

We can find in the *giddy and non-apprehensive character of the fallen heart* a further cause of shortcoming in
praise. How much giddiness remains in even thoughtful
people of God! They suffer themselves to be whirled
along from one thing to another, without pausing to
think of how much they owe to God in all these circumstances and events. There is thought in all the music
of the grand masters of olden time; the strain may be
simple, but it is thoughtful; for want of thought we fail

in praise. The non-apprehensive character of the human heart is a further sore impediment to praise. Events are continually occurring in which God's gracious and merciful dealings with us *are to be seen,* but *we do not see them,* because we are weak in apprehensive power, and the consequence is we do not praise. No wonder if we do not praise, when we do not see what we have to praise for. It may be that many of these things will come to light hereafter; that in eternity we shall read the history of our past lives, with all God's mercy both in giving and withholding, in ordering and restraining; and then being gifted with apprehensive power of the keenest nature, we shall be able to praise with full deep meaning in our songs.

Let us consider further—*the deadness of the atmosphere* in which the human heart has to live and to beat. It is very hard for the body to feel elasticity and exhilaration in a dull and heavy atmosphere; when oxygen is scarce the spirits soon begin to flag. We know by experience the effects of atmosphere; there are dull heavy days when we are fit for scarce anything, when our arms droop by our sides and we drag our feet along, and when it would be intolerable exertion to sing; such an atmosphere as this is very often round about the soul, its weight oppresses the heart. It is hard to praise when we "dwell in Mesach and sojourn in the tents of Kedar;" "how shall we sing the Lord's song in a strange land?" Our own family influence may be depressing, the aspect of religious and congregational affairs may be gloomy, the people we are thrown into company with may be uncongenial, and thus, without any immediate sorrow closing our lips, we may find that

they are closed, and that we cannot open them in praise.
For this there is one remedy, and but one. As the
diver when deep beneath the waves draws his supplies
from above, so must we; we must seek for something
purer and better than that which we have to breathe
around. We may get this purer air in two ways; the
Lord may enable us to climb to some height where we
shall be above the rolling fogs or cold and clammy
mists, or He may leave us amongst these and yet supply
us immediately from Himself, just as those who are
floating upon the water supply the diver who is beneath.
Man can be thus supplied, God can breathe into him,
He can command a connecting medium between His
oppressed servant and the atmosphere of heaven, and
through that medium the exhilarating atmosphere of
what is pure and holy may be breathed. When we
complain of what is around us, let us remember that
although we cannot alter our surrounding atmosphere,
still the fault that we have no better is with ourselves;
we gasp, we languish, we are depressed yet all the while
it is possible to be so happy as to sing a song of praise.

Now all this entails loss. Man was made to be a
praising being, and he cannot come short without there
being loss. There is always loss when God's design is
not carried out. Man was originally designed more for
praise than for prayer, it is since his fall that he has
become the reverse, more a being of prayer than praise.
It is difficult to imagine what Adam could have wanted
to pray for in Paradise; he had everything that could
conduce to his good, or that he could imagine to conduce
to his good; if he had no want, if he felt none, what
was there to call forth prayer? But there was a great

deal to call forth praise; every tree and herb, every animal and insect was wonderful; the flowers with their perfumes, the fruits with their varied flavours, the very enjoyment of existence both in body and soul, all called forth the song of praise; we can conceive of no other worship in Paradise before the fall, except this of praise.

But God's design is not to be for ever marred by the Devil; His people are made for His praise; praise is His revenue, and He will not remit it because man has fallen. Prayer has come in, but prayer does not dispense with praise; prayer should travail in birth to bring forth praise.

Well then, since God still requires praise from man, and since He has given him abundant materials for praise in "his creation and preservation, and all the blessings of this life, but above all in His inestimable love in the redemption of the world, by our Lord Jesus Christ, in the means of grace and in the hope of glory," we may well expect to find loss, unless His requirement be carried out; and the loss in this case will be very similar to that which is entailed in the matter of Ministry and Testimony. God's honour is robbed, the aspect in which His people present Him and His service to the world is one of gloom; He is misrepresented in the eyes of those who are on the watch for everything that can detract from His claims for service; they say, "look at that long-visaged creature, with his head bent down, and his eyes lustreless, and his breath all spent in sighs, there is what religion does for a man, come along with us, you see religion cannot do much towards making a man happy." Besides which, God is robbed directly; He hears the praises of the angel and the archangel; all around His throne are possessed with a praising spirit; the souls of those in blessedness are full of praise and joy; on earth alone there is silence, or it may be here and there the scanty notes of isolated song. On earth! and who are to be found on earth? Men who are daily and hourly helped by Him; men who have been saved from perdition by Him; men who were purchased at the price of the bloodshedding of His own Son; men who have outstretched before them a glorious eternity; surely from such God might well claim the song of praise.

The world also suffers. We are bound to impress the world, so far as we can, so far as our influence and example reach; and what impression do we leave in this matter of praise? Can we say that we have given any company in which we have been, or any individual with whom we have associated, the idea that it is a pleasant thing to serve the Lord? Have we been whining and complaining Christians, or tart and twisted Christians, or stiff, starched Christians, or mourning and melancholy Christians, any, every kind of Christian, except a praising one? We have met with Christians of all the above mentioned kinds; we believe they were real Christians, but some of them, as has been well remarked, it would be quite time enough to know when we meet in heaven. Well, what have we been? What, dear reader, have you been? Has your union with Christ ever lit up a brilliant light in your eyes, or made a sweet smile play around your mouth; such a light as no artist ever painted, such a smile as no sculptor ever chiselled. And did men say to themselves "That is a happy man;" and did they feel that your smile and your cheerfulness recommended religion, and did they begin to think that religion opened the door to enjoyment, and not to misery and woe? These are important questions, and it will be well for us to think what our influence upon our fellow men really has been. A Christian may often do more with one smile than with fifty frowns; more with one song of praise, than with a thousand denunciations of woe. How can the world believe that religion makes men happy, unless it sees that it does so? We cannot expect the world to walk by faith; it walks by sight; it judges by the seeing of the eye, and by the hearing of the ear; and that being the case, let us give it a smile to see, and a song to hear.

And now let us turn to ourselves. We lose grievously by not having a praising spirit. We have not that elasticity and spring which, as was shewn in the chapter on "Heartiness in Action," would make us bound forward on our heavenward journey, and set cheerfully about our spiritual work. The sailors give a cheery cry as they weigh the anchor; the ploughman whistles in the morning as he drives his team; the milkmaid sings her rustic song as she sets about her early task; when soldiers are leaving the town in which they have been quartered, and their spirits are supposed to be likely to be affected at leaving friends behind, they do not march out to the tune of the "Dead March in Saul," but to the quick notes of some lively air. A praising spirit would do for us, all that their songs and music do for them; and if only we could determine to praise the Lord, we should surmount many a difficulty, which our low spirits never would have been equal to, and we should do double the work which can be done if the heart be languid in its beatings, if we be crushed and trodden down in soul. As the evil spirit in Saul yielded in olden time to the influence of the harp of the son of Jesse, so would the spirit of melancholy often take flight from us, if only we would take up the song of praise.

The spirit of merriment is, above all others, the most infectious. It spreads from one to another in company; if it once commence, it generally rapidly increases in an individual; and thus should it be in the holy joy and exhilaration of the heart, it should spread over the soul. "Bless the Lord, O my soul, and all that is within me bless His holy name." Thus sang the Psalmist. Thus should we sing too. We should with him issue this, which is one of the grandest invocations which can be uttered, and which is addressed to one of the noblest audiences that can be convoked. The Psalmist peals a summons through all the courts and chambers of his being, and calls forth every capacity of his nature, that one and all, they might join in a vast chorus, of which the name of God should be the theme, and the glory of God the end. It seems as though he gathered into some one vast inner chamber his powers of thought, and memory, and hope, and fear, and love, and that he gave charge to his soul to be the leader of this choir, yea, to be the very soul to it, breathing life and sense into its melody, to give the key note to its chants, and to rule its song. Yes! as David did, so let us do also. Each man has within his own bosom the materials for a choir, as tuneful as any which ever stood in surpliced array beneath the cathedral's fretted roof; a choir with full, deep, rich voices, whose anthems can swell, whose choruses can peal upwards—upward, upward, far above the din and turmoil of the earth, until they float into the presence of God Himself, and mingle, it may be, with the myriad voices of those whose praises are ever heard around the throne.

Let us turn now to *some of the particulars for which the Psalmist declared that he would praise God.* We shall confine ourselves to such as we find mentioned in the verses at the heading of this chapter, and to the points immediately connected with them. The first which we are to notice is that found in Psalm cxxxix, 14. "I will praise Thee, for I am fearfully and wonderfully made."

We think but little of our *personal creation,* and it may be that we have but very seldom really praised God for His wonderful dealings towards us in our physical frames. The Psalmist saw enough in his own body to excite his praise; so might we in ours, and that without going very deep into the anatomical mysteries of muscles, and bones, and nerves.

The daily powers of enjoyment which we possess in our bodies should excite our praise. It seems, no doubt, a small and common operation enough, to eat one's breakfast, dinner, or supper, and we generally thank God, by means of a grace, for the provision; but does it ever strike us, how much we have to be thankful for, in the bare fact, that we are able to digest that food? The horrors of indigestion are many, and take a multitude of forms. We are told by physicians that uneasy sensations of all kinds, heart-burn, lassitude, weariness, headache, sickness, broken sleep, loss of appetite, horrid dreams, irritable temper, are some of its accompaniments; and if we were to trace them any further, we should see them assuming the dimensions of evil of a most formidable kind. Many a man's life has been made a burden to him, from the simple fact, that his digestive powers were bad. Well! if you, dear friend, can eat common food, to make no mention of dainties, do you ever think how much you have to be thankful for, and how much you ought to praise God for? See what has to take place, before that common process of digestion can be satisfactorily and comfortably accomplished. Before your food descends into the stomach it must have prepared, and in readiness to receive it, a sufficiency of that important fluid known as gastric juice. When the food is dissolved by this gastric juice, and changed into the greyish or whitish pulp called chyme, your food, thus dissolved, is slowly conveyed, by a curious motion of the stomach, to its right and lower extremity, which is called the pylorus; *i.e.*, the door, or outergate of the stomach, or, as some call it, the door keeper. That pylorus or door keeper, is in itself a wonderful study; it seems to exercise a sort of choice; for if anything present itself there, which is not proper to be conveyed into the system, or not well adapted for making blood, it does not for some time suffer it to pass. After this the chyme has to be mixed with the bitter fluid called bile, which comes through a small pipe from the liver, and also with another liquor resembling saliva, proceeding from what is popularly called the " sweetbread." The chyle is now conveyed along in a number of minute vessels, which all meet in a common trunk or receptacle, upon the first or upper vertebra of the loins. From this receptacle one or more pipes carry it upwards, on the right side of the spine, towards the top of the left shoulder, where, meeting the great vein which brings back the blood from the left arm, it empties its contents. Then the chyle mixes with the blood, which immediately descending into the heart, passes through the lungs to undergo a peculiar and important process, which we cannot enter on here.* When we take all this into account, and bear in mind how fearfully and wonderfully we are made, and how many evils are averted from us in this one matter, surely we shall see that we have cause for praising God.

Then take the air we breathe. Perhaps it seems a small thing to some of our readers that they have air to breathe, and it is an equally small thing that they are able to breathe it; but let them look at the man afflicted with asthma, gasping, fighting for a breath, to whom it would be almost heaven upon earth to breathe freely even the air laden with what we should call the most nauseous smell, and such a sight would do them good; they would then see that well might some of their breath be spent in praising God, seeing to Him they owe every breath they draw.

Look also at the almost continual immunity from pain which many of our readers enjoy. By far the largest number have little more than an occasional ache, just enough, if they used it aright, to shew them how great their mercy is, in daily exemption from suffering. Suppose when you have a toothache, it were to become permanent; suppose when your head were racked with this pain, you also had what a holy man who suffered excruciatingly, called, "the toothache in his back!" in a word, suppose you were a continual sufferer, instead of

* See a very interesting and intelligible little book called "The House I live in."

being as you are, and were reduced to saying as one of old did, "thank God for four-and-twenty hours without pain," then you would know how much you had to shew a praising spirit for, when you were simply free from pain. The body of man should be like a well-tuned harp, every muscle and nerve should be like an harmonious string, and from them all, the thankful soul should draw God's just tribute of thanksgiving and of praise; and be it so, that there are some strings which He has touched with a chastening hand, even from them in a minor key may be heard a sound of song; praise that pain is no worse, praise even from them; praise that support is given for bearing it; praise that a time is coming when there shall be pain no more, neither sorrow, nor crying, for "God shall wipe away all tears from their eyes."

Our daily powers of enjoyment in common things, to say nothing of countless extraordinary favors, should stir our hearts, when we consider how fearfully and wonderfully we are made. Think, dear reader, of this; and remember that God can teach men to praise, not only by pleasure, but by pain; this latter is often the discipline of the rod, a messenger just sent to remind us of mercies for which we forget to praise.

If we pass from our personal creation to our *daily powers of enjoyment*, how much have we here also to stir our praise? Let us look at the sky over our heads, what a lovely prospect have we even there! Had God chosen, He might have made the sky of a dull and leaden hue; if the atmosphere were duly supplied with oxygen, we could live under a leaden sky, as well as under one of the most gorgeous tints; there is no absolute necessity for the beauty, and oftentimes the splendour which meets our eye when we look up. At one hour we see the sky a deep liquid blue, without a cloud or spot; then we have presented to us pillared masses of resplendent cloud, reminding us of the great white throne which shall be set; and then the scene changes again, and the pillared cloud is removed, and smaller clouds, all glittering in the sunshine, with swift yet stately motion, traverse that field of blue, and we think of the armies of heaven which follow Jesus on white horses. Oh! that sky is a grand and noble object of contemplation, and if only God teach us by His own handiwork, our hearts may be elevated indeed by looking at its glories. There go the pall-like clouds with their golden fringes, and their silver linings, telling us that there is wealth attached even to our darkest sorrows; there lie scattered all over the heavens the dappled masses of silver and gold, as though the Lord of glory had Himself passed by that way, and it had been strewn for His feet by adoring angels' hands; yonder the heavens are overspread with a burnished sheet, as though the sun would remind us as he set, of what shall be the portion of the Lord's people after their life's sunsetting, even the city of gold. Times there are when the jasper, the sapphire, the chalcedony, the emerald, the sardonyx, the sardius, the chrysolite, the beryl, the topaz, the chrysoprasus, the jacynth, and the amethyst, seem all flung in wild confusion abroad upon that sky; or when, amid its ever changing hues, they seem to melt into, or give place to one another; and if we look at this sky as it is, and as it might have been, is there not cause for praise, even as we look up? But it is impossible to sum up man's

daily powers of enjoyment; let the reader just lay down
this book for a few moments, and bethink him of what
has fallen to his lot, and he will see that he is acting an
ungrateful part, if he will not praise.

Nor must we forget God's gracious provision for His
people, in suffering. There are many of God's suffering
ones on earth. They are laid on beds of sickness; they
have hours of solitude; their food is like bitter herbs;
their drink like vinegar; their clothing is, it may be, the
bandages of their sores, and each breath they draw is
sorrow; but if they be God's suffering ones, then, despite
all this, they have cause to praise. We have met the
suffering ones of the Kingdom up in attics, almost above
the hum of the crowded street; down in cellars, almost
beneath the vibrations of the loaded waggons; we have
seen them in the morning, and they were suffering, and
at noon, and they were suffering, and at eventide, and
they were suffering: but we have also seen them happy
and praising, in the morning, and at noon, and at eventide again. And how was this? They were not left of
God, because they had not received one kind of blessing;
no! He had given to them largely, only in another way;
they had the sick man's blessings—blessed foretastes of
what was laid up for them at their journey's end; high
thoughts of how they were glorifying God in suffering;
special communings with Jesus, and comforts from the
Holy Ghost. And good cause for praise have many
suffering ones, when they think of how much and how
truly they can glorify God in simple endurance. God
can be as much glorified in *endurance* as in *action;* there
is often more action in endurance than meets the common
eye. We would say to the dear afflicted children of God,

"you occupy a real and an important position in the army of God, and you are taking an effective part in the great operations which are being carried on." The rifleman in his sombre suit, is hidden away from sight in the waving corn, or behind a tree or stone, but he is taking part in the engagement, as much as the artillery-man who stands to his gun, or the dragoon whose polished helmet, and glittering sword, are seen flashing in the charge; and the garrison who defend an important fortress, and keep watch and ward for long days and nights, and at the utmost but resist assault with success, are as truly engaged in the great conflict, as those who fight and are seen in the more open field; so the suffering ones of God, hidden away from sight, engaged in bearing pain without a murmur, in exercising patience as for Jesus, and in the presence of evil spirits, are just as much engaged in the great conflict between good and evil, as the minister who is occupied in more public ministrations, and whose name, as a devoted man of action, may be well known throughout the church of God. Encourage the suffering ones of the Lord with this thought; say to them, "every day you are fighting in the presence of evil spirits; every day you may win fresh glory to your celestial crown; every day you also are on the great battle field, and shall have part in the distribution of the spoil." Such a view of illness as this, will cheer some desponding friend; he will no longer say, "I am left alone;" he will have a fresh motive in suffering patiently; he will feel all the interest of an active position; he too, he will feel, is a soldier on active service; and even amid the groanings of the flesh, will be heard the praisings of the spirit. There is deep reality in the notes of sick-bed praise.

Let us now turn to the Psalmist's praise for God's " *bountiful dealing*." " I will sing unto the Lord, because He hath dealt bountifully with me." Psalm xiii, 6.

The position in which we find this verse is worthy of remark. We find it coming in at the end of a Psalm, almost every word of which is about danger and sorrow. Many trials are spoken of and recognised, but they are not allowed to hide out the bountiful dealing of God. Now it often happens that we fail to recognise God's *bountiful* dealing, when we have had some recent trial. We allow the trial, with its thoughts and sorrows, to swallow us up, and to hide the bounty of God's dealings towards us. We are tempted to act by God, just as man in a petulant temper, often acts by his fellow-man; we forget in a present refusal, all former gifts—in what we think a present slight, all former favours. We are like the Israelites, who as soon as they came into some temporary difficulty or distress, were forgetful of all that God had done for them, in bringing them forth from the land of Egypt. This is a point in which we must be on our guard; Satan will be sure to fix our minds upon this recent trouble; he will in effect say, " What! with this before you, while you are actually smarting from it, can you talk of the bounty of God?" Even so; with this actually before us, actually pressing upon us, ours must be the spirit which says, "The Lord gave, and the Lord hath taken away, blessed be the name of the Lord."

We must be on our guard also against *a readiness to detract from God's dealings with us*. This spirit of

detraction is only too common, and it has a most baleful
effect upon the spirit of Praise. It hides out the
greatness of God in action; it mixes up His dealings
with circumstances; and we, ever looking at the seen
rather than the unseen, dwell upon the persons and
circumstances brought into play, and not upon God, who
put them into motion, to produce the desired result.
For example, I need a sum of money—say a thousand
pounds—to carry out some design for God; I seek it from
the Lord; I do not seek it from man, but simply and
directly from God; surely, if it be sent, the praise should
be given to Him alone. In answer to prayer the needed
sum begins to drop in; now in pence, now in pounds,
now in larger sums; Satan however is at hand to detract;
he says, "yes, it is true this money is coming, but then
it is by natural means; God is not to be so immediately
praised and thanked as you think; that pound came from
a person who knew you, and who never would have
given anything but for that; and that cheque came from
a man who never would have given it but that he is
personally connected with the place;" and thus Satan
goes on trying to account for every farthing, and by
producing human agencies endeavours to rob God of
the praise which is His due. We may be able to account
for almost every farthing; but if the money had been
sought from God, and not from man at all, the very fact
of its having come, should draw forth our praise, for the
right hand of the Lord has brought mighty things to
pass. So, if we have a dear friend, for whom we have
prayed, restored to health, Satan whispers, "It was
Dr. ——— who cured him, what a clever man!" Or
"it was such and such a medicine; recommend it to all

your friends!" and thus the means are made to detract
from the One by whom the means were given, and by
whom the use of the means was taught. If we are to
have a praising spirit, we must be on our guard against
these detractions of Satan's, or very soon we shall find
ourselves giving to the creature that which belongs to
the Creator; instead of the praise of God we shall be
engaged with the praise of man. We must fix our eye
steadily upon Him; we must say, "This comes, O Lord,
from Thee; to Thee, and Thee only, be the praise."

There are certain seasons *when the dealings of God
are apparently unbountiful,* and we must be on our
guard, lest, at such seasons, Satan deprive us of a
praising spirit. We are often not permitted to have our
own way; we are not given what we wish for, perhaps
what we think we want. When this is the case, we are
very apt to think that God is not bountiful in His dealings towards us; and however much we may be resigned,
we can hardly attain to a spirit of praise; but what is the
issue of this? We are kept from some evil—stopped
upon a road at the end of which is a precipice; or God is
preparing to deal far more bountifully with us than we
should have done with ourselves. The issue of all God's
dealings with His people must be bountiful and good;
happy is that man who has faith enough to praise while
the issue is being worked out. We may rest assured
that God never yet dealt with any of His people with a
close and niggard hand.

Let the believing reader look, however, at what the
Lord has done *for his soul,* and there indeed, he will
find evidences of bounteous dealing. Well might he
think of "the riches of God's grace," and say, " Return

unto thy rest, O my soul, for the Lord hath dealt bountifully with thee." Never let any man who knows the salvation of the Lord detract from His character as a bounteous dealer, because of some present afflictive dispensations, or because he is permitted to be exercised in any spiritual trials; let him look at the rich dealings of God with his soul; let him see hell escaped, heaven prepared, glory purchased, an abundant entrance opened to everlasting life; then let him see at what a price all this has been procured, and let him look at what he himself is, even at the best; and let the story of God's bounteous dealing ever be in his mouth. Oh, that the Lord's people could ever dwell in full realization of how bountifully they have been dealt with, then, instead of fretting over every little thing, their mouth would be filled with God's praise and honour all the day long. If you, dear reader, know the Lord, stir up your heart to rejoicing because of this bounteous dealing; do not let your dull laggard heart alone; say, "Come, wake up, bethink thee of thy mercies, 'make a joyful noise unto the Lord,' the Lord must be praised, and thou must praise Him." Perhaps the heart is heavy and sleepy, but we must wake it up out of sleep; we must blow up the slumbering embers upon the altar, and wave the incense censers, until the perfumed smoke curls upward to the skies; the sacrifice of praise and thanksgiving must be offered, and bounteous dealing must be the story of its accompanying song. O my soul, "give unto the Lord the glory due unto His name." "Bless the Lord, O my soul, and forget not all His benefits." "Bless the Lord, O my soul, and all that is within me, bless His holy name."

Giving of Help is another of the mercies which stirs the Psalmist's praise. "The Lord is my strength and my shield, my heart trusted in Him, and I am helped, therefore my heart greatly rejoiceth, and with my song will I praise Him."

The reception of help issued in joy of heart; and joy of heart issued in praise. Now we also, like the Psalmist, have received help; as with him so also with us, we have had joy of heart when we were helped; but has our joy like his, issued in praise? There is scarce any one who does not know what it is to have felt an exhilaration of spirits, when some threatened calamity is passed; or when something has been endured which had been greatly feared; when a door of help has been opened; when the weight which pressed has been removed. As soon as all had come right, and the nightmare which bestrode our heart had taken its departure, we could sing for joy; everything seemed delightful; we felt in good humour with every one; we had a gentle intoxication and effervescence of spirit; in that effervescence we seemed to get rid of a great deal of acid, which, perhaps, for some time, had made us rather sharp and tart. Now, we must not go out of our way to look for great events; those of which we are now speaking are to be found strewn tolerably thickly all over the face of our daily life. Men of business have received payment of bills, which were very shaky concerns, and yet upon which their own credit had involuntarily been staked; they have found those who could help them in a pinch, ready to do so, when they went to them with fear and trembling, not knowing but that they would decline to give the needed aid; women have been delivered from

the pain and peril of childbirth;* children have been
brought through illnesses and so forth; and has the joy
of heart, and the sense of relief, obtained on these
various occasions, and such as these, led the heart to
praise? If God be not traced in everything, of course
it has not; but if He be, how comes it to pass that we
allow our joy to evaporate in mere exhilaration of heart?
There are many who are no better than the Amalekites,
of whom we read in 1 Samuel xxx, who "were spread
abroad upon all the earth, eating, and drinking, and
dancing;" the joy of the world is carnal; it never issues
in the praise of God.

May the people of God, who read these pages, be on
their guard against omitting praise when they are helped;
they cannot fall into this error without greatly displeasing
Him. Ingratitude is odious in God's sight; and this is
ingratitude of no trifling degree. Let our joy take the

* We cannot pass this subject by, without expressing deep
regret at the mere ceremony which "The Thanksgiving of Women
after Child-birth, commonly called, the Churching of Women,"
too often becomes. Some cannot go out to a ball, or to a
theatre, &c , until they have been churched! and we have often
been pained by the evident want of feeling displayed. The words
in the Psalm read upon the occasion, are supposed to be those
(certainly not of the officiating minister, but) of the woman who
has recently received the mercy, but they often end in mere
sound, and nothing else. "What reward shall I give unto the
Lord, for all the benefits that He hath done unto me? I will
receive the cup of salvation, and call upon the name of the Lord."
Alas! this so called thanksgiving is too often nothing but solemn
mockery; the clerk says, "Amen," and perhaps the woman says,
"Amen," and there the matter ends; in what way such persons
"take the cup of salvation," as we cannot perceive ourselves, so
we must leave them to determine with God.

distinct form of praise; praise to God—acknowledgment
that it is from Him we have received the blessing, and
that to Him the praise is due. A favour is doubly sweet
when it comes from one we love; if we feel God to be
our Father, and if we love Him as such, will it not be
doubly sweet to us to receive the blessing from Him?
"General praise" will never do; we must offer "specific
praise," for specific blessings; an act of praise for each
act of mercy, each help, each blessing as it comes.
When we have been helped, or received a blessing, it is
well to stand up before God in the privacy of our own
room, and look up into the sky, and try, as it were, to
pierce to His very Throne, and offer up a special thanksgiving, naming that very blessing just received, by its
common name; for example, (to refer to a matter already
touched upon) if money be needed, it is well to pray for
it with our hands open, and in the attitude of a person
putting out the hand to receive; that is very helpful,
especially if we look at our hands as then empty; then
when the Lord sends what we need, either for His cause
or for ourselves, it is well to take it, and to put it into
the palm of our hands, and kneel down or stand up before the Lord; and after stirring up our minds by looking
at it there, and thinking how it came there, to praise
Him, and say, "I thank Thee, Lord, that Thou hast sent
this into my hand." There is something very distinct
and well-defined in such an act as this; and there is a
reality which we believe to be acceptable to God. When
a preacher has sought for help in his day's ministry, or in
preaching a sermon, it is well, when he comes home, to
go into his study, and then and there thank God for that
help; and far indeed was that good woman from being a

weak minded or silly person, who, when she had dressed
and laid upon the table a dinner for a large party, sur-
veyed it all, and as she did so, thanked God, who had
enabled her to do her cooking well.

The loving-kindness of the Lord was another subject of
the Psalmist's praise. He says, "I will praise Thy name
for Thy loving-kindness, and for Thy truth." (Psalm
cxxxviii, 2.) There are two beautiful thoughts brought
out here; one is, "God's condescension in thought;"
the other, "His tenderness in action." These are both
included in "loving-kindness." And both of these are
shewn by God to His own people. He humbleth Himself to behold the things of the children of men; He
condescends to men of low estate; of the blessed Jesus
it is said, that "though He was rich, yet for your sakes
He became poor, that ye through His poverty might be
rich." (2 Cor. viii, 9.) Who can tell the depths to
which God condescends in loving thought? We are
told that the very hairs of our head are all numbered;
and if the hairs of our head, then surely all else beside.
God, as the Heavenly Father, takes an interest in every
thing about His people; He takes this interest in
matters which they think beneath His notice, or of
which they, from their ignorance, do not know the
importance. The mother may draw whole stores of
comfort from a realization of the condescending thought-
fulness of God. He will be interested about her babe;
if she commit it to Him, He who made the universe
will, with His infinite mind, think upon her cradle and
the helpless creature that is rocked to sleep therein.
The sick man may draw whole stores of comfort from
the same source, for he can believe that the ONE by

whom the body was fearfully and wonderfully made, will think over the sufferings of that body, and alleviate them, or give strength for the endurance of them if they must be borne—condescension of thought marks all the dealings of God with his people.

And hard following upon it comes *tenderness in action*. Now this " tenderness in action," is a great part of the loving-kindness of God; it is meet that a thoughtful mind and tender hand should go together in the perfection of love. God is not only energetic, but tender also in action; He is the God of the dew-drops, as well as the God of the thunder showers; the God of the tender grass blade, as much as of the mountain oak. We read of great machines, which are able to crush iron bars, and yet they can touch so gently as not to break the shell of the smallest egg; as it is with them, so is it with the hand of the Most High; He can crush a world, and yet bind up a wound. And great need have we of tenderness in our low estate; a little thing would crush us : we have such bruised and feeble souls, that unless we had One who would deal tenderly with us, we must soon be destroyed. There are many soul diseases, to which a tender hand alone can minister; just as there are many states of body which need tender and patient nursing, and which cannot otherwise be successfully dealt with, even by any amount of skill. This tenderness we see continually in action in woman's ministrations in ordinary life. Her voice has notes more sweet and soft than can be distilled from any instrument of music; her hand has a touch more delicate and fine than even the breath of any summer's breeze; it is to her man carries the stories of his sorrows; it is she that has to pillow his

aching, heavy head; well as he thinks he can do without
her, in the more exciting scenes of life, he finds that he
is not independent when the time comes for suffering
and grief. And what makes woman equal to sustaining
the heavy burden thus cast upon her? How comes the
ivy to be able to sustain the oak, around which it used
to cling, ornamenting it, while it owned its lordship and
strength? She does all in the power of the tenderness
of her nature; rugged and uncouth would life indeed be
if such tenderness were withdrawn. But pass away to
divine things—from woman, to Him that was born of
woman—and what do we find, but tenderness of action
in Him? That tenderness, which in any of mankind is
but as a spark from the fire, is perfect in His bosom;
its fulness is there; and it is continually being shewn to
them. The good Samaritan not only binds up the
wound, and pours in oil and wine, but sets the wounded
man upon his own beast, and says "take care of him."
We have often felt this tenderness of action on God's
part; we have been gently restored when we went
astray; we never received a heavy chastisement when a
light one would do; we never had a chastisement prolonged one moment beyond the needed time. Has not
Christ given us a balm in many times of sorrow? Has
He not spoken to us with a gentle voice, when one of
thunder would not have been too loud for our deserts;
and have we not here good cause for praise? Expect
loving-kindnesses from the Lord, enjoy them, but oh! do
not allow them to pass by unnoticed, because of their
delicacy; their very tenderness, their very delicacy is
their beauty. O, my soul, be all grossness of vision

removed, and thine be the Psalmist's words, "I will praise Thy name for Thy loving-kindness."

We would not altogether pass over the *Truth of God* as a subject of praise, although to go deep into it would be altogether beyond the limits of the present volume. We would only draw the reader's attention to "the coming out of God's intrinsic character," as brought before us here. He is a truthful God; He has been, from time immemorial, tried and proved by His people as such; and that truth should be one subject of their praise. But let us remember God's intrinsic character; let us praise Him for honouring and answering the dependence which we have placed upon His word; let us not lose sight of His character, in the gracious acts which have proceeded from it. We rested upon God's truth; truth has not disappointed us, and for it we should praise. The redeemed in glory praise God for His truth; they have attained the land of blessedness, simply because they reposed upon that truth; a shadow of variableness in God might have ruined them all; but with Him there is no variableness nor shadow of turning, and they are saved. What have we to depend upon, but simply *the truth of God?* We have nothing to lean upon, but His simple word. "He that believeth shall be saved," is our only security for eternal life, but that is enough. "God is not a man that He should lie, nor the son of man that He should repent;" and it is the truth of God that is to carry the believer safe to heaven. As we rest, then, upon this truth; as we feel it equal to all our need; as we see the gigantic interests at stake— and yet not at stake—for they are safe; well may the

Psalmist's words be ours, " I will praise Thy name for Thy loving-kindness and Thy truth."

Escape from the triumphing of the ungodly, stirred also the spirit of praise. "I will extol Thee, O God, for Thou hast lifted me up, and hast not made my foes to triumph over me." Psalm xxx, 1.

If ever there was a man who had reason to thank God in this respect it was David. He was hunted like a partridge upon the mountains; those of his own household lifted up the heel against him; and there were some seasons when it seemed almost impossible that he could escape even with his life. David was in this a type of Christ; the enemy was continually upon the watch for him; fraud and violence combined to take away His life; but the enemies of Jesus had no triumph over Him; they never attacked Him without a defeat, and when at last He died, *He laid down* His life. An apparent triumph was gained over David when he fled from his palace, a fugitive from the violence of his own child; and an apparent triumph was gained over the Saviour, when He hung upon the cross, but David was restored, and Jesus was raised from the dead, and the triumphing of the wicked was but short. The truth is, Satan defeats himself; his energies are not destroyed by God, but they are neutralized; God does not always prevent his working, but He does make his efforts turn against himself and on behalf of those of whom it is said, "All things shall work together for good." Romans viii, 28.

Satan no doubt often strikes the people of God, but the arrow that he shoots recoils upon himself, and inflicts upon him and his cause, the injury he thought to inflict on them. The persecution of the early Christians scattered them throughout the world, and spread the gospel throughout the nations; and now the very talk which there often is against the truth, but serves to make some enquire, and to spread its influence more and more. It is true the enemy may rejoice for a season—the beast that ascendeth out of the bottomless pit may make war against the witnesses, and overcome them, and kill them; the peoples, and nations, and kindreds, and tongues, may rejoice over them, and make merry, for three days and a half; but their triumphing is only short, for " after three days and a half, the spirit of life from God enters into them, and they stand upon their feet, and great fear falls upon them which see them." We must distinguish between temporary and final triumph. The first is allowed to the enemy, the second is not; the foe is permitted very often to rejoice for a while, but the final triumph is never left with him. Let us remember this in our own conflicts with the Evil One, in many of which we seem to be worsted: on such occasions we lose all heart; we believe that there is truth in all that boasting with which he presses us so hard; we think that he will follow up his victory, until we be utterly destroyed; but all this is only for a season; let us cast ourselves on God, let us say, " Consider and hear me, O Lord my God; lighten mine eyes, lest I sleep the sleep of death; lest mine enemy say, I have prevailed against him, and those that trouble me rejoice when I am moved;" and we shall have cause with the Psalmist to say, " I will extol Thee, O God, for Thou hast lifted me up, and hast not made my foes to rejoice over me." With the exception of the blessed Lord Jesus Christ Himself, there never lived one over whom the Devil had not temporary triumphs; that

they were only temporary is due to preserving grace.
Let us consider the histories of olden time, and we shall
see that they all witness this. The triumph over Joseph,
over David, over Daniel, over Shadrach, Meshach, and
Abednego, over Mordecai, and all such, was but short,
it was a triumph, but only for a while; so is it with us,
it shall not last. And let this encourage any of us who
are greatly depressed under some present defeat, which
involves a corresponding triumphing of the Evil One. He
now meditates further proceedings against us; his design
is to press us; to go on from one victory to another over
us, but God can lift us up. We have cast ourselves
down, but He can lift us up. He (if we cast ourselves
upon Him) will make the case His own, He will enter
into conflict with our foe; He will lift us up so that we
also shall be as it were set upon our legs again to fight,
and we shall win back the ground, the loss of which gave
the enemy occasion to blaspheme. The Psalmist declared
that God prepared a table for him in the presence of his
enemies; and what He did for him, He will do for us;
only let us not forget to praise; the Psalmist said,
"Thou hast lifted me up, Thou hast not made my foes
to rejoice;" we must say the same—we must extol God,
attributing the victory to Him, for by Him it has been
won. Not to recognise Him in action, not distinctly to
give the praise to Him, will be to put the enemy in the
way of rejoicing over us by a further fall.

There remains one point more which we would especially notice, and i.e., praise for *hearing prayer*. "I
will praise Thee, for Thou hast heard me." (Psalm
cxviii, 21.) In this point, almost above all others, God
is frequently robbed of His praise. Men pray; they

receive an answer to their prayers; and then forget to praise. This happens especially in small things; we should ever remember that whatever is worth praying for, is worth praising for also. The fact is, we do not recognise God in these small things as much as we should; if we do praise, it is for the receipt of the blessing, with which we are pleased, leaving out of account the One from whom the blessing has come. This is not acceptable to God; we must see Him in the blessing, if we would really praise. The Psalmist says, "I will praise Thee, for Thou hast heard me;" he praised not only because he had *received*, but also because he had been *heard*—because the living God, as a hearing God, was manifested in His mercies. And when we know that God has heard us, let us not delay our praise; if we put off our thanksgiving until perhaps only the evening, we may forget to praise at all; and if we do praise, it will in all probability be with only half the warmth which would have animated our song at first. God loves a quick return for His blessings; one sentence of heartfelt thanksgiving is worth all the formalism of a more laboured service. There is a freshness about immediate praise which is like the fragrance of the early morning, which is like the bloom upon the fruit; its being spontaneous adds ineffably to its price.

Trace, then, dear reader, a connection between your God and your blessing. Recognise His hearing ear as well as His bounteous hand, and be your's the Psalmist's words, "I will praise Thee, for Thou hast heard me."

CHAPTER XX.

THE DIFFERENT ATTRIBUTES OF PRAISE.

Psalm ix, 1, 2. "*I will praise Thee, O Lord, with my whole heart.*" "*I will be glad and rejoice in Thee.*"

Psalm xxxiv, 1. "*I will bless the Lord at all times, His praise shall continually be in my mouth.*"

Psalm lxxi, 14. "*But I will hope continually, and will yet praise Thee more and more.*"

Psalm cxix, 7. "*I will praise Thee with uprightness of heart, when I shall have learned Thy righteous judgments.*"

Psalm cxliv, 9. "*I will sing a new song unto Thee, O God.*"

Psalm cviii, 1. "*O God, my heart is fixed, I will sing and give praise, even with my glory.*"

IT will be well to consider for a short time some of the attributes of real praise, so that we may not only praise, but praise aright. If we be rightly instructed, we shall aim not merely at the possession of any Christian grace, but at perfection in it.

The subject then upon which we are now to dwell is, THE ATTRIBUTES OF PRAISE.

And first let us mention *Heartiness in praise.* There is something pre-eminently miserable in faint unliving praise. Amongst men a half-hearted praise is considered almost akin to blame, and we may rest assured that no great price can be put upon such praise in heaven.

Lip-service—the mere duty of praise, is of little worth; praise is of that nature that unless it be accompanied by feeling it must be dead and flat, and cease almost to be itself; the feeling may not always be the same, it may be gratitude, or admiration, but still it is feeling, and as such gives life to praise.

Let us bring this matter home to ourselves, and we shall understand it better by our own feelings than by any arguments or words. Let us suppose that our children felt it a duty to come and praise us every morning, that they came near either singly or collectively, and with drooping eye, and unimpassioned face, and hands hanging listlessly by their sides, they began to recite or sing in a monotonous tone their obligations to us for letting them sleep beneath our roof and eat our food; or suppose we had just given one of these children something it had long desired, or saved it from some accident, and that it came before us, and in the same dull attitude began to repeat some particular form which it had evidently got by heart, should not we feel utterly disgusted at such a would-be exhibition of gratitude as this? And yet this is the kind of praise which we too often offer to God. Such is not the praise of which the Psalmist speaks here, when he says, "I will praise Thee, O Lord, with my *whole* heart;" he had meaning, he had feeling in his song; and better would it be for us to hum a psalm tune with a feeling of springing of heart to the Lord, than to offer up a Te Deum or Jubilate under a cathedral's roof, unless our souls pass upward with it to the throne of God.

Impressed then with a belief of the nothingness of this mere "duty praise," let us seek distinctly to have our hearts stirred up to thankfulness, and to heartiness in praise. We may do much for ourselves in this matter by the help of the Spirit, for a good deal of our formalism in praise comes from not thinking, from our not entering individually into it. Let us think and reason with ourselves somewhat in this way—

"Why should *I* receive this mercy which God has now bestowed? Are there not hundreds of others whose need is as great as mine, and they have not received as much? My pain has ceased, while theirs continues day after day; my comforts are many, whilst theirs are but few; I have not deserved this relief in any way; I have received it as a gift; then stir thyself, my heart, to praise.

Moreover, let us think, what might have been our state if we had not received such and such a blessing. Had not God mercifully arrested a cough it might have turned to consumption; had He not sent us such and such pecuniary help at such a time, we might have been beggared and bankrupt before now; had we not been sent to such a place, or been kept back from going to some other place, might we not have met with ruin or death?

Thoughts such as these would have another good effect, viz., that of keeping us in a thankful spirit, and from a grumbling and repining one, when things do not fall out exactly as we should wish. How do we know what great mercies are hidden in these apparent crosses? If I am hindered from going to a place, how do I know but that if I had taken the journey, I might have slipped getting in or out of the train, and have broken my leg, if not my head? how do I know but that if I had gone at that particular time to that particular place, I might have trodden perhaps upon an orange peel in the street, and have had a fall which might have confined me to my bed for weeks? If I see nothing good coming out of what happens, I believe in the warding off of something bad; and let a circumstance appear never so provoking, we may still find plenty of cause for cheerful praise, for, if we be God's children, it must be working together with other things for our good. But in order that such thoughts as these may induce us to praise heartily, they must be something more than mere speculations; we may speculate as much as we please as to the particular good to be had or the evil to be averted, but we must have a deep belief that good *is* given and evil *is* averted; the depth of our belief will give heartiness to our praise. An unthinking spirit is always an unthankful one. But the grand influence is that of the Holy Spirit: when He stirs within our hearts, warming and vivifying us, we feel rise within us the spirit of praise. Just as the birds which have been silent during the winter, sing when they feel the influence of the spring, and as they break forth when the morning dawns and the shadows of the night have hastened away, so the soul which could neither sing nor praise for perhaps many a long hour of coldness and darkness is stirred on the incoming of the Holy Ghost. The Spirit of God is a Spirit of praise; no doubt He is a convicting Spirit, and One who can make thunders roll and lightnings flash throughout the heart, but He is also a Spirit of genial influences, presiding over and evoking the harmonies of the soul; yes, even more than this, creating them, as the Spirit of praise. That praise must be hearty indeed, which has its origin from God, it must be acceptable as it returns to God again; may we have it more and more; may we seek it more and more; we must have God Himself to help us, if we would praise Him aright.

The Psalmist speaks further of the *Continuance of his Praise.* "I will bless the Lord at all times; (or in every season) His praise shall continually be in my mouth." "I will sing unto the Lord as long as I live, I will sing praise to my God while I have my being." "I will extol Thee, O God, my King, and I will bless Thy name for ever and ever."

There are some who can praise only at certain seasons, *i. e.*, when they have received some mercy; it is true what might be called a small mercy will make them praise, but they must always have a finger upon their heart's spring, or they have no heart for praise. Each fresh mercy winds them up like a musical box, and they play their tune, and have done with it; when another mercy comes, they will be set off again for one tune, but for no more; they want a *living* motive power, and on that account there are such long gaps in their sounds of praise. And there are others, whose song cannot be called forth, except for some very great mercy; they must be startled into praise; they must almost escape from the jaws of death or ruin, before they can see how much they are indebted to God. The intervals between the praises of such persons are long indeed; what might be called their minor mercies go for naught, and they pro-voke God to teach them the real greatness of these "minor mercies," by the removal of them. Others there are, who can never praise when an affliction is upon them; any sad dispensation is enough to quench their spirits, to break their harp strings, and to make them hang the harps themselves upon the willows; they can-not put deep meaning into those words, "The Lord gave, and the Lord hath taken away, *blessed be the name of the Lord.*" There is shortcoming, however, here, which the child of God must endeavour to avoid; when we are in affliction, God is unchanged in His relationship to us, and we are unchanged in our relationship to Him; and praise is in point of fact as much His due in the time of sorrow as of joy. No doubt it is hard to practice this; this is a point of attainment to which many a true believer has not reached, but grace can easily raise him to praise even in all his pains. Thus was it with a poor old widow, who ejaculated thankfully, "How favoured I am!" under circumstances in which we, perhaps, should have thought ourselves accursed.

"She was a poor widow in the decline of life, and supported herself with the most rigid economy by knitting.

"I saw her in the intense cold of last winter. The house was one upon which time had made such sad ravages, that one room only could now be inhabited: and in that she dared not have a fire when the wind blew hard, because the chimney had become unsafe.

"'How favoured I am,' she said, 'for when it has been the coldest, the wind didn't blow much; or there was so much snow on the house I could have a fire without danger. *I cannot be thankful enough!* And then,' she continued, 'Joseph has been at home nights almost all the winter, and he could get my wood and water, when there was so much snow I could not get out.'

"'But do you not feel very lonely while Joseph is away?'

"'Oh, no; I get along very well through the day;' her Bible lay upon the table by which she was sewing, 'and when I can see the neighbours' lights in the evening, it is company for me. I have thought a good deal about sick people this winter; and then I think *how favoured I am*, that I can go to bed and sleep all night in health.'

"I saw her again to-day. Rheumatism had disabled one foot, and she sat still sewing, with the swollen, painful limb raised upon a cushion. 'How favoured I

am!' she still exclaimed: 'when my poor Lydia was
alive, I lost the use of *both* my feet for a time, and she
took care of me; but now I can get about by moving
my foot upon a chair, and I make out to do my work
and get Joseph's meals ready nicely. I can't help
thinking, What if it had been my *hands?* How
favoured I am!'"

Amid all the varying experiences of life, there ought
to be no break in the continuity of our praise; the
verse of the well known hymn should be indeed our
rule:

> " Through all the changing scenes of life,
>   In trouble and in joy,
> The praises of my God shall still
>   My heart and tongue employ."

If we cannot ever praise when affliction is upon us, it
is as much as to say, " now that I have not the good
things of God, I have not God Himself; I only knew
Him in His good things, and now that they are away,
I cannot recognise Him any more." He who would
continue in praise, must see God in Himself; he must
see that though things change, He changeth not; that,
although they perish, He endures; though they wax old
as a garment, He is the same; God is to be praised, not
only for what He *gives*, and what He *does*, but also for
what He *is*; and never, probably, can purer or more
disinterested and genuine praise arise on this account,
than in the time of our sorrow and pain. We have
seen some afflicted ones thus praising, and that, with no
small measure of joy in hours of severe distress; the
lips were often compressed with excruciating agony, but
they opened to praise the Lord; a sigh, a groan, would
come forth to ease poor burdened human nature, but

that was the voice of the suffering flesh, and not of the sanctified spirit, which was ever ready with its thanksgiving, even though the parched and quivering lips were scarce equal to the task.* Oh! how are many of us rebuked by such sights and sounds as these; oh! how shocking does our ingratitude appear, when we recall to mind the wasted form, the sunken eye, the parched and burning lip of the poor invalid, unable to turn in bed, unable to sleep, unable to eat, unable to breathe without pain, and yet able to praise. Surely such praise must be of exceeding price in the sight of God, it must be like the music of a difficult piece played with a master's hand; it must be counted fit for the ear of the Monarch, fit for the court of heaven; and so it is. May we learn from the sorrows of others, if we will not from our own joys, and praise the name of the Lord.

Let us not forget, that the Psalmist declared, that he would praise more and more. "But I will hope continually, and will yet praise Thee more and more." Psalm lxxi, 14. Heartiness in praise is good, and so is continuance therein, but we should not be content with these, we should aim at *an increase of praise* also.

Let us remember that an unthankful spirit is a very growing one; like all evil weeds it grows apace; unthankfulness for little mercies soon spreads to unthankfulness for greater ones, and then to unthankfulness for the greatest of all. We ought to have an increasing spirit of praise owing to the law of life. That law, as we have already observed, is progression, and wherever life is strong, praise will be loud. We can easily account

---

* The author has heard continual praises from a tongue half eaten away with cancer—what use, beloved reader. are you making of your tongue?

for this. The child as he progresses in life, and develops in his faculties, increases amongst other things in perceptive power; this increase awakens admiration, wonder, thought; he perceives the uses of things, their beauty, their construction, their bearing upon himself, and so forth, and his other faculties are brought into play by this increase of perceptive power. The child of God was never destined to stand still; he was given life, with the intention of there being after growth, and that in praise as well as anything else. How then, it might be asked, do we find ourselves getting on with reference to growth in praise? Do we feel our perceptive power increasing; do we find ourselves able to trace God's hand more and more; can we see the bearing of certain dispensations upon our good; çan we see that there is blessing wrapped up in ordinary, common place experiences; can we perceive more and more how much cause we have for praise? If we be thus increasing in perceptive power, surely the accumulation of our mercies ought to affect us; we should every year we live praise more and more! The more we praise for mercies past, the more shall we have cause given to us to praise, by mercies yet to come. God will honour a spirit of praise, even as He honours every grace which His Spirit gives.

All that now remains is that we should briefly notice

THE DIFFERENT KINDS OF PRAISE, of which the Psalmist speaks. These are *Singing to the name of the Lord, Manifesting, Blessing, Extolling, Thanksgiving, Exalting.*

Just as the stem which is full of sap throws out many branches, so the believer who is full of a spirit of praise will give vent to it in many different forms. Let us consider some of these. There is

Manifestation. "I will shew forth all Thy marvellous

works." Psalm ix, 1. God is greatly praised when His people exercise a manifesting spirit—when they speak of the good things which He has done for them—when they give Him the glory due unto His name. In this, however, they are often deficient; they do not indeed try to take credit to themselves, but they do not give the praise to God; they are silent, and by their silence the Most High is robbed of His praise. It is no wonder that the people of the world know so little about the Lord, when He is so little brought before them by His own people. We ought not to be continually receiving good things from God, without ever speaking of them; for example, if a child has been grievously ill, and we are congratulated on his recovery, and we know and feel that we owe that recovery to the Lord Himself, we should not allow our friends to go away without our distinctly recognising *before* them, and *to* them, the gracious working of God; without " shewing forth His marvellous work." How often do we allow the physician, and the medicine, and the change of air, and all such means to be spoken of, and we are silent about the One from whom they derive their efficacy; we do not shew forth God's marvellous works. Who can tell what a blessed effect this recognising praise would have upon many of our relatives and friends? When they heard us continually bringing before them the good things which God has done for us; when they heard success in any enterprise, escape from any danger, and so forth, ever traced to the one Almighty hand, they would perhaps begin to think; and by our reiterated praise, and manifestation, they might be led to believe; and so, our blessings would be put out to interest for God, and doubtless would increase and multiply to ourselves.

When we have received any special good thing from the Lord, it is well, according as we have opportunities, to tell others of it. When the woman who had lost one of her ten pieces of silver, found the missing portion of her money, she gathered her neighbours and her friends together, saying, "Rejoice with me for I have found the piece which I had lost." We may do the same; we may tell friends and relations that we have received such and such a blessing, and that we trace it directly to the hand of God. Why have we not already done this? Is there a lurking unbelief as to whether it really came from God; or are we ashamed to own it before those who are perhaps accustomed to laugh at such things? Who knows so much of the marvellous works of God as His own people; if they be silent, how can we expect the world to see what He has done? Let us not be ashamed to glorify God, by telling what we know and feel He has done; let us watch our opportunity to bring out distinctly the fact of His acting; let us feel delighted at having an opportunity from our own experience, of telling what must turn to His praise; and them that honour God, God will honour in turn; if we be willing to talk of His deeds, He will give us enough to talk about.

"*Extolling*" is another form which the believer's praise will take. "I will extol Thee, O Lord, for Thou has lifted me up," &c. Psalm xxx, 1. "I will extol Thee my God, O King." Psalm cxlv, 1. To extol is to set pre-eminently on high; to exalt above all others; it is the expression of the greatest possible admiration; it is letting others know our high opinion of a person, and endeavouring to win them over to it. The man who has such a high opinion of another as to induce him to extol him, will not be likely to rest without bringing forth into prominent observation the object of his praise.

This surely suggests an enquiry to each of us; have we this extolling spirit? do we feel an earnest desire that God should be magnified, yea, rather do we feel an earnest desire to magnify Him ourselves; not only that His name should be set on high, but that it should be set on high *by us*. That God's name will be exalted and extolled, we may be sure, for He will not lose His glory; but this may be done, without being done by us. "Extolling" is something more than the faint praise which is given to God, even by many of His own dear people; it is pressing upon men His excellencies; it is attracting their attention by unusual praise. Let us not be afraid of doing this; let us make men *think*, by what we have to say of God; let them say, "there is a reality in all this; these men must have had some experiences out of which they speak and sing." Our earnestness, our energy, would doubtless impress many with the reality of our religion; it may be they will ask about the dealings of the One we extol; and while they are investigating His claims to our praise, feel constrained to praise themselves.

This "extolling the Lord" will accomplish one of the great ends of praise, viz., His exaltation. "Thou art my God," says the Psalmist, Psalm cxviii, 28, "and I will praise Thee; Thou art my God, I will exalt Thee." It is true that God both can and will exalt Himself, but it is at once the duty and the privilege of His people to exalt Him. His name should be upborne and magnified by them; the glory of that name is now as it were committed to them; what use are we making of the opportunity and the privilege?

Henceforth, may we be more animated with the spirit of praise; henceforth may we shew the world more of the joy of the believer's life, and of the blessedness of the One the believer serves; we shall impress by telling what the Lord *hath* done, when we may entirely fail by declaring what the Lord *can* do; the world will pay more attention to us when we are *praising* God for a *small* mercy, than when we are *praying* to Him for a *great* one. There is an operative power in praise; let us not lose the reward which we might have gained by rightly using the power of praise. It may be that they who have here done work the best for God, shall have appointed to them the most glorious work hereafter; that they who have praised the most amid the scoffers of this world, shall be heard the loudest and the sweetest in the choirs of the redeemed. There is perhaps a reward in kind, as well as in degree.

Let the time past be sufficient for our silence, and for neglect of praise. Let us now invoke the Spirit to stir within us the sounds of holy song; let us string anew the harps which have been hung upon the willows; let us listen attentively, and God Himself will give us the key note for our song; let us but be willing to praise, and God will teach us how to praise, yea, by fresh mercies He will quicken us in praise. "My heart is fixed, O God, my heart is fixed, I will sing and give praise. Awake up my glory; awake psaltery and harp, I myself will awake right early. I will praise Thee, O Lord, among the people, I will sing unto Thee among the nations. For Thy mercy is great unto the heavens, and Thy truth unto the clouds. Be Thou exalted, O God, above the heavens, let Thy glory be above all the earth." Psalm lvii, 7, &c.

CHAPTER XXI.

The Willing Spirit, and the Weak Flesh.

Matthew xxvi, 41. *"The spirit indeed is willing, but the flesh is weak."*

SUCH were the words of our blessed Lord, as He contemplated the slumbering forms of His weak disciples. They have in them much that is humiliating, they have in them something that is comforting also. Jesus recognises the willing spirit, albeit it is hidden in the weakness of the flesh. And as the Saviour did of old, so does He now, so will He do by the reader, who desires to make the Psalmist's "I wills" his own.

Let the reader, then, of these "I wills" be encouraged to pronounce in the Psalmist's words his fixed determinations both as to endurance and action. Deeply conscious of the weakness of the flesh, let us invoke the help of the Holy Ghost, and He will energize it for all it has to bear or do. Be it our part to bear and do, leaving all results with God.

This willing spirit shall be acknowledged by God in

perfect independence of all outward results; whether the willing spirit make a trial, yea, many trials, and fails; or whether no opportunity of making a trial be given to it at all. Were it not thus, the labour of the man of God would be unsatisfactory indeed; for the results are very often not commensurate with his efforts much less with his will. The question of results need not be entered into at all. Had the man a willing spirit, and if an opportunity were afforded to him did he embrace it? If so, although every plan of usefulness failed; although from a long life of ministry he never saved a soul; from a long life of teaching he never made one understand unto eternal life; from a long life of truest charity he never reclaimed a single wanderer, or left one continuing impression for good upon his ungodly neighbours; the willingness of his spirit shall be recognised in the courts of heaven, and not a tittle of the blessing shall be lost. And is not this full of sweetness for such as have very willing spirits, but have comparatively few opportunities of acting openly on behalf of Christ. At times, such reproach themselves, and feel irritable, that while others are privileged to do so much, they have scarce an opportunity of doing anything at all. They say, " these few shillings are all that I can give ; these few hours are all that I can offer; my self-denial has been strict to accomplish even this; but alas! what is it before God?" Rest assured that God will take all your circumstances into account; and as He once gave a wondrous blessing to her who had done what she could, so will He give a wondrous blessing to you. There are some to whom this statement will be of value; their hearts are their witnesses that they are willing in spirit; their deeds, though small in themselves give a concurrent testimony, because under the circumstances they are great. You are not excluded from the greatness of the reward; the willing spirit shall never want the glorious crown.

We need no wide-spread sphere on earth, in which to shew the willing spirit, and win its high reward.

The willing spirit is seen in sickness, bereavement, and poverty, in prayers, and strivings, and watchings of soul, in perseverance in our difficulties, self-denial in our characters, and victory over our sins. And many of God's people shew that in all these particulars they have the willing spirit; imperfect, they all doubtless are, but they are willing; Christ's words most fitly describe their state. That man who lies all day long afflicted on his bed, who recognises a Saviour's loving hand in every pang, and wishes to bear for His sake, and mourns when a throe of acutest agony has wrung from him an impatient word, or stolen from him an impatient look— that man has a willing spirit.

That man who has suffered bereavement, upon whose heart wild waves have dashed, and wild winds blown, who has suffered, who is suffering, and who, fearful of himself, clings close to Christ, and says, " O Jesus, Thy will be done, I am not strong enough to make my praise heard above this storm, but Thy will be done; " that man though his heart cling to fond memories, and his sorrow cut the very marrow of his soul, has a willing spirit; and against him there shall not be brought any weakness of the flesh.

That man who in poverty is compelled to bear, because it has pleased God to ordain; who is not fretful and impatient; who calms the risings of his soul with the knowledge of the simple fact that the One that loves him has ordered this; such a man has a willing spirit, and may such a spirit be vouchsafed to us.

Oh may the Holy Ghost Himself strengthen your courage, deepen your endurance, and increase your self-denial. Oh! may He so pervade all your powers of action, that they may become willing powerful instruments to work out the commands of a willing and a powerful spirit—and who can tell what a glorious picture, poor and weak as we are, we shall present to the world, if only the Holy Ghost will give us strength? Perhaps we shall be able to deny all for Him, to bear all for Him, to do much for Him; our "Prayer," our "Trust," our "Action," our "Ministry," our "Praise," will be full of life from heaven, and the picture presented to the world will be Jesus rejoicing over our energy and devotion: instead of Jesus standing over our forms prostrated and in slumber—testifying in sorrow, that "the spirit indeed is willing, but the flesh is weak."

THE END.